Azriel Harnowitz

Conservative Judaism

Conservative
Judaism

An American Religious Movement

NEW, AUGMENTED EDITION

MARSHALL SKLARE

SCHOCKEN BOOKS · NEW YORK

To My Wife
Rose

Preface

THE value of quite a number of the researches devoted to
one or another small Jewish community, or concerned
with the attitudes of a group of Jewish college students,
has been limited. Such efforts have frequently not succeeded in clarifying the problems of "Jewish living," or
in elucidating sociological principles of wider application.
The restricted contributions made by many such a piece
of monographic research are not wholly traceable to limitations on the part of the investigator. Rather, in seeking to
find a suitable research design, the student may have nar-
rowed his horizon to such an extent that he stands little
chance of encountering highly significant problems or very
surprising data.

Thus a sizable proportion of those who are confronted
with the dilemma of manageability versus significance
have erred in the direction of the former tendency. It is,
however, our feeling that the latter path is the preferable
alternative at present. Accordingly, we have endeavored
to investigate what is perhaps one of the central problems
in the area of the sociology of the Jew, and to do so against
a rather broad canvas. It is true that some local community data have been utilized, as well as public opinion

materials. But on the whole, the type of social movements approach which we utilize has precluded the focusing of attention upon special populations.

As a consequence of our framework for analysis, it has not always been possible to achieve as great a degree of precision as would be desirable. Also, we have not always been able to gather data on various supplementary points of interest. Furthermore, generalizing may involve the committing of violence against one or another party. Some of our readers may object to certain statements by saying that: "In my town it's different," "Our congregation doesn't have the type of program which you outline," and "Speaking as a rabbi I don't believe you have a full appreciation of what I do and think." While some limitations in the area of precision, exhaustiveness, and typicality are perhaps inevitable, it is our feeling that the results justify the procedures which we have adopted.

This volume represents a revision of the author's doctoral dissertation done at Columbia University. A large number of stylistic changes have been made for this version, and at a relatively few points some new materials have been introduced. In addition, various portions of the original manuscript which could interest only readers with very highly specialized interests have been deleted. Scholars concerned with bibliographical details, methodological problems, a comparative treatment of data, and critiques of the works of other investigators, will find that all of these subjects are treated in the original version.

Among those who have assisted me in this research, it is a particular pleasure to record the name of Prof. S. M. Lipset. This would indeed be a far different work if not for his encouragement as well as for the insights which he contributed so freely. In addition to the significant comments conveyed to us by Prof. Salo W. Baron, the writings

and lectures of this scholar constituted essential preparation for our study. The interest and encouragement of
Prof. Herbert Hyman and Dr. Charles Y. Glock is acknowledged.

Thanks are also due to Rabbis Theodore Friedman,
Simon Noveck, and Solomon S. Bernards; the help of Ruth
Hickerson, Marc Vosk, and Dr. Salo Rosenbaum is also
gratefully acknowledged. Dr. Emil Lehman of the United
Synagogue was helpful in providing needed data and records. The Jewish Reconstructionist Foundation and the
American Jewish Archives have also assisted with needed
materials. Through the good offices of the late Rabbi
Solomon Goldman, a sum of money was made available
for this project which helped in the payment of some of
the initial clerical costs. Many others—rabbis, scholars, lay
people—have contributed to the study in various ways. Although they shall remain anonymous, their cooperation
has been essential. Of course, the responsibility for the
interpretations found in the pages which follow is ours
alone.

My wife was both a source of encouragement and good
advice, and a helpmate in the arduous details of manuscript preparation.

Marshall Sklare

New York City
April, 1954.

Contents

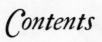

Contents [13]

C. THE PROBLEM OF THE RABBI
D. THE "IDEOLOGY" OF CONSERVATISM
E. THE SHORTCOMINGS OF THE CONSERVATIVE
   "IDEOLOGY"
F. IS THE CONSERVATIVE MOVEMENT SPLITTING?
G. RECONSTRUCTIONISM

VIII. *Retrospect and Prospect*   **246**

 IX. *Recent Developments in Conservative*
     Judaism   253
     A. THE PRIMACY OF CONSERVATISM
     B. THE PROBLEM OF CONSERVATIVE MORALE
     C. THE CRISIS IN CONSERVATIVE OBSERVANCE
     D. THE NEXT CONSERVATIVE GENERATION

Notes   283

Index   325

List of Tables

Introduction

MUCH of the ground covered in this book constitutes a *terra incognita*. Except for historical treatments, there has been much speculation but little careful investigation of Jewish religious movements. One writer comments that: "The nature of these divisions [Reform, Conservative, and Orthodox] in the American synagogue is a perplexing problem to sociologist and theologian alike." [1] A prominent teacher and official of the Conservative movement states: "The unresolved, recurring question at every convention [of the Rabbinical Assembly of America, the professional association of Conservative rabbis] was: What is Conservative Judaism?" [2]

Analyses of so-called "internal" developments in the Jewish community, such as the present study, are of little worth unless they deal also with the impact of "external" phenomena. The inability to grasp this point may well be one of the reasons why the evolution of the American Synagogue has been such a puzzling phenomenon. *Changes in Judaism have their origin in changes in the lives of Jews.* Since these changes result from interaction between

Jews and *non-Jews,* the nature of the general American community becomes one of the determining forces. It will serve as a second focus for our analysis. Set in this broader perspective, the present study may be considered as a case history of the development of a particular American religious group.

Our framework will be *sociological.* We assume that religious movements are accessible to study much as are other social phenomena like voting behavior, patterns of consumption, or juvenile delinquency. Assuredly, the methods for investigating these varied problems are not identical. Nevertheless, all can be studied with presently available research tools—some no doubt more successfully than others.

The sociological study of religion does pose a unique problem, however. Religion *is* different from other areas of human behavior, for it is an object of sacred rather than secular concern. Its values are not relative—they are not commonly thought of as changing. They are ultimate, or *suprasocial.* Approaching a suprasocial phenomenon as a social datum seems suspect inasmuch as the procedure appears to "debunk" the movement under study. The believer may question the assumptions made by the sociologist: that it is possible to penetrate this area of experience, and that religion is related to social structure. But even if the sociologist should offend, the believer cannot help but be intrigued. If the person is an adherent of Conservative Judaism—a movement which we think is particularly amenable to sociological investigation—he must find himself reflected, albeit imperfectly, in the pages which follow.[3]

In this work the *origin* of religion is not systematically investigated. Those pursuing this problem have been forced into studying the function of religion in the life of preliterate tribesmen. In a "simple" culture, presumably one might find the key to the puzzle of how and why this aspect of human behavior began; the investigator would be able to fathom the "true" meaning of religion. Thus if we were interested in the problem of origins, ours would be a wrong starting place—the present research is devoted to the religious life of a highly sophisticated folk. When we bypass the origins problem we do not mean to imply that by so doing we deny that it constitutes a crucial question for research. In the present context, however, the problem is only of minor interest.

This research constitutes something of a departure even among studies of present-day religious life. Probably the majority of the scientific articles and monographs which utilize more or less contemporary materials (aside from those investigating the rise of Protestantism) are devoted to an analysis of religious behavior among the socially disadvantaged. Such individuals characteristically join sects rather than denominations. Although the behavior of middle-class groups like the one under study is not very picturesque by comparison, it is not thereby any the less significant.

It must be admitted that the investigations done thus far into the religious life of the socially privileged have been less interesting and less suggestive than the investigations in the field of sectarian behavior. Perhaps research on denominational churches has suffered from an overdose of practicality. Many of the investigations of Protestant churches, for example, have been subsidized by religious agencies. They were made with the object in view of increasing institutional effectiveness.[4] Their scientific usefulness, and thus even their long-, if not short-range practical utility, has been limited.

Some readers will ask whether *this* study is of practical

significance. It was *not* written with the end in view of improving the effectiveness of religious institutions. In spite of this, those who are personally involved either as professionals or lay-people may well discern practical suggestions at one point or another. Whether or not they succeed in doing so, it will be generally conceded that knowledge of the type derivable from the present analysis is a precondition to serious thinking about the future of Jewish religious life in America.

I

The American
Jewish Community:
Changing Needs and Values

MOST present-day Jewish congregations designate themselves as either "Orthodox," "Conservative," or "Reform."
In addition to different institutional loyalties, it is commonly felt that adherents to these groups are distinguishable by certain religious practices and presumably by special approaches to Jewish theology as well. The Orthodox
may be considered the rightists, for they wish to retain
the maximum possible number of traditional practices and
they also profess the most conservative theology. Reform,
which advocates extensive changes in Jewish tradition,
may be categorized as representing the liberal or radical
wing. Judging from the position which spokesmen for
Reform take on theological issues, marked similarities can
be discerned as between it and several of the liberal de-

nominations in the Protestant family of churches. Conservative Judaism—which will constitute the focus of our analysis—may be designated as the mediating approach which combines elements drawn from both of the polar groups. As the centrist wing, it caters to those who cannot accept Orthodox traditionalism, but who at the same time find themselves alienated by Reform radicalism.

What are the historical forces and events which help explain the growth of these divisions? In order to suggest an answer to this question, a brief review of certain aspects of American-Jewish history is required.

A.

SOME HISTORICAL CONSIDERATIONS

Jewish immigration to the United States before the year 1914 is conventionally divided into three "waves." The Sephardim came earliest. They were Jews whose home had once been on the Spanish peninsula, or in some other country located on the Mediterranean coast. The second wave, consisting of German Jews, was a nineteenth-century immigration which originated both in Germany itself as well as in some neighboring countries where the middle-class Jews of the large cities had been attracted to German culture. The last group to come, arriving chiefly during the period 1880-1914, were the East European Jews. This category included individuals from Russia, Poland, and other territories ruled by Czarist Russia, or from certain sections of the Austro-Hungarian Empire. Even today, many East European Jews have seldom met a Sephardic Jew, or even a German Jew who was not a "refugee." This is not surprising if we realize that over 90% of the Jewish immigration from Colonial days to World War I originated in Eastern Europe. Although accurate statistics about the Sephardim and the German Jews are lacking, it is undeniable that these earlier groups were inundated by the third wave of immigration. Jewish life as it is commonly encountered in the metropolitan community is a derivation chiefly from East European patterns.[1]

The problem of all three immigrant groups was basically similar: The adjustment of a traditional Jewish system whose practices were in harmony with a medieval "closed" society, where Jews frequently occupied the status of a pariah people, to a new system characterized by a secularized social order—an "open" society where Jews exercise the rights of citizenship. To this common problem, the groups made different types of adjustments. The reasons are traceable to varying cultural traditions, dissimilar environments in Europe, and differences in numbers. Also, because Jewish immigration stretched over three centuries, each group encountered a unique type of "America" when it settled here.

The Sephardim, having had a long history of contact with European and Islamic culture, were the most advanced group. Historically, their social status was the highest of all the European Jewish groups. Long residence in this country, small numbers, and the lack of a strongly different culture, resulted in tendencies in the direction of assimilation.

It is noteworthy that Sephardic Jewry did not create any new Jewish religious movements here. The group had already adjusted somewhat to the modern world before arriving in the United States. Although there are examples of Sephardic Jews who have affiliated with Reform, most of their synagogues (of which there are only a handful) have remained rather traditional. The Orthodox rituals of the Sephardim are unique for the Jewish community. Lacking any of the earmarks of lower-class behavior, they strike the observer as highly dignified and grave. Orthodoxy among the Sephardim did not suffer the stigma of being connected with backwardness and degradation. Rather, public—if not always private—observance of traditional rituals became a mark of self-respect. Non-observance meant, in one sense, to leave the family—to show contempt for the distinguished line of one's forebears. Sephardic Orthodoxy did not appeal to the average German or East European Jew.[2] It is essentially an Orthodoxy growing out of a special tradition, and having strong insular tendencies.[3]

German-Jewish contact with European culture took place chiefly in the nineteenth century. While most German Jews who came to this country had but recently left the ghetto, they were living in what was at the time the most dynamic country on the European continent. Germany was not a multi-ethnic nation. During much of the last century it was on the road to political unification and a strongly centralized administration—all this being connected with the growth of a pervasive nationalism. These conditions encouraged assimilation. They gave impetus, in turn, to the development of a counter-movement, what is known today as Reform. This type of Judaism represents, as we noted previously, a radical adaptation of traditional norms and practices. Some German Jews had experience with Reform before arriving here. The majority, however, were still formally Orthodox, but they were on the way to emancipating themselves from the cultural background of which Orthodoxy was an expression. Only in America could Reform Judaism develop unfettered by government regulation, Jewish communal pressure, and the dead hand of tradition.

It would be a mistake to identify *all* German Jews with Reform. A handful did remain loyal to traditional practices. On the other hand, we know of some (it is difficult to determine the exact number but it is certainly larger than the traditionalists) who lost all contact with Jews and Judaism. In addition, one further group is distinguishable: those who lost their identification with the Jewish religion but who retained some bonds with their fellow Jews. The existence of such a tendency is evidenced by the fact that certain country and city clubs, philanthropies, private schools, even certain dancing classes, balls and other social events, have drawn a public composed largely of German Jews. Many participants are not distinctively Jewish if one judges them on the basis of observance of holidays, attendance at worship, or providing their children with a religious education. Theirs has been chiefly an "associational visibility."

Notwithstanding these centers of integration outside of the religious sphere, Reform Judaism remains the most typical expression of the German-Jewish group.[4] It has exercised a definite influence in the Jewish community as a whole. The Sephardim were an unknown quantity, but the more numerous German Jews—already in the public eye because of their striking success in business and professional life—drew the attention of the East European masses. While strong resistance and ridicule might have been accorded their Reform Judaism, its high social status and "American" quality made it a form of Jewish worship and practice to be reckoned with.

East European Orthodoxy was different from the system known to the Sephardim or encountered by the German Jew during childhood in a Bavarian village. It grew out of the peculiar conditions of East European life. Most of the adjustment of the East European Jew to the modern world had to take place in America. Coming from those parts of Europe where many remnants of the feudal social order still existed, the attempt of the East European to

transplant his Orthodoxy inevitably meant disorganization. The Sephardic pattern was unknown to him, and
without immediate appeal in any case. Reform could not
attract all East Europeans, for there were two blocks to
their affiliation. The first was that of class and status: The
position of the German Jews was far above that of the
newcomers, and there were no Reform congregations with
a constituency compatible—in terms of social level—with
the new arrivals. Also, since Reform Jews were eager to
preserve their status, they were not a missionary group
and gave very little encouragement to the formation of
new congregations for the East Europeans. The second
factor was cultural or religious: Reform beliefs and practices contrasted very sharply with East European Orthodoxy. Since the gap between the two systems was so wide,
it discouraged even those alienated from Orthodoxy from
making a readjustment of the type represented by Reform.
The extent of the hiatus between East and West European
Jews in America is evident from a statement made by
Oscar I. Janowsky:

Between 1880 and 1920, American Jewry was completely
transformed. In 1880, they numbered about 250,000, approximately one-half of one per cent of the total population. . . .
In 1920, about 3,500,000 of the 106,000,000 inhabitants of the
United States were Jews—nearly 3½ per cent of the population. Moreover, in 1880 the relatively small number of Jews
blended with the American environment. They were members of the respectable middle class, not too concentrated in
any particular locality, and at home in the language and
mores of the country. However, during the last two decades,
and especially after the turn of the century, as the flood of
east-European immigration continued, the mass of American
Jewry became conspicuous as an immigrant element. In several large cities, they lived huddled together in "ghettos,"
spoke their own tongue and perpetuated customs and ideas
which appeared alien to many of their co-religionists. . . .[5]

It would be desirable to conclude this historical introduction with some statistics about the growth or decline of Orthodoxy, Conservatism * and Reform. While membership figures for a few religious bodies are adequate, the Jewish statistics—like those of some other American religious groups—are of questionable worth. The Jewish Statistical Bureau, for example, gathers population data but does not differentiate those who are unaffiliated with temples or synagogues, or who do not attend worship.[6] Also, each of the national synagogue unions appears to adjust its figures in the light of those published by rival bodies. Probably the number of adherents of Reform, Conservatism, and Orthodoxy is roughly similar at present.[7] Some expert observers believe that Conservatism is the fastest growing of the three movements, and the one which in future decades may well be *the* regnant form of American Judaism.[8] Whether or not such predictions eventuate, its rapid rise does indicate that Conservatism possesses some peculiar appeal which the other two groups lack.

B.

MOBILITY, ACCULTURATION, AND THE CHARACTER OF THE SACRED SYSTEM

Two key concepts emerge from our introductory discussion. The first is social mobility; the movement of persons up and down in the hierarchy of classes. The second concept is acculturation: the process involved when groups of individuals having different cultural heritages come into contact. Commonly, when the interaction is that of a dominant group and a minority group, the increased

* We shall frequently employ the term "Conservatism" since it is more convenient than the usual designations such as "Conservative Judaism" or "the Conservative movement."

similarities produced by the contact results from the modification of the *minority* culture. Assuming that the phenomena of acculturation and mobility are related, does mobility follow acculturation or vice versa? For American ethnic groups the rate of their acculturation appears to depend to a considerable degree upon the *tempo of their social mobility*. Such a relationship may, however, be absent in less dynamic societies.

Comparing the Jews * with their sociological counterparts—ethnics who arrived at the same time and in about the same numbers—we find that the Jews have been more mobile than any of their fellows. What type of evidence exists to substantiate this assertion? Since the Federal Census does not include questions about ancestry or religious preference, it is necessary to rely chiefly upon (1) polls, and (2) community studies.

Although no special polls have been conducted on the problem of Jewish mobility, in some of the studies which include questions on socio-economic status respondents have also been asked to designate the religious group with which they affiliate. Community studies might be expected to yield even richer data than could be obtained by polling, but in terms of our purposes such studies have produced only limited results. Because an area must be chosen that can be fully covered with the resources at hand, most investigators prefer to study rather small communities. Important ethnic groups like the Jews are frequently missing from communities of this type, particularly if they are located outside of the Eastern part of the United States. In addition, most opinion and community studies do not differentiate between East European and other types of Jews. Furthermore, since Jews lacked a

---

* From this point on, except where the content specifically indicates otherwise, "Jews" will mean East European Jews.

peasant class in Europe, their mobility may seem deceptively high in comparison with peasant-descended ethnic groups. The absence of a sizable number of Jewish farmers in the United States also makes it more complicated to draw significant comparisons. Because of these considerations, it is necessary to handle the data with caution. But the main facts about Jewish mobility are hardly in doubt.

An example of the public opinion type of investigation is one of the nation-wide polls conducted in 1948 by the American Institute of Public Opinion.[9] From a review of the data it becomes apparent that the class structure of American Jewry is closest to that of the following religious groups: Presbyterians, Congregationalists, and particularly Episcopalians. These denominations have high status because of the class levels of their adherents: The preponderant majority of their membership is "old American." Jews outrank the Catholics, a denomination which includes many ethnics who came here contemporaneously with the Jews. Even Protestant groups like the Lutherans, composed of ethnics most of whom arrived in the United States before the Jews, have occupations which rank them lower than the Jews. Results of community studies are in agreement with poll data. The one done in "Yankee City," for example, shows that Jews occupy the highest position among all the ethnic groups in the community.[10]

Since rapid mobility has been characteristic of an entire segment of the Jewish population, a *larger* middle class was created here than in any other comparable ethnic group. In the others slow mobility has characterized the group as a whole; this has been coupled with rapid mobility on the part of exceptional individuals. The fact that among Jews rapid mobility has been a group rather than an individual phenomenon has resulted in the crea-

tion of a public whose level of acculturation was such as
to make them feel strongly alienated from Orthodoxy.
If mobility had been very gradual, it is conceivable that
Orthodoxy might have adjusted itself. However, where
mobility is *so* rapid, the tendency is for an institution to
be outstripped in its adjustive efforts by its public. The
constituency develops new needs to which the old institution cannot adapt itself without making too great a break
with the past.[11] Elderly individuals who have been successful economically but whose main socialization took
place in another culture (and thus upon whom the American acculturative process has less impact), as well as those
who are left behind in the mobility process, become the
chief reservoirs from which Orthodoxy must draw its followers.[12]

In addition to its rate, the impact of mobility depends
on: (1) the type of culture characteristic of the dominant
group and (2) the nature of the minority's own traditional
system. If the culture of the minority has strong similarities with the one held by the dominant group, the original system may be less disvalued; the operation of the
acculturation process will not suddenly upset the original
system. However, should the culture gulf be wide, it will
be increasingly difficult to bridge the chasm being expanded by the social mobility. Since narrowing must take
place chiefly by means of a modification of the minority
group's culture, changes in their traditions will have to be
profound. It may not be possible to maintain the fiction
that the changes are "natural" (i.e., that they are compatible with the tradition). Minority-group members may recognize the claim of tradition at the same time that they
feel the impossibility of adherence to it. In this situation
they tend to abdicate their claim to orthodoxy and use a
new designation to describe themselves.

The traditional Jewish system is deviant in Western civilization to the extent that the Christian heritage forms one of the basic cultural influences. Leaving the problem of *Weltanschauung* aside and confining ourselves to the more narrow field of religion, we find that in addition to doctrinal distinctions between Christianity and Judaism, important divergencies exist in the area of religious *practices*.[13] Although it originated in the same culture area as did Judaism, Christianity—by its very desire to differentiate itself from the Hebrew religion—made any number of important changes in the field of ritual. Furthermore, in Europe it became "Westernized." While the Jews lived in the West for centuries, they continued to elaborate and observe their Eastern traditions. All this is not to deny that some cultural interchange *did* take place between the two groups, and that the Jewish system underwent some degree of metamorphosis.

In order to illustrate the problem, let us take one of the most obvious symbols of Jewish "Easternness": the segregation of the sexes during worship. According to tradition, women must be confined to a separate part of the synagogue which is curtained off or somehow separated from the main section occupied by the males. Women have no role in the performance of the rituals. While the male is required to observe a multitude of commandments and prohibitions, the formal religious obligations of the woman are only three in number: [14] following the female ritual purifications, lighting the Sabbath candles, and *hallah*.* This Eastern pattern was acceptable in the *shtetl*, the small town in Eastern Europe whose population consisted of a relatively high proportion of Jews. In such areas the non-Jews were divided into three groups:

---

* That portion of the dough of the Sabbath loaf which is dedicated to the Lord.

a mass of peasants, a small number of government officials, and a sprinkling of aristocrats. Characteristically, there was no Christian middle class.[15]

One additional example will be helpful. The Jewish community has traditionally constituted a "sacred society." Under such circumstances the distinction between sacred and secular is nonexistent. Accordingly, in addition to ritual, religious custom, and morals, the Jewish legal system seeks to regulate behavior in areas which to the Western mind are of secular concern only. They include "personal" matters like the fiber content of clothing and the type of food and beverages consumed, as well as "social" matters like the method of payment of employees.

The position of the spiritual leader in such a sacred society is unique. His power derives not from priestly functions as in the Western tradition, but rather from his mastery of the intricacies of the sacred code and his ability to make the system viable by dealing with novel situations through the use of established canons of interpretation. Similarly, the ideal layman also deviates from Western standards. The pious Jew is not an individual necessarily engrossed in prayer and contemplation who proceeds to develop "inwardness," or even someone who devotes himself to the performance of good works. It is rather he who is punctilious in his observance of the code and who has mastered it so perfectly that he understands the reasoning behind each commandment and prohibition. Since the study of the sacred system is so highly esteemed, the religious virtuoso is not the saint but the *scholar*. It is a matter of individual preference whether or not the scholar chooses to exercise the rabbinical office, to make his living by some other means, or to be supported by family or patrons.

These particular features of the Jewish system were

already under attack in late nineteenth-century Eastern Europe. Their incongruity even in a chiefly peasant, only semi-secularized Roman Catholic or Russian Orthodox milieu was apparent to some. Brought to a secular, industrial environment, dissolution of the integrity of the system was a foregone conclusion. Warner and Srole note that:

Judaism . . . is a unitary system of legislation sanctified and revealed by God. Transgression of the minutest edict is a sin and offense to God. The moment that one edict is questioned, the authority of the entire system is challenged.[16]

A need consequently arises for a new system which will mediate the crisis brought about when social mobility produces high acculturation. It must reduce the incongruity between a *Western, Protestant, secular* environment and the *Eastern, Orthodox, legalistic* Jewish system. Reorganization may proceed in two directions: (1) Continuation, reinvigoration, or reformulation of *selected* elements in the system which fulfill certain continuing needs and which do not conflict seriously with American norms. (2) The growth of *new* functions both within the old institutional framework as well as outside of it. These are in the nature of compensatory mechanisms filling the void which has resulted from the undermining of the previous system.

The resulting cultural system is no longer a truly sacred one, for it now consists of a number of folkways allowing for considerable deviation. It may be thought of as a subculture whose flexible patterns offer a variety of ways of being "Jewish." Many difficult problems arise in the process of the transition from the "unitary system of legislation sanctified and revealed by God," to the new subcultural system. Their existence is manifested by conflicts which take place between the first and the second generations, by institutional disequilibrium, and by what may be called "religious disorganization." Conservatism, we may assume, is one of the resultants of the organization-disorganization-reorganization cycle.

C.

DESIRE FOR SURVIVAL

In addition to the rate of social mobility and the character of the traditional system, several conditions are required before an adjustment of the Conservative type can be set in motion. The first is the desire for survival: group members must feel that although acculturation is acceptable, *assimilation* should be prevented.

It was once thought that each ethnic group would—in the space of a few decades—leave their "ghetto" and fuse into the melting pot. Sociologists conceded that groups which came here fairly late, against whom discrimination was practiced, or whose original culture was strikingly different from the dominant one, might be more cohesive than others. But assimilation was considered inevitable. At present it is becoming increasingly evident that ethnicity still remains a significant basis of social stratification. For example, an investigation in New Haven, Connecticut, discloses that Swedes and Danes—who came here earlier than many other groups and whose culture was not strikingly deviant—still constitute recognizable entities in that city.[17] Does this result from prejudice, from rejection by the dominant group? [18] Is it traceable to the influence of ethnic survivalists who are strongly attached to the old culture and who preserve the sub-community by influencing marginal individuals to remain loyal? Is it that the content of the original culture, once it is adapted to American conditions, retains a degree of attractiveness?

Or is it because ethnic solidarity now serves a new purpose: protection from *anomie*—the atomization and disorganization characteristic of present-day society which results in a loss of the feeling of social solidarity?

This last suggestion is a particularly intriguing one since the problem of *anomie* exists for all peoples who live in a society characterized by mobility, by the segregation of kinship, occupation, and leisure-time roles, by shifting norms, and by clashing social systems. One of the structures which compensates for this characteristic feature of modern life is the voluntary association. These groups help to create for the individual additional primary and secondary relationships. Viewing such bonds as a "defense" against *anomie,* it is apparent that they can be elaborated on various levels: class ends, shared life experiences, similar play interests, or *common descent*. While the present-day ethnic is no longer in need of a therapeutic instrument to reduce the trauma resulting from encountering radically new norms and values (as was the case with his father or grandfather), he *is* in need of meaningful social relationships. Participation in the affairs of his ethnic group may be a convenient way of meeting this requirement. The "defense against *anomie*" theory may well help to explain why some of the sub-communities preserve a degree of integration in spite of the participants having shed many old-world culture patterns.[19]

Rejection, the influence of the survivalists, the adapted culture, and the *anomie* problem are undoubtedly all factors which operate to retard—although perhaps only temporarily—the assimilation of ethnics. With the amount of knowledge which we have at our disposal, it is difficult to decide just how much weight should be assigned to each of these forces, as well as to others detailed below. Whatever the situation in other groups, it will be conceded that Jews have shown themselves *particularly* desirous of retaining some form of group identity.[20] Marden has gone so far as to state that "The prospects for Jews in American society appear different from those of any other minority . . ." [21] for he doubts whether the other groups will be able to persist indefinitely. Marden explains that while Jews have been subject to much acculturation, this process has not led to the further step of assimilation:

> The acculturation of Jews, however, presents some striking differences to that of other immigrant groups. In many ways the Jewish group became more rapidly and successfully adjusted to life in America than the other immigrant groups. This has been true with reference to economic success, participation in civic life, and educational achievement.
>
> . . . increasing acculturation has not led to complete assimilation, nor are there any indications . . . that it will ever do so. The Jewish community within the larger gentile community, modernized and adaptive as much of its cultural content is, still remains distinct.[22]

A full explanation of this almost unique desire for survival will not be attempted here. Some of the causes have already been cited. In addition there is the fact that Jews still possess a feeling of superiority, although more in the moral and intellectual realms now than in the area of spiritual affairs. While the feeling of superiority is a factor which has received comparatively little attention from students of the problem, it is of crucial importance because it operates to retard assimilation. Leaving the group becomes a psychological threat: such a move is viewed not as an advancement but as cutting oneself off from a claim to superiority.[23] However explained, the "will to live" serves to encourage the making of experiments, like Conservatism, which aim to discover a *modus vivendi* for the Jewish community.

D.

THE ETHNIC CHURCH AND RELIGION AS A VEHICLE

Judaism constitutes an *ethnic church*:[24] a fellowship whose members are differentiated from those belonging to other denominations by virtue of their special *descent* as well as by their doctrines or practices.[25] In America the uniqueness of this type of church is its articulation of ethnicity and religiosity in a multi-ethnic society where ethnic groups are essentially minority groups, i.e., subordinate to a majority group presumed to be non-ethnic. In addition to Jews and others, this type of body is found in the three divisions of Christianity: the Protestant, Roman Catholic, and Eastern Orthodox Churches. To illustrate for the Protestant group, special Lutheran bodies and synods exist for the Danes, Finns, Germans, Hungarians, Icelanders, Norwegians, Slovaks, Swedes, and others. Special nationality parishes have been established in the United States for Roman Catholics who come from Armenia, Croatia, Italy, Poland, Portugal, the Ukraine, and many other places.[26]

These groups are first of all *churches*, for like all religious organizations they seek to provide ". . . a way of facing the problems of ultimate and unavoidable frustration, of 'evil', and the generalized problem of meaning in some non-empirical sense, of finding some ultimate why." [27] But concurrently they have an additional task: the preservation of a particular sub-culture or ethnic group. Note that the language used in sermons, liturgy, or hymns may be the one spoken in the homeland; that certain rites and holidays are observed which are celebrated only by members of the special ethnic group; and that celebrations commemorate events unique to the history of the group.[28] The ethnic church commonly makes special educational arrangements designed to teach its youth those special loyalties necessary for group survival. This frequently includes some training in the language of the homeland. Understandably, the ethnic church appears to be a highly sectarian institution to those who do not possess loyalty to a sub-culture. H. Richard Niebuhr, for example, has complained that:

. . . many an immigrant church became more a racial and cultural than a religious institution in the New World. Its parochial schools were fostered not only that the children might receive instruction in religion but also that they might learn the mother-tongue and with it the attitudes and social ideals of the old homeland. In many a Sunday School German or Swedish readers were the only textbooks; in many a pulpit the duty of loyalty to the old language was almost as frequent a theme as the duty of loyalty to the old faith. So the churches of the immigrants often found a new and additional reason for their separate existence. They now represented racial sectarianism. . . . They became competitive conflict societies, intent upon maintaining their distinction from other groups, no matter how closely these might be akin to them in doctrine, polity and piety.[29]

Leaving aside consideration of the polemical tone of his statement, Niebuhr is correct in suggesting that these churches have become an important mechanism for the preservation of ethnicity. Religion easily recommended itself for this role. The church was one of the few institutions of the original culture capable of re-establishment in the new land. Also, since the ethnic church is the counterpart of non-ethnic institutions of the same order, it would automatically receive identical formal recognition, although of course its status position may not be on the same level. Furthermore, while ethnic separatism is not

very highly valued in our culture, religious distinctiveness is allowable—even esteemed in a way because it is
"American." Given the attraction of national culture patterns which have slowly but surely impressed themselves
upon the ethnic, group distinctiveness could be preserved
—even if emptied of much of its content—under the ban-
ner of religion. Thus, because of the challenge to group
survival, ethnicity has tended to retreat and to reappear
in a very different form.

In summary, the forces working toward the continuation of the special function of the ethnic church con-
verge from the following two directions: (1) From the
dynamic of the institution itself. Since the future of the
church generally hinges on the persistence of the ethnic
group, it must promote ethnic group solidarity in order
to survive. (2) From ethnics who—whether consciously or
not—realize that religion is an acceptable method of group
differentiation, that church functions may include much
more than the dissemination of the word of God. Such
individuals see suprasocial differences as legitimating the
perpetuation of divisions in the social structure. While it
is true that in some cases group persistence has been in out-
right ethnic form, in other instances the main index to
continuing ethnicity is to be found in the survival of
churches whose membership is relatively homogeneous.
Most of the group are still descended from individuals
who come from the same homeland. American ethnic
groups are tending to change their outward appearances.
They can preserve themselves as religious groups.

On the whole, Jews in the United States choose to be
regarded as members of a religious denomination. However, the various groups in the community who have arrived at this consensus are differently motivated. There
are, of course, those who feel (as well as act) that religion

is the prime expression of Judaism. The religious designation is, therefore, expressive of their true ideological preferences. Another segment of the community has wider
Jewish interests than simply religion (or even possess other
Jewish interests which serve to replace religion), but they
feel nonetheless that—given American traditions—*religion
must become the main expression of Jewish identification
as well as the guarantor of Jewish ethnic survival.* At the
very least, they would contend that the designation of
the Jewish group as constituting a denomination is a highly
convenient fiction which it is wise to cultivate. Lastly,
there are those whose feelings of Jewish identification are
weak or conflicted, and whose survivalistic urges are consequently questionable. Nevertheless, because of public relations considerations, they feel that it is essential that Jews
stress the religious designation. The middle group seems
to be the predominant one at present. While few Jews—
particularly those in the middle group—could succeed in
verbalizing their feelings as we have set them down, there
is ample evidence available pointing to the existence of
these trends.[30]

It is significant that although overall Jewish identification has remained at a high level (and while synagogue
affiliation appears to be greater than previously), Jews
today hardly seem very observant of religious practices.
Their day-to-day religious behavior is readily apparent
from data gathered in a poll conducted by the National
Opinion Research Center during 1945. This survey re-
veals that only 6% of those who identify themselves as
Catholic state that they seldom or never attend religious
services, 19% of the Protestants make this statement, but
no less than 32% of the Jews are found in this category.
Of the Catholics, 69% attend religious services once a
week or more, 36% of the Protestants do likewise, but a

mere 9% of the Jews attend. Worshiping at least once a month are 81% of the Catholics, 62% of the Protestants, and only 24% of the Jews.[31] It would seem then that many wish to identify themselves as being members of a religious group while at the same time they lack much religious interest. Because of such a trend, one student of Jewish problems speaks of the ". . . paradox of the concentration of Diaspora survivalism on religious channels in the face of increasing weakening of religion." [32] Although the fundamental tie in the Jewish community continues to be on the level of common ethnicity, many apparently share Mordecai M. Kaplan's viewpoint that ". . . [the synagogue] is the only institution that can define our aims to a world that will otherwise be at a loss to understand why we persist in retaining our corporate individuality." [33]

All of this results in the strengthening of the religious structure in spite of increasing secularization. As we noted, reinforcement comes from different directions. The ethnic survivalists concentrate upon religion as the most satisfactory means of Jewish identification, and the more marginal group seizes upon it as a protective device which will help to raise status, draw allies to the Jewish cause, and in the long run serve to decrease the virulence of anti-Semitism. Both are forced into "making good" on the stereotype by according some support to religious causes. Whatever their real feelings, their very desire to project the stereotype means that they have to concede a responsibility for supporting religious institutions. Additionally, the stereotype—once it is successfully established—reacts back on the Jew himself. Whether because of impressions conveyed by Jews, or because of factors which operate independently of minority-generated pressures, Gentiles may begin to convey that they consider the Jewish group as just another religious denomination. At this juncture, the

Jew may find himself propelled into fulfilling the image projected by the Gentile. Although he himself may not actually believe the stereotype to be wholly valid, he feels that he must act like the type of "good Jew" which the Gentile imagines—the Jew who is loyal to his rabbi, interested in his synagogue.

Such developments do not prepare the ground for any kind of true religious revival. Attendance at services may not even grow very substantially. However, religious institutions will receive increasing financial support and community esteem, particularly if they offer a program which includes non-religious activities and is strongly oriented toward ethnic values. We can assume that Conservatism resulted in part from the feeling that the Orthodox synagogue was inadequate to meet the demands of the environment—that ethnic solidarity would have to be perpetuated chiefly under religious auspices and that consequently a new type of institution was required.

E.

CONGREGATIONALISM

The final general factor involved in the growth of Conservatism is the type of religious organization, or *polity,* found in the Jewish group. Religious institutions vary from those characterized by the highly centralized episcopal type of structure to those organized in the congregational form where local bodies retain much of their autonomy. Largely because of the conditions of Diaspora living, Jews in the United States are extremely congregational—they stress the independence and self-sufficiency of the local synagogue. As one student of religion has stated: "Within the local [Jewish] congregation there is full independence. There are no synods, assemblies, or hierarchies

of leaders to control anything whatsoever in the synagogue." [34] The directors of each congregation determine
their own ritual; ethnic bonds make it well-nigh impossible to read any group out of the fold regardless of its
deviant behavior.

What is the importance of this in connection with the
growth of Conservatism? It is conceivable that the movement would never have started if a different type of polity
existed. Had Judaism been organized along episcopalian
lines, dissent might have been driven underground, instead of eventuating in the establishment of new kinds of
synagogues. But one could object by saying that the demand for change was too vigorous to stifle. If this were
true, the strife that would accompany the split from Orthodoxy would result in a far different type of Conservative
movement. Ideological clarification and organizational
centralization, both of which—as we shall see—are decidedly
absent in Conservatism, commonly result during the initial period in the growth of movements when their opposition to the *status quo* is most marked. In a situation like
the Jewish one where over-all organization and authority
is so amorphous, deviant types of congregations can hardly
be said to be in "revolt" against the system; they have
merely effected a compromise adjustment which does not
threaten the *status quo* in the ordinary sense.

Although congregationalism promotes differentiation, it
is far from being wholly dysfunctional in its consequences.
Differentiation permits the retention of over-all loyalties
to the group and to the religion at the same time that it
promotes the fragmentalization of tradition. In addition
to such general perspectives, it is significant to note that
extreme congregationalism works toward the simplifica-
tion of our analysis. Making allowance for certain types of
rigidities, it is apparent that the form which the local

congregation takes is generally an excellent index to the needs and feelings of the community, or at least that segment of the group which is active in a particular synagogue. Of course, since the congregation is unrelated to any larger entity except by the unstructured bonds of ethnicity, its board of directors is free—if it so wishes—to preserve the *status quo* by conducting its activities along time-honored lines and thereby disregard the defections of the synagogue's more mobile and acculturated periphery. But any clique which is dissatisfied is free to establish its own synagogue.

Among Jewry every congregation must appeal for community support and is entirely on its own resources. In contrast, even the congregationally-inclined Protestant denominations extend help to local units, and frequently subsidize needy congregations for considerable periods of time. They may have available loan funds to assist in the building of churches, and they also frequently possess a network of field offices which help in the organization and counseling of local congregations. Special provisions may be made by denominational agencies to keep alive church units which could not exist but for outside aid.

While Jewish philanthropy is renowned, in the main it has not entered the field of religion except to endow rabbinical seminaries and other educational enterprises. Thus the congregation is not an object of philanthropy of a city- and nation-wide character.[35] It is conceived of as a neighborhood enterprise; its constituency take upon themselves the complete obligation for maintenance when they organize on a formal level. If it is a popular and growing synagogue it has apparently gauged the state of public opinion and is expertly serving the needs of its constituency. The Jewish institutional structure presents few blocks to free congregational development or decay.

II

Orthodoxy in Transition

A.

INTRODUCTION:
THE IMPACT OF INSTITUTIONAL STRAINS

THE failure of adequate adaptation on the part of the traditionalists helped create the pressures which resulted in the development of Conservatism. Orthodox adherents have succeeded in achieving the goal of institutional perpetuation to only a limited extent; the history of their movement in this country can be written in terms of a case study of institutional decay.

All religious groups face the following problem: the rate of change characteristic of their institutions is notoriously *slow* compared with those of other areas.[1] In a period of high social change such as the one which witnessed the emigration of hundreds of thousands from the *shtetl*, the strains on such a resistant institution as the Orthodox synagogue were immense. This type of synagogue was in adjustment with the social structure of East European Jewry, described previously as a sacred society characterized by the kind of primary and kinship groups peculiar to village life. The Jewish minority was subordinate to the non-Jewish majority. Very limited social mobility existed for both groups.[2]

Brought to a highly different culture area, there were instances where the Orthodox synagogue flourished for a time. It functioned as a cultural constant in the life of the disoriented newcomer, as a place of haven in the stormy new environment. However, as the integration of the immigrant proceeded apace, the disparity between the two cultural areas was highlighted. East European Judaism had been adjusted to a system where piety and devoutness pervaded *all* groups and where the intercourse between Jew and non-Jew was chiefly limited to a type of "antagonistic cooperation." The lack of such a relationship here and the absence of a high degree of general religiosity helped to speed alienation. Unparalleled social mobility resulted in fragmentalization of the former East European class and status lines with which the religious system had been intertwined. The secondary group relationships so typical of urban life also played a part in discouraging observance of the Orthodox type. The general American environment, characterized by all that is implied in the term "secularism," symbolizes the challenge which the Orthodox synagogue was forced to meet.

Under these conditions Orthodoxy did make adaptations, but the great demands occasioned by the new environment resulted in these changes being incomplete. The process of adjustment was complicated by the rigor and the high degree of elaboration characteristic of the Jewish sacred system. In addition, the following factors help account for the amount and type of adjustment which was made: The lack of any hierarchical organization which could encourage adaptation, and the relative absence of an Orthodox bureaucracy with strong ambitions and a high degree of morale; the possibility of setting up *bona fide* congregations without authoritative fiat; the lack of really large investments in plant or equipment; the prosperity of certain Orthodox Jews; and the rapidly changing character of urban neighborhoods.

The most obvious adaptation was based upon an experience common to all of the immigrant groups: the lessening or disappearance of loyalties founded on localism. Thus most contemporary Orthodox synagogues are no longer integrated around common sentiments which have their basis in village, or even regional, loyalties. Although the name of a congregation may still indicate the town from which its founders hail, the membership tends to be mixed. Worshipers commonly include immigrants (or the children and grandchildren of immigrants) who originated from such diverse places as the Ukraine, Hungary, Galicia, Poland, and Lithuania. This decline in localism is one of the factors making possible the growth of the large Orthodox synagogue. Such synagogues contrast sharply with the very numerous, and generally small institutions of the immigrant era. Although the newer synagogues inevitably betray a weaker pattern of interaction among their membership, presumably they are stronger institutions and as such are better able to meet the challenge of the environment.

Secondly, a pattern of Orthodoxy has emerged which for all practical purposes overlooks certain of the requirements of the sacred system. While synagogue procedure has been kept intact, a strategic compromise has been effected by disregarding the degree to which the congregant adheres to the sacred system while *outside* the sanctuary. Congregations which refuse to overlook untraditional behavior and in some way restrict the participation

of non-Orthodox individuals are rarely encountered except in certain neighborhoods of New York City. Demanding adherence to the traditional code both outside as well
as inside the sanctuary would have resulted in organizational suicide. Thus the so-called non-observant Orthodox
Jew * has actually been admitted without much protest.
In very recent years, Orthodoxy has also perceived that
it may adapt modern techniques of organization and administration, as well as certain Western standards, to its
own purposes.[3]
For those who have remained loyal, American Orthodoxy is apparently a viable system. *By serving the needs
of a special group, the Orthodox synagogue has been able
to continue an attenuated existence.*[4] Although now and
then it may project plans to win back large numbers to
"Torah-true Judaism," the majority of its adherents recognize that the defections are permanent. In one sense losses
represent an advantage to those in control: it may prevent
any challenge to the present leadership. In essence, Orthodoxy is becoming a sub-cultural system within the larger
Jewish order, for those who continue to observe the traditional norms with some degree of rigor are now actually
sectarians. The current picture is in contrast to Orthodoxy's historic role (assuming that we may call pre-emanci-
patory Judaism "Orthodoxy"), which has been that of
being *the* regnant form, with only a comparatively small
number of dissenters on the fringes. Many such dissenters
either returned finally to the ranks or placed themselves
outside of the community by converting to Christianity or
Islam.

---

* Someone heterodox in personal behavior but who, when occasionally
joining in public worship, prefers to do so in accordance with traditional
patterns.

B.

THE ORTHODOX SYNAGOGUE
IN THE AREA OF SECOND SETTLEMENT

Since the stresses experienced by Orthodoxy provide clues to some of the factors responsible for the development of Conservatism, it is worthwhile to study them in some detail. This can be accomplished by observing community patterns in one of the larger cities.[5] In Chicago—the particular metropolis which we studied—East European Jews have moved into at least three different ecological areas.[6] Students of urbanism describe this progression as follows:

a) *Area of first settlement.* This is the district populated by those immigrants who are "just off the boat." The area typically adjoins the central business district, it was occupied previously by an earlier ethnic group, and it is considered a slum. With the decline in immigration since the 1920's, many such districts have lost their Jewish population.[7]

b) *Area of second settlement.* This is an adjacent district where the immigrant or his children move during the process of raising their class level or improving their social status. Acceptance of residence here is indicative of the impact of acculturation. The district has no tenements. Its inhabitants reside in medium-priced apartments or small homes.

c) *Area of third settlement.* This is the most fashionable ethnic settlement and is composed of the offspring of the more successful immigrant families. It is typically located near the city limits. Residence here symbolizes the attainment of solid middle-class position or better, and is indicative of a relatively high level of acculturation.[8]

In the first area, sometimes designated as the "ghetto," the synagogue was Orthodox.[9] In structure, function, and content it resembled its *shtetl* counterpart.[10] Its size, as well as the fact that frequently it was a *landsmanschaft* synagogue (i.e., composed of individuals from the same European community), has already been noted. Wirth described it as follows:

> In January, 1926, there were 43 Orthodox synagogues on the near West Side [of Chicago]. Most of these are small, only a few having over 100 members. They are made up largely of immigrants who originated from the same community in Europe. They are open daily and are frequented by a small group of elderly people who gather for prayer and for a discussion of the Talmud. . . . They are equipped with a basement, which is used for daily services and meetings, while the main floor is occupied only on Sabbath and holidays.[11]

In contrast to other groups, social mobility in the Jewish community frequently begins with the first rather than the second generation. As the Jew leaves the working class, he changes his place of residence and moves into the area of second settlement. His new synagogue differs somewhat from the type of institution characteristic of the "ghetto." Bonds of localism decline. The institution is the prototype of the large Orthodox congregation as yet relatively unaffected by the competition of Reform and Conservatism. Since many founders of Conservative synagogues spent their childhood or early adulthood in second settlement neighborhoods, a detailed description of the patterns characteristic of such districts is required.

The discussion that follows constitutes an analysis of one such area in Chicago—the "Lawndale District." Although we shall describe Jewish life in Lawndale in the present tense, our analysis is more typical of some thirty years ago when the area served as the leading center for Jews and Judaism in the entire community of Chicago.

1. *Characteristics of Worship*

Worship is the chief function which takes place in the second settlement synagogue.[12] Services are held three times each day, on the Sabbath, and on the festivals and holidays. In general, the content and form of these services still resemble those modes current in Eastern Europe at the time of immigration. Procedures vary from service to service, but some general characteristics can be indicated.

Worship is conducted by either a cantor or a lay person. The participation of the rabbi is essentially the same as that of any other pious member of the congregation. The services are highly informal as in the *shtetl* synagogue where:

The coming and going, the murmur of voices . . . are not felt as disrespect. . . . As long as the minyan, ten adult male Jews, is present from the beginning of the reading (of the Torah) and six are there at the end, all requirements have been satisfied. The synagogue is literally the Home of Prayer, and one moves freely there as in the home of his father.[13]

Worshipers cover their heads during prayer, usually by keeping on the same hats they have worn in the street. Males wrap themselves in the *talis,* or prayer shawl, and during morning services also don *tefillin,* or phylacteries.

In contrast to the practice followed in many contemporary religious groups, little emphasis is placed on the sermon. Addresses are given from the pulpit, but they are chiefly fund-raising appeals. Some are for causes not connected with the congregation itself. At certain times, "honors" giving the worshiper the privilege of participating in the Torah service (during which the chief object of adoration—the Torah scrolls—are removed from the ark) are auctioned off. Participation in the Torah service generally obligates one to make a special contribution either to the congregation itself or to some charity.

Hebrew is the exclusive language of prayer. Most of the speaking which is done from the pulpit is in Yiddish. Congregational business is generally transacted in this language. Unlike many ethnic churches which hold different services with a consequent shift in language for the foreign-born and native-born, there is generally only one service for all.

2. Functionaries

Several functionaries are needed for the operation of a large second settlement area synagogue. The *shammes,* or sexton, is a personage of real importance. He spends his time making arrangements for the services, distributing the honors, keeping equipment in order, collecting money, and assisting the laymen in administrative matters. Since the synagogue seldom has an office in operation, much of the business that would normally be transacted there is handled by the sexton. He is perhaps the most permanent member of the staff.

The *chazzen,* or cantor, is another important functionary. His vocal attainments, and the particular style which he employs in chanting the important prayers, is of great interest to the congregation. Some institutions hire famed virtuosi who appear at their services only a few times each year. Lesser cantors sing more frequently, for they may lead the prayers at Sabbath services. Each synagogue advertises its High Holiday services widely. The cantor is the featured attraction. Competition for "name" cantors results in the payment of large sums for the few who excel in this art.

The rabbi is far from being the leading functionary in such synagogues. Indeed, his position is ambiguous. In the *shtetl* he served the entire community and was not connected with a particular congregation. As we noted, his main function was religious study. Unless he had an assistant, he also rendered a related and very necessary service: answering queries about the tradition. Religiously speaking, he served as the "ornament" of his town.

The shift in community structure and the pronounced weakening in adherence to the sacred system is reflected in the functions performed by the spiritual leader in the area of second settlement. Here the rabbi may lead a *chevra,* an adult study group, but frequently a layman is able to give the necessary instruction. While the rabbi may preach, this is not an important duty of his office. Since he has no formal training in public speaking, frequently he is not very successful in this role. His limitation in the English language, although possibly shared by the majority of the congregation, is the subject of critical comment. Not only is the rabbi untrained, but in addition the worshipers are not very receptive. They are more interested in the delivery of the liturgy than in the inspiration of his message.[14]

Of prime significance is the fact that the rabbi receives a constantly diminishing number of inquiries about ritualistic and legalistic matters. While the immigrant synagogue frequently lacks a spiritual leader, the synagogue in the area of second settlement generally employs one, if only for reasons of congregational prestige. However, the rabbi usually receives only a very nominal salary. A substantial portion of his income must be derived from various emoluments, from fees for rendering certain special services, and from compensation for supervising the manufacture and handling of foods and beverages which need special care to insure their ritual correctness. Being attached to a prominent congregation aids the rabbi in procuring income from these sources. Considering the roles of the sexton, the cantor, and the rabbi in the area of second settlement, we find that they are still very distinctive to the Jewish community. Like the procedure followed during worship, they have not been Westernized.

3. Congregational Activities

Outside of worship, the program of the synagogue is insignificant. Study of the Jewish legalistic tradition by the adult males, which in Eastern Europe had been a very important function frequently taking place on synagogue premises, has lost much of its appeal. It is still held daily although attendance is very limited. In the *shtetl* such groups were numerous and they were distinguished according to varying levels of scholarship.[15] The relatively scarce study groups of the area of second settlement index the decline in this once highly esteemed activity. Almost all devote themselves to rather simple texts, or they discuss the problems of Talmudic law on an elementary level.

The traditional benevolent societies, such as those for the making of loans or for the burial of the dead—integrated with the synagogue structure and still a force in the immigrant community of the first settlement—are on the decline. Their services are provided either by business establishments or by well-financed, city-wide, Jewish charities operated from outside the neighborhood. While the second settlement congregation owns a cemetery, it is managed by a small number of individuals and hardly provides a significant focus for participation.

Since little thought is given to age and sex grading, affiliated organizations are few. In keeping with traditional modes, the synagogue does not provide special activities for young people since it is thought that they should take their place in the program of worship and study. There is no voluntary association for adult males. Their socializing must take place before, during, or after the services, and at the study circle. Adult males do gather at the meetings of some organizations which still use synagogue premises. A number of congregations also hold annual dinners. However, because of the unelaborated structure, it is generally difficult for the man to have any close tie with the congregation if he does not participate in the study circle or is not a faithful attendant at worship.

Women are in a somewhat different situation. Their position is in the process of transition from the station which they occupied in Eastern Europe to one more in conformity with American mores. In those activities which are sacred in nature, few changes have been made. During services, women are seated only in the balcony. They are not present at daily worship and have no active part in the Sabbath or holiday services. They are still not eligible for any of the honors distributed in connection with the reading or handling of the scrolls. Indeed, their presence at services is not particularly encouraged, and the number of seats available for the men in the main sanctuary is generally larger than the number provided for the women. The traditional pattern of separation of the sexes and subordination of the woman is also underlined by the fact that no arrangements are made for the study of the sacred system by the adult women.

Women *have* entered the congregational sphere, however. This development has occurred through the organization of an association: the ladies' auxiliary. The change does not challenge the sacred worship practices, and at the same time the women are accorded some measure of recognition. Although the congregation frequently derives financial benefit from the activities of its auxiliary, such associations typically have little voice in synagogue affairs.

The influence of the women must still be exercised through their husbands.

In addition to its limitations as a community center, the second settlement congregation is also generally inactive in the field of Jewish education. As in Eastern Europe, the local congregation is not thought of as being responsible for religious education on the primary level. Children who receive their education from other than private tutors generally attend an afternoon Jewish school known as a "Talmud Torah." Some of these institutions, it is true, are affiliated with congregations, but the connection is only nominal. Their boards are generally independent. The Talmud Torahs have extra-congregational sources of income.

4. The Synagogue and the Community

The synagogue is increasingly being displaced as the institutional center for individuals who participate in the sub-culture. While the congregations appear to flourish on several of the holidays, a much larger number of potential worshipers live in the area than could possibly be seated in all the synagogues at any one time.[16] Even if we disregard those who are alienated from religion, it is still apparent that the majority join in worship at most only a few times each year. A comparatively small segment of the population participates in the services held between the main holidays, and it has previously been noticed that study of the sacred system is of interest to only a specialized group. Nevertheless, the second-settlement-area synagogue adds nothing to its program which would compensate for the decline in worship and study.

New agencies arise to fill the institutional vacuum. The Jewish community center located in the neighborhood is larger than any single synagogue. It sponsors a varied list of leisure-time activities. Its athletic program, little theatre, and adult classes (mostly devoted to courses of general rather than specifically Jewish interest) have a large following. The center is supported mainly from outside the community. Contact between this institution and the synagogues is minimal.

The area is rich in clubs and organizations. Some of them meet at the center, others at rented halls, homes, or in the synagogues. For the most part, the varied associations are not articulated with the congregations. Unless associations have a distinct religious purpose (such groups exist only in limited numbers), they have little real contact with the synagogue. True, most organizations hesitate to schedule meetings on Jewish holidays. To do so would incur communal disapproval. Many also have such distinctively Jewish purposes that it is questionable whether they could be labeled as "secular" groups. Also, the associations assist in preserving group identity and thus serve as indirect reinforcement for the religious structure. From the religious perspective, however, their *immediate* effect is disintegrative.

One of the main foci of activity around which the organizations build their programs is philanthropy. The giving of charity is highly esteemed. Although this activity has religion as its ultimate sanction, it is now organized separately. The synagogues may still engage in fundraising for non-institutional purposes, but this is done generally on behalf of the smaller charities with special aims. For the general-purpose city- and nation-wide drives which interest all Jews, it is obvious that superior results can be obtained if the bulk of the funds are gathered outside congregational channels. Parenthetically, it is significant that the shift in communal activity has been noted by the leaders of the Democratic Party who are in control

of the political structure of the area. While as public-spir-
ited citizens they may give financial support to the congregations, they are really free agents. The politicians have
been able to consolidate their power without much assistance from officials of the religious institutions.

The interaction of the congregations with the non-
Jewish community is small. Since the majority of the population of the district is Jewish, and also due to the fact
that the non-Jews in the surrounding neighborhoods are
frequently ethnics who occupy the same or even lower
status, at least in the conduct of religious life the influence
of the non-Jewish world remains limited. Second settlement Jews have few social identification problems. They
are "Jewish" Jews even if they are irreligious.[17] The state
of intergroup relations does not trouble them deeply.
The ethnic character of the district works to dispel any
fears about the strength of loyalties to the group. Reactions which take place when a sub-culture is threatened
with extinction hardly arise.[18] Although the rabbi and
the pious layman decry the habits of the younger generation, many individuals expect violations of the sacred code
as the price which they or their children must pay for
having come to America. The conditions which would
lead, on the one hand, to anti-religious movements, or,
on the other, to the formation of new religious groups,
are absent. Apathy, rather than antipathy or religious
zeal, characterizes a certain sizeable section of the population.[19]

C.

MEETING ATTEMPTS AT ADAPTATION

In actuality the religious situation is not as static as
has been suggested by our analysis thus far: Attempts *have*

been made to modify the structure and content of Orthodoxy. For example, now and then congregations will hold Friday evening lectures and some claim to operate a "social center." One synagogue founded a club for young adult males. Another named a new functionary: a director of activities. However numerous, these tendencies never reach fruition because of the presence of strong institutional blocks. Such resistances are traceable to the strength of the "push-pull" factors at work.

Second settlement areas—like many other types of neighborhoods in the large city—are highly unstable. During its early period (1900-1910) as well as through its heyday (1911-1925), Lawndale was considered a middle-class area. In its period of decline (1926 to the present), the level of the neighborhood dropped to lower class and lower-middle class. Many of the remaining residents plan to leave as soon as other housing is available, particularly since sections of the area are being settled by Negroes. Thus during the early and middle periods of their history, second settlements serve essentially as zones of transition for families originating in the immigrant community who are on the way to establishing residence in the more stable areas of third settlement.[20]

Because exodus from the neighborhood is so rapid, the synagogues are generally under the control of individuals whose *status* aspirations are limited. They have little desire to climb any further since such mobility would involve considerably more acculturation on their part. This would entail a definite sacrifice and thus it is not surprising that some middle-aged and elderly Orthodox people prefer to continue residence in a community where they are widely known and esteemed, even though they can afford more comfortable and prestigeful quarters. While limited in their status drives, it is consequently apparent

that their *class* level is definitely third settlement. As a
group they can afford to cover any congregational deficits
which result from waning community interest; the income from the sale of High Holiday seats continues to provide funds for basic congregational expenses.

In addition to these wealthy leaders whose acculturation has reached a ceiling, the functionaries also seek to
block any change. The rabbi in particular is threatened.
Regardless of the possible theological objections which
he might have to doctrinal or procedural revisions, such
changes would invariably work to his detriment. Indeed,
his position as a professional is already somewhat ambiguous. Although innovations might benefit the *institution,*
they would succeed in further outmoding the skills of the
present spiritual leaders.

Demand for change originates from young, socially mobile individuals who may not observe all commandments
of the sacred system but who have, nonetheless, strong
religious and ethnic loyalties. In spite of their pressure,
the congregations generally remain in the hands of the
elders. The following personal document prepared for this
study by a perceptive layman details the history of a synagogue located on the border of a second settlement district. Here an ambitious program of innovations was attempted:

The synagogue was governed by its more prosperous members, middle-aged business men. When the synagogue was organized, they brought over Rabbi A from Russia to act as
the spiritual leader of the congregation. Rabbi A was a pious
man with a long black beard: deeply religious, scholarly, and
non-secular. He delivered sermons in Yiddish and conducted
special classes for the scholarly few. Services at the synagogue
were "disorganized" in the traditional Orthodox sense. Every
member had his own prayer book and prayed at his own pace.
The only unifying force was the singing of the cantor. Many

members, however, did not always keep up with the cantor. The rabbi, then, did not *conduct* services. The officials had to discipline the congregants frequently.

During the early 1930's, a new group began to take over the leadership. These were young business and professional men who were less prosperous than the old guard but zealous in their efforts to modernize the synagogue. They wished to retain the values of Orthodoxy and yet to make the services meet the needs of the younger, American-born element. One such man, Mr. B, was elected to the presidency of the congregation over the bitter opposition of the old guard. First Mr. B introduced Friday evening "services" which were followed by a social hour and the serving of tea and cookies in the community hall. The service was not the regular evening service traditionally held at sundown before the evening meal. This service was held *after* dinner and featured noted Jewish lecturers, book reviewers, Jewish singers, symposia on current topics—all conducted in English. This move met with great success.

Mr. B and his group then began to change the regular services themselves. He attempted to institute the use of a uniform prayer book and periodically to announce the page on which the cantor was praying. The synagogue purchased a microphone so that speakers could be heard. All of these innovations widened the breech between the old guard, which included the rabbi, and the new group. While the new leadership was popular with the rank and file, the old guard had more money, and also more prestige as they were the founders of the congregation. The rabbi, if not held in great affection, was nevertheless respected. He evoked a response in every Torah-loving person because of his scholarliness and piety. He reminded people of their fathers and grandfathers—bearded Jews who had shared his love of learning.

The cleavage turned to real conflict. It became clear that Mr. B and his group wanted to oust the rabbi, who had nothing to offer the young, and to replace him with an English-speaking spiritual leader. The rabbi thereupon began to refer to Mr. B as the "shagitz"—the Gentile. Mr. B would be quick to deny this and then by some deed he would make it clear that the rabbi was being excluded more and more. His group

proposed making Rabbi A emeritus. Rabbi A and his followers fought back. Rumor had it that they hired thugs to bring
bodily harm to Mr. B and his group. Gradually the old guard
took over again. The new group, worn out and defeated, gave
up the synagogue as a lost cause and moved out to new and
brighter neighborhoods.

The old guard, having the largest stake in the community, fights hardest to block deviations from that pattern
of Orthodoxy with which it is identified. More mobile
individuals, whose roots are not very deep, always have
the option of moving to an area of third settlement. Many
others of their kind have already made this change. In
the newer neighborhoods where Orthodoxy is not well
entrenched they are experimenting with non-Orthodox
forms.

D.

NON-ORTHODOXY IN THE AREA
OF SECOND SETTLEMENT

Thus far we have simplified our analysis by disregarding any other institutionalized religious behavior but that
found in the Orthodox group. However, there is one Reform Temple in this second settlement neighborhood in
Chicago, and steps have been taken to establish a Conservative synagogue there as well. The Reform institution was founded in 1913 by business and professional
men dissatisfied with the Orthodox mode of worship. In
addition, they felt that the community needed a program
of social activity for young people. At the beginning their
institution attracted some attention because of the nov-
elty of its Friday evening services. The Sunday school
which it conducted also grew rapidly since it filled a need
among the middle-class elements then resident in the

neighborhood. Many of this group sent their sons to the Talmud Torahs or arranged for private instruction, but —in accordance with tradition—they generally were not interested in providing intensive instruction for their daughters. Hence the Sunday school met the educational needs of the girls. The Temple also experimented with activities for young people, but when the community center was opened this facet of the program diminished in importance.

Growth was brief. Neither the popularity of the Temple's service nor its educational and recreational facilities contributed greatly toward strengthening the institution. The group which it tended to attract lived in the area for only a short time and the Temple has always been short of funds.[21] Its existence has hardly been any threat to the Orthodox congregations. They have not modified their programs as a result of the establishment of this institution.

During the 1920's an attempt was made to introduce Conservatism into the community. The plan was to conduct High Holiday services in the hope that this would give impetus to the organization of a permanent congregation. Apparently this effort met with little response, for with the exception of the following brief notice in an official publication, information about it is lacking:

Plans are being completed for conducting High Holiday Services for young folks in the West Side of Chicago . . . up to now [we have] not been represented in that section of the city which has a Jewish population of about 100,000 Jews. . . . These services are to be held in an auditorium of one of the local public schools and no charge for admission is to be made.[22]

The same plan was tried again during the 1940's.[23] The initiative for this effort originated outside the community, as was perhaps true of the previous attempt. The services were aimed at interesting returned veterans. Again no charge was made for admission.[24] The High Holidays were followed by Friday evening services which featured sermons by some of the most prominent Conservative rabbis in the city. These efforts finally eventuated in the organization of a small and relatively inconspicuous congregation whose impact on the community—as in the case of the Temple—has been very limited.

E.

NORMS: IDEAL AND REAL

So much for the role of the deviant religious groups. Returning to Orthodoxy, one other factor is needed to complete our study of the patterns characteristic of the second settlement. The "non-observant Orthodox Jew" was mentioned in Chapter I, but the implications of such deviations require more thorough consideration here. While the non-observant Orthodox individual is a special type, and in one sense an extremist, he illustrates a *general* tendency.

Second settlement Jews conduct themselves in a traditional manner when they pray, but even those who are considered Orthodox deviate in the religious life which takes place outside of the congregation. Already, American norms are observed in much extra-synagogual behavior. For example, the female purifications are not widely practiced. A *mikveh* (ritual bath) is located in the neighborhood, but it is patronized only by a handful. From the viewpoint of the sacred system, most of the young and middle-aged married women in the community commit a major sin by not observing the laws of purification. However, their ritual uncleanliness is not only generally disregarded, but in many circles the very concept has become a subject for cynicism and humor. Such a reaction is understandable toward a tradition which varies so widely from Western religious norms: according to such norms impurity results from a *moral* rather than a ritualistic transgression. While rigid separation of the sexes is still enforced inside the synagogue, it has broken down outside of the house of worship where these avoidance patterns apply as well.[25] It may also be noted that in activities other than worship or study sponsored by the synagogue or taking place on its premises, separation of the sexes is rarely enforced.

Furthermore, all edibles served in the synagogue are *kosher* and the food taboos are still being followed with some degree of rigor in many of the homes. On the other hand, this aspect of the sacred system has broken down outside of the family and the house of worship. The majority of the restaurants in the neighborhood (as well as those located in other areas which are heavily patronized by community members) are either non-*kosher* or serve non-*kosher* food prepared in what is known as "kosher style." Thus the food taboos—another marked deviation from American norms—are being violated in the public restaurant, the place where un-Orthodox behavior can be practiced with a minimum of guilt and family conflict.

Other aspects of the sacred system, such as the Sabbath, could be the subject of extended inquiry. However, enough has been said to indicate that while the patterns followed in the synagogue are still highly resistant to modification, much of the behavior taking place outside of the sanctuary deviates from Jewish custom and law. It is true that norms followed in different areas may vary widely, and that a sacred system is subject to re-specification as to what is considered sacred and what non-sacred. "Ideal" norms exist and ". . . established institutions may thrive upon a relatively large amount of passive conformity and discreet deviation. . . ." [26] But a viable system does demand *some* articulation between institutional areas, particularly in light of the tendency for different patterns of behavior to influence one another. Interpenetration cannot be delayed indefinitely, and this process is clearly observable in the next area of settlement. There, religious behavior is not strongly isolated from other areas.[27]

To summarize, several factors were suggested to account for the strength of Orthodoxy and the weakness of Conservatism and Reform in the area of second settlement:

1. The second settlement district is an area of transition. Many Jews who might form a public for the Conservative movement do not continue to reside in the community for very long. Conservative synagogues come into existence by one of two methods: the founding of an avowedly Conservative congregation, or the modification of an Orthodox institution, i.e., its gradual metamorphosis into a Conservative synagogue. Given such prominent Orthodox institutions, development by the latter method is not feasible. The former alternative apparently demands more enthusiasm than is found in the community, for even the initiative for the founding of the present small group had to come from outside of the neighborhood.

2. Even though this area is not the "ghetto," the majority of the population is Jewish. This results in many ghetto-like features. The influence of non-Jewish religious practices, as well as the problem of ethnic identification, is still at a minimum. Individuals are not as yet sufficiently alienated from the "ghetto" to encourage the growth of nostalgia. As a consequence of their lack of social distance,

they are still resistant to religious movements of a mediating character.

3. The very large and seemingly prosperous Orthodox synagogues display much institutional rigidity. Although there is considerable religious apathy in the community and a great deal of violation of Jewish norms, the Orthodox synagogue may continue momentarily to exist on its "capital"—the authority gained through centuries of observance and the resistance to changing what are thought of as age-old traditions.

4. Jewish activities taking place outside of the synagogue are abundant. They absorb much of the time and energy of individuals who, under different circumstances, might utilize synagogue auxiliaries for their associational interests. The Orthodoxy of the synagogue is sustained, but at the price of transforming the synagogue into a sectarian Jewish institution. An attempt to rechannel leisure-time interests by elaborating its own associational structure would mean the modification of synagogue traditions. Residence in a neighborhood where Jews are in the majority does not encourage the concentration of ethnic survivalism under the sanctions of religion.

III

The Development

of the Conservative Synagogue

A.

CHARACTERISTICS
OF THIRD SETTLEMENT AREAS

IT IS significant that all of the ten congregations in Chicago belonging to the United Synagogue of America (the congregational union of Conservatism) in 1926 were located in third settlement areas.[1] Most of the synagogues were established during, or soon after, World War I—the period when settlement of these areas by East European Jews took place.[2]

What are the unique features of the third settlement which are relevant to our problem? The first striking factor is that the third settlement is not a predominantly Jewish neighborhood. Generally speaking, Jews constitute about 10-15% of the population. As a consequence they are less able to withstand the pull of American norms than previously.[3] In addition to the simple fact of ratios, it is important to note the *character* of the non-Jewish majorities. It will be recalled that in first and second settlement areas, Jews were surrounded chiefly by other ethnics who were their contemporaries in terms of date of arrival here. This population was overwhelmingly Catholic. However, since Jews are more mobile than their fellows, they reach third settlement areas much faster than others.[4] Since they tend to overtake those who arrived previously, their new neighbors should be mostly Protestant "old Americans," or "old ethnics" such as Scandinavians and Germans. This is in fact the situation found in the Chicago third settlement areas. Whereas Jews had hardly felt any status deprivation when they compared themselves to their peasant-descended Italian or Slovak neighbors in the first and second areas, the situation was different in the third settlement. Although the *class* position of Jews compared favorably with that of their neighbors, Jewish subordination in terms of *status* was apparent. The importation of the Orthodox synagogue to areas of third settlement would not help to reduce this status hiatus; it would in fact only serve to underline it.

East European Jews encountered another situation which affected the development of their institutions. In some of the neighborhoods they had been preceded by German Jews. Whereas the East Europeans were the first group in the second settlement and consequently established the pioneer institutions, German-Jewish Reform temples had been organized in some of these districts long before their arrival. While the majority of the East Europeans were not attracted to these institutions, they could not avoid being influenced by the temples even if they preferred not to join them. The status of the comparatively few Reform Jews found in the second settlement was not much higher than that of many Orthodox Jews, for both groups were East European in origin. But in the third settlement the picture is very different. In one such neighborhood in Chicago, for example, the membership of the Reform temples included a group of German Jews who played a leading role in the economic and cultural life of the metropolis. Through his Conservative synagogue the traditionally-minded East European Jew thereby created a prestigeful institution which could compete status-wise with Reform.

Minority status, the character of the surrounding population, and the presence of a group of Jews of higher social position all helped to speed acculturation. The simplest index to this process is the shift in language patterns. The use of Yiddish rapidly declines; its employment in daily life is avoided. While Yiddish words and phrases are considered appropriate in certain contexts, the Jews of the third settlement pride themselves on being English-speaking. Given the thorough knowledge of Yiddish possessed by most of the adult population, it can be assumed that this avoidance is functionally significant. The evasion may be viewed in part as an attempt to emphasize the separation from the culture pattern of the former area, and to reinforce the claim to higher status both to oneself and to other Jews, as well as to Gentiles.[5] However the declining use of Yiddish must be placed in the proper perspective. As over against other ethnic groups where avoidance of native languages may be significant in that it presages increased assimilation, this factor does not have similar functional significance in the Jewish community. The decline in Yiddish is an index to acculturation, not assimilation. In the same family where the use of Yiddish is at a minimum, the child may be encouraged to study Hebrew, while at the same time the parents are active participants in a congregation.[6]

That acculturation rather than assimilation is the keynote of the third settlement area is also borne out by other evidence. There is no proof, for example, that here a smaller percentage of children receive a Jewish education than in the second settlement—in fact more may attend than previously. But a qualitative difference does exist: the Jewish education typical of the area of third settlement is less intensive than before. The Jewish school is affected by the Protestant Sunday School pattern, frequently as it is reflected by Reform Jewish education. Parents demand that the Jewish curriculum be arranged so that children will not miss their normal mealtime, and that sufficient leisure remains for sports, hobbies, instruction in music and other skills, medical appointments, etc. They no longer require the facility in Jewish subjects which results only from long hours of study. The Talmud Torah, identified with the type of intensive instruction popular in the first and second settlements, is not found here.

This leads us to a consideration of the extent of religious observance. The tendency in this ecological area is to achieve some compromise between complete adherence and complete non-adherence. On the one hand observance is lower than before. In many cases, however, families establish minimum standards—a floor to non-observance as it were. Rituals are practiced chiefly in two places: in the home and in the synagogue, with the latter constantly bulking larger. In other situations Jewish distinctiveness is diminishing. The feeling of guilt about deviations, used to advantage in the second settlement by Rabbi A, is largely absent. The sacred system is now viewed as a discrete body of folkways and group patterns. The multiple dependencies existing between institutional areas now extend to the field of religion. In a personal document prepared for this study, a Conservative rabbi categorizes the practices of his congregants as follows:

> One of the characteristics of Jewish religious observance in America is the absence of what we normally call "consistency." The "either-or" attitude towards ritual and ceremonial has disappeared among the bulk of synagogue Jews. Thus, many are very faithful in their attendance on the High Holy Days, and are equally diligent in absenting themselves throughout the remainder of the year. In many a home the Sabbath is welcomed by candles and Kiddush, but cooking and work go on within the home and avoidable Sabbath violations outside of it. American Jews are exercising selectivity in the realm of traditional customs.
>
> Perhaps nowhere is this tendency more pronounced than in the vast area of the dietary laws. Time was when a home was either Kosher or "tref" [non-Kosher]. Today, among members of my congregation the question: "Do you keep a kosher home?" is very likely to be answered: "Well, what do you mean by a 'kosher' home?" If we pursue the conversation further, we soon realize that there are degrees of observance ranging from the completely observant home to the one which serves meat of forbidden animals. In between, we might find such unorthodox combinations as: (a) dietary observance, except for the absence of two sets of dishes and utensils; (b) some [who purchase Kosher meat] may eliminate "kashering" [the ritual salting and soaking]; (c) some buy Kosher meat, but pay no further regard to the dietary laws; and (d) some buy only meat of permitted animals, but not from Kosher stores.
>
> These divergencies are by no means exhaustive, but they indicate the innumerable potential combinations—all of which, I dare say, exist. It would be quite safe to say that complete observance and complete disregard are of about equal incidence—less than 10%. The bulk of my congregation would be distributed between these extremes.[7]

So much for changes in the areas of ritual observance, Jewish education, and language. An even more significant feature is that in spite of acculturation and secularization, the bonds of ethnicity continue. Jews still lead a segregated social life. Since they are now in a minority, there should be greater opportunity for closer contact with non-Jews. True, we find much more secondary association with Gentiles than previously. This of course is based on the factor of propinquity. Nevertheless, primary relationships and close friendships are still limited chiefly to the Jewish group. Participation in voluntary associations is a convenient form of measurement of this phenomenon, and it appears that third settlement Jews are affiliated predominantly with Jewish rather than non-sectarian organizations.[8] Jewish voluntary associations in this area do differ from previous types, however. *Landsmanschaften* are no longer popular. Lodges which stress burial insurance, sick benefits, and other forms of assistance needed by a lower-class population decline. Rather than practicing self-help, many organizations orient themselves around philanthropic endeavors on behalf of less fortunate brethren.[9] But whatever shifts take place in the character of the voluntary associations because of changing economic levels, Jews do continue to associate largely with other Jews just as they did before.

The problem of Jewish identification bulks large in this area. We have already indicated that this has been handled by underlining the religious character of Judaism and by seeking to further the identification of Jews as one of the three American religious groups. Consequently, avowedly secular Jewish institutions are not predominant in third settlement areas. When they are established, they may be explained away as being the Jewish counterpart of the Christian "Y". Frequently there is an adjustment and combination of synagogue and center. Which emphasis is the stronger one may well depend on the ratio of Jews to non-Jews. In sum, the local synagogue becomes the Jewish badge of identification to the neighborhood at large.

B.

ORTHODOXY AND REFORM

Jews in the area of third settlement are confronted with two alternatives: continuing with Orthodoxy or adopting Reform. Their rejection of Orthodoxy is particularly significant. It is reflected by the very physical appearance of the synagogues: While the Orthodox congregations in the second settlement are large structures which dominate the boulevards, in the area of third settlement they are generally inconspicuous institutions housed in modest structures located on the less important streets, or even on noisy commercial thoroughfares. The majority of the Orthodox public frequently consists of neighborhood merchants as well as elderly individuals who have moved into the district because of the mobility of their children or the desires of their family.[10] The neighborhood merchants are a special group inasmuch as they did not venture into the area because of achieved status; their migration was motivated by the search for business opportunity. They own small retail shops and service establishments.

During the first twenty years in the life of the third settlement, the Orthodox synagogue serves as a haven for those who are alienated from the culture of the area. Its clientele consists of individuals whose pattern of acculturation is in keeping with the one typical of the previous area of settlement. Hence the Orthodox synagogue must accept a subordinate role and pursue its course as a sectarian institution catering to the needs of the few. Aside from those who form its regular clientele, it may be patronized now and then by men who wish to recite the prayers for the dead or by others who desire to celebrate the various *rites de passage,* and annually by individuals who are attracted by the modest charge which it makes for High Holiday seats.

To the socially mobile, Orthodoxy bears the stigma of the "ghetto." They feel that Orthodox procedures are out of keeping with the type of behavior expected of the middle class, that Orthodoxy will not raise their status among fellow-Jews of higher social position, and also that Orthodoxy will not help to improve Jewish-Gentile relations. The language which it uses, and with which it has become identified, is the Yiddish which they avoid. Being un-Orthodox in their observance, they are not inclined to follow within the sanctuary all of the laws which they persistently violate on the outside; at least they do not care to be lectured about their derelictions. They see no evidence that Orthodoxy is attempting adaptations which will meet the pressures which they experience. They find little interest in the traditional program of worship and study. Orthodoxy may serve as an unwelcome reminder of the culture from which they would prefer to disassociate themselves. Consequently Orthodoxy is found *in* the area of third settlement, it is not *of* it.

Turning to Reform, we find that a very different picture emerges. In contrast to Orthodoxy, one of the important motivations of many who join the established Reform congregations is the feeling that such affiliation can be used as a social elevator speeding a rise to higher status. One observer comments on his visit to a Reform temple as follows:

The faces I saw were those of Russian Jews whom I had known not so long before as dwellers of the West Side Ghetto! These Jews could only recently have become members of the Temple! . . . it could not have been by the process of evolu-

tion that these people had advanced mentally to the stage
where they sought a more rational and esthetic form of worship. The transformation had come too soon to be convinc-
ing and the only logical explanation was that they were
socially ambitious. . . .

It became not uncommon for a West Side Jew who had
acquired wealth and was eager to obtain social prestige, to
move . . . [to an area of third settlement]. If he happened to
be the father of marriageable children, his next step was to
join a Temple.[11]

During the period from World War I to the 1930's, the
East European Jew had to accept Reform largely on its
own terms. However, German-Jewish congregations did
not exist in all third settlement areas, and thus a number
of temples came to be founded by East Europeans. In
these institutions small but nevertheless significant compromises were made. But the "old-line" congregations
hardly effected any concessions calculated to ease the adjustment from Orthodoxy to Reform. There also have
been frequent charges that, in addition to having to adjust
to a different ritual, the East European Jew was excluded
socially in some of the high-status Reform congregations.[12]

In summary, until Reform congregations modified their
ritual and program as occurred in the last two decades,
their procedures represented too great a transition for
many East European Jews. The large status differences
existing between those whose families came from Western
and from Eastern Europe reinforced the hiatus in ritual
and thought. Between what was for them the too-highly
adapted Reform temple on the one hand, and the under-
adapted Orthodox synagogue on the other, middle-class
East European Jews established congregations which de-
viated from the pattern of both groups.

C.

THE PATTERN OF CONSERVATISM *

The language problem offers a convenient starting place for obtaining an over-view of Conservatism. The Conservative synagogue, like the Conservative home, is English-speaking. One of the basic requirements of these congregations, and as we shall see an important influence on the movement as a whole, has been the hiring of only English-speaking rabbis. One who can speak the language without a foreign accent is preferred. All congregational business in transacted in English. Yiddish words and expressions are used in sermons, in private conversations, and in the telling of stories and jokes. Until recent years, the rabbi might occasionally deliver a talk in Yiddish to elderly congregants. However, the use of Yiddish in these situations only serves to emphasize the predominance of English and the break with former patterns.

Worship is the next important area. Conservative religious services must be "Jewish" enough so that there will be continuity with previous experience, but at the same time they must take the new norms into account. The most popular adaptations have proven to be those which are in keeping with the spirit of the tradition, but whose *form* is different from the one followed in the immigrant synagogue. Conservatism mediates between the demands of the Jewish tradition, the feeling of both alienation and nostalgia toward first and second settlement areas, and the norms of middle-class worship. It must in effect borrow something from each of these elements and synthesize them into a new pattern.

* This section is meant to serve as an introduction to the remainder of the volume. The points suggested here are developed and documented in Chapters IV-VII.

Even if the newly devised ritual could satisfy the norms
of very different cultural systems, there is a limit to the
amount of interest which would be manifested in worship. Protestantism seldom aims at getting most congregants to attend more than one religious service per week.
With secularization proceeding rapidly in the Jewish community, the most that can be hoped for is to match this
schedule. (Secularization also means that the traditional
type of study circle, if it exists at all, is unimportant in
the congregational program.) But the conducting of services, no matter how adroitly designed, would not enable
Conservatism to gain much community support. A *multi-
functional* agency under the congregational form is a type
of compromise absent before, but in the third settlement
this structural adaptation becomes standard. It results in
the creation of powerful synagogues able to deal, at least
in part, with the challenges present in the area.

The most obvious unfilled need is suggested by a fact
which we noted previously: the Talmud Torah was not
extended further than the area of second settlement. Given
the need for some agency to provide for Jewish education
in the third settlement area, this function was taken over
by the congregation—the strongest Jewish institution in
these districts. Since the directors of Conservative schools
were merely agents responsible to the board of the congregation, who were in fact exceedingly vulnerable to
local pressures, the directors were prepared to go much
further in making adjustments in the curriculum than
was true of the more independent Talmud Torahs.

The flexible structure of the Conservative education
has proven to be highly popular. It has provided a Sunday
school curriculum for the children of minimalist parents,
as well as a reduced Talmud Torah program for those

interested in more intensive training. Thus whatever the desires of parents, except if they belong to that small minority which insist on a very thorough Hebrew education, their needs can be met. If the boy attends Hebrew school, he can be taught enough so that he will be competent to perform at the *Bar Mitzvah* rite, the ceremony which symbolizes the attainment of adulthood. He will also be able to follow the prayers during services. Confirmation, a ceremony devised chiefly for girls, serves as the equivalent for those whose education is confined mostly to Sunday school. This combination of patterns has typically not been present either in Reform or in Orthodoxy until recently.

The synagogue school represents more than a convenient way of meeting needs not filled by any other institution in the area. It also helps to provide much reinforcement for the individual congregation. The educational program for the young serves to compensate for the declining interest in worship among the adults. In addition, the parents of the children who are registered in the school represent a group which can be enrolled in the congregation. By entrusting the education of their children to the synagogue, they have acquired an interest in its affairs. Just as the conscientious middle-class parent joins the public school Parent-Teachers Association to help better school conditions, to gain a more thorough understanding of his child, and to participate in the educational process, the same procedure may take place in Jewish education. Parents whose first contact with the institution was made in the effort to provide their offspring with the training needed to orient them to the group rather than for the purpose of serving their own religious needs, can later be involved in a host of synagogue activities. By stressing a child- and youth-centered program, the Conservative synagogue profits from one of the main emphases of American culture.

Serving educational needs represents more than simply teaching the young the language and ideals of their people, or a technique of enlisting their parents. The congregational school is also a means of insuring the continuity of Conservatism in general and of the local congregation in particular. It will be recalled that the founders represent a ghetto-bred generation which experienced rapid embourgeoisment and speedy acculturation. There will *not* be a large-scale replication of these conditions, and thus in the future Conservative synagogues must be peopled, at least in part, by children of the present adherents. To survive, institutional loyalties must be implanted and some type of ideological expression cultivated. Thus the Conservative-bred generation, moving further than present third settlement areas and building homes in the suburbs, presumably would be motivated to establish new congregations there. Although this generation will not be subject to the same cross-pressures (it is doubtful, for example, whether their class position will be any higher than that of their parents), due to indoctrination, Conservatism may seem to them to be the "correct" way to practice their Judaism. Instead of having only *relative* validity and therefore bound to wither when social conditions change, the congregational school may aid Conservatism in assuring its institutional continuity by enlisting adherents who possess an absolute commitment. Under these conditions both layman and professional tends to make his particular synagogue an end in itself and to strongly encourage activities which will be helpful in furthering self-maintenance. The children of congregational members offer a readily available public for this purpose which can be reached without heavy expenditures of time, money, and scarce personnel. Because of status ascription, no class or status problem exists with these adherents.

One additional function is assumed by the congregation to compensate for the declining interest in worship. We noticed previously that although highly acculturated, Jews in the area of third settlement carry on their social life largely in association with other Jews. Requiring the continuity of the ethnic group for its continued existence, the Conservative congregation encourages members to spend much of their leisure time within its precincts. Leaders of the movement have recognized that it is problematic whether in the majority of cases this will lead to greater participation in worship. However, *the synagogue as an institution will be strengthened and ethnic bonds reinforced.* The social program, particularly in those phases which affect young people, is an attempt to fortify the institution by making it a multi-functional agency. But more significantly it represents a response to what is thought of as the threat of assimilation existing in the area of third settlement. The older generation, having moved out of the so-called "Jewish" neighborhoods and having accepted much acculturation, fear that their offspring—lacking their own background—will extend acculturation to the stage of assimilation. They are, therefore, anxious to encourage the participation of young people in the synagogue, for they feel that such activity will help arrest this process. The elders are aware that the maximum number can be attracted by emphasizing sports, entertainments, dances, social clubs, and similar activities.

The Conservative synagogue aims to serve others besides the young. Through the organization of affiliated bodies, it is capable of offering satisfying leisure-time activities in a dignified atmosphere to adults as well. Women are the most enthusiastic participants in this program. We noticed that they were already enrolled in the voluntary associations which existed in the second settlement. But although the second settlement woman does some charity work, she still confines most of her activities to the home. It is in the third settlement that the Jewish woman begins to cultivate "interests" during her leisure. The program for women not only serves to give them a place in the structure of the synagogue, but significantly their participation is possible without any ideological commitment. Given the desire to associate with other Jews, one is accepted into the sisterhood as a fellow-ethnic. Initially at least there is no pressure to join the congregation or to participate in the religious services. Interest in the institution may grow in time, and the woman may draw in her husband and other family members. Although her original objective was social, ultimately she may take her place at worship, particularly if it incorporates features stressed in the leisure-time program.

Social activities in Conservative congregations call for much grading along age, sex, and interest lines. This policy represents a realistic attempt to meet recreational needs. Orthodoxy did little in utilizing this interest for organizational survival; Reform also seems to have been relatively more inhibited than Conservatism. Apparently the status pretentions of Reform served at times to make it fearful that large-scale recreational programs would attract many lower-middle-class individuals into its institutions. Developments along these lines have also been limited somewhat by Reform's lack of stress on ethnic survivalism. As a consequence of the development of a multi-functional agency encompassing worship, social and recreation activities, and youth education, Conservative congregations describe their functions as being three-fold: (1) a *Beth Tefillah* (house of prayer), (2) a *Beth Keneseth* (house of assembly), and (3) a *Beth Midrash* (house of study).

Enlargement and change in function to the point where the synagogue satisfies multiple interests involves a shift in the roles of the professionals. The crux of this modification is a rapid rise in the position of the rabbi. Like his Reform colleague, the Conservative rabbi must play a crucial role during worship, supervise the educational program, and interest himself in the social activities. He must serve as a pastor to his congregants and represent the Jewish community to the non-Jewish world. While other officials such as principals, activity directors, and executive secretaries are found in many of the larger congregations, they are generally subordinate to the rabbi. Although the rabbi may delegate authority, he is the individual who is held responsible by the laymen for the efficient operation of the congregation in all its departments.

The cantor is frequently a member of the permanent congregational staff, but he also ranks below the rabbi. Conservative congregations avoid hiring virtuoso singers, and the very preeminence of the rabbi helps to diminish the importance of the cantor. Much of the modernization of the synagogue has been accomplished at the expense of the traditional institutionalized role of the sexton. Although most Conservative congregations still employ this official, he is no longer a crucial functionary. The rabbi has taken over the management of the important religious services, and congregational business is now handled by office personnel. Since the rabbi's role is so decisive, in order to understand the movement it is not sufficient to analyze the development and patterning of the Conservative synagogue alone. We must also attempt to gain an understanding of how the Conservative rabbi came into being—how it happened that there were men *qualified educationally* to assume these new functions, as well as *prepared psychologically* for their roles.

IV

Religious Worship in the Conservative Setting

SINCE Conservative Judaism is perhaps best known by the character of its religious services, this area will provide us with a convenient starting place for detailed analysis. First to be considered is the *form* of worship. This includes external appearances, the language of prayer, synagogual arrangements, and the manner in which the Deity is addressed. There is next the *program* of worship: the public observance of the traditional holidays, festivals, and prayer services. Special interest centers about whether or not any new—and hence untraditional—occasions for divine convocation have been created. Lastly the *content* of worship, or the ideological framework of the prayers, services, and rituals, must be analyzed. Since the forces working towards stability or revision of the liturgy are of particular significance, they shall be treated at some length.

By separating form and content we mean only to suggest a distinction helpful in the setting up of an analytical framework. Actually there is an inseparable link between the two categories. Content defines form, while changes in form—made without apparent desire to change ideology—may deeply influence content. Form grades imperceptibly into content, content into form. Dividing these two categories does not constitute a denial of the many interrelations and fusings which take place in actual fact. But the distinction is very helpful in making an introductory analysis. Full monographic treatment of the problem, however, would involve stressing interrelationships, fusings, and "unanticipated consequences."

A.

THE FORM OF WORSHIP

It was established previously that Orthodox Jewish forms differ widely from those common in the West, particularly in Protestant countries. In addition to this overall factor, it is notable that behavior during Orthodox worship is not at all in keeping with the particular cultural norms observed by the American *middle class.* Among Jewry, extreme informality in the religious setting and the continuance of "secular" behavior in "sacred" situations originally had no social class referent—such manners were exhibited by members of all classes in Eastern Europe. In the United States, however, with former lower- and lower-middle-class Jews adopting middle-class ways, and with the Jewish upper class no longer adhering to the tradition, the old deportment comes to be thought of as *characteristic* of Orthodoxy as a system. Consequently, the individual is motivated to break with previous patterns not only because of possible theological objections, but by the very fact that his mobility has served to stigmatize much of his previous behavior—including that in the field of religion—as lower-class and hence inappropriate to his new station.

Furthermore, since traditional Jewish worship is *actually* characterized by so many patterns which are, according to American norms, typed as being lower-class, the identification of Orthodoxy and social inferiority has been especially pronounced. While the ends of Jewish worship are approved by the general community inasmuch as they are considered to be identical with the goals of Christian devotion, some of the *means*—or devotional practices—used to attain them do violence to the conventional norms and aesthetic standards observed by middle-class persons. Were the traditional patterns of worship continued, middle-class Jews would be alone among middle-class people generally in practicing rites of a lower-class character. This disparity, then, introduces a strain in the institution and a readjustment becomes necessary. If the synagogue is to retain its middle class, standards during worship must at least approach those in general use. Essentially, new means must be devised or appropriated to enable old ends to be served. The following quotation illustrates the way in which Conservative Jews themselves have conceptualized this problem:

When the Conservative Movement was organized, the Rabbis and the laymen, in order to build a Synagogue which would attract the young American Jew, were confronted with the problems of developing a service, which would be traditional and at the same time modern so that the American Jew would find himself at home.[1]

The form of worship may be studied under three headings: (1) changes in the status of *woman,* (2) introduction of *decorum* at services, and (3) reduction in *"commercialism"* during worship. Our analysis of these factors will highlight the view that the changes introduced by Conservatism constitutes a Western, bourgeois version of Jewish tradition necessitated by rapid upward social mobility and acculturation, and that furthermore the development has aided in the maintenance of some measure of equilibrium in the sub-community.

1. The Status of Woman

Perhaps the single most disruptive force, or "strain," to American Jewish Orthodoxy has been the position of woman. We explained previously that female subordination constitutes an important violation of Western norms. Here we must introduce a related—although analytically separate—consideration: The inferior position of woman is not only alarming when considered strictly normatively, but—viewed from the standpoint of institutional survivalism—it also presents a vital *organizational* threat. This is a consequence of the fact that males do not evince the same degree of religious interest as of old. Were they actively participating in worship and religious study, female subordination might constitute a serious annoyance, but it would hardly threaten institutional integrity. The gradual withdrawal from worship and religious study on the part of the male creates a void which must somehow be filled; women represent the logical group which can bridge the gap. To encourage their participation, the norms of Judaism must be modified. Considered technically, the subordination of woman, inasmuch as it contributes to institutional instability, constitutes a "dysfunctional" element in the traditional system. Even though change will entail a serious violation of the religious code and the overcoming of much resistance, a *status quo* position would mean organizational suicide.[2]

It is highly significant to note that varying with class

and other factors, religion in Western culture is predominantly an activity of *females*. For example, Robert and Helen Lynd found that women tend to take religion more seriously than men. Some 62% of the membership of Middletown's largest church, they discovered, was female.[3] Leiffer has estimated that ". . . the average [Protestant] church has about 50% more women than men in its membership." [4] Fichter suggests that the same situation is found among Catholics: women outnumber men by approximately 7 to 3 in partaking of the spiritual activities of the parish.[5]

Unlike Christianity, Orthodox Judaism has not been able to make much use of the tendency in our culture for religion to maintain itself by appealing to a female public. While second settlement Orthodox synagogues, as we noted, accept some financial assistance proffered by their ladies' auxiliaries, institutional rigidity prevents the utilization of any really large-scale reinforcement. It may well be that by the second settlement the Jewish woman is already more faithful in complying with the requirements of the sacred system than is her spouse.[6] One may observe that, unlike their husbands, some Orthodox women are reciting prayers or reading devotional literature faithfully each day (as females they are not under any religious obligation to do so). Indeed they receive no encouragement—formally or informally—for participating in such spiritual exercises. Their devotions are held in private and if not practiced on what could be described as a secretive basis, certainly the prayers are said in real seclusion. The same rituals are being performed concurrently at the synagogue by a diminishing group of males. It seems safe to say that the inability of Orthodoxy to use this "spiritual reserve" for the strengthening of its institutions, rather than permitting the effect of the activity of women to be dissipated because of highly informal structuring, has helped contribute to its own decline.

Against this background, the importance of the following observation is manifest: The overwhelming majority
of Conservative synagogues seat men and women together.
This is known as "mixed seating," or the family pew system. The adjustment of woman's position is an outstanding feature of the Conservative synagogue as well as the
most commonly accepted yardstick for differentiating Conservatism from Orthodoxy.[7] This change is taken by the
woman as symbolic of her new status, and was regarded
by both sexes at the time of its adoption as a concession
of crucial significance.

We are interested in some of the effects of this shift.
Since the Friday evening service forms the backbone of
the year-round worship program in Conservatism, the sex
distribution at these services can be taken as a measuring
rod.[8] According to the figures submitted by local synagogue officials, women already predominate among the
worshipers. In 39% of Conservative institutions women
now form between 25% and 49% of the congregation on
Friday night, while in 54% of the congregations they constitute from 50% to 74% of those attending.[8a] While it
is admittedly difficult to measure whether or not the revision in woman's status has had real "functional" value—
and if so to what degree—we suggest that it *is* helping in
institutional maintenance. Women in the Conservative
synagogue are taking up the slack produced by the male,
whose decrease in attendance may well represent his acceptance of the general American pattern in the field of
religious behavior.[9] The sex distribution during worship
in Conservative synagogues may soon approach Western
standards. The new norms, responsible as they are for the
destruction of the unity of the Jewish sacred system, have

provided a compensating factor. Jews are beginning to follow a pattern new to their group but implicit in the *American* system: much concern on the part of women for religion—an interest for which they are presumed to have a special affinity.

It is notable that as the Jewish woman reaches a new class level and becomes acculturated, she can turn to religion (or, more exactly, to attendance at public worship and participation in synagogue activities) as a leisure-time interest and as a symbol of newly won status. Under these conditions, the synagogue may serve as the focus for "deflected achievement" on the part of its female public. However, at the same time that this participation is taking place, the woman is neglecting the performance of many of the prescribed rituals (such as certain laws relating to the food taboos, or to Sabbath observance) which are incidental to her activities. Paradoxically, the strength of organized religion is augmented while personal behavior becomes increasingly secularized.

It should not be inferred that women in Conservatism are accorded perfect equality with their spouses. Although the sexes do sit side-by-side during worship and the women take part in all the responses indicated in the liturgy, they are still excluded from certain worship activities. To take the most significant instance, the ritual surrounding the handling and reading of the Torah scrolls is still generally reserved for males. This varies, however, according to the sanctity of the service. During the High Holidays the exclusion of females from the pulpit is almost complete. The procedure is modified at times during the less awesome Sabbath morning service. Women are frequently allowed considerable freedom at Friday evening worship, for the Torah scrolls are not particularly important in this service.

Thoughtful laymen have maintained that these variations indicate an inconsistency in the Conservative approach. For example, a leading Conservative figure in the Midwest stated that:

A generation ago the young architect, the young engineer, the young doctor, the young lawyer, the young business man saw in Conservative Judaism a chance for genuine religious self-expression integrated with the best of thinking in the world at large. We saw the opportunity of giving equality to the women within the framework of our religious life. We gave them seats beside us, and since then, we have spent most of our time wondering about how we ever dared to be guilty of such a deviation. Our congregations still argue about the question of a mixed choir, not to speak of . . . calling a woman to the Torah. In this instance and in so many others, we feel that the past twenty-five years have not brought the fruition . . . to which we looked forward with such eager expectancy.[10]

But there has been no widespread agitation for perfect equality. Conservative women have generally been satisfied with their limited status—a great advance over the age-old segregation. Furthermore, the pattern of formal equality coupled with limited participation follows the model of many Christian denominations where the rites central to worship are also performed largely by males.

2. The Problem of Decorum

We have already discovered that in Orthodoxy, quiet or intense recital of prayers and a "worshipful" attitude are not considered to be the only appropriate modes of religious behavior. In fact should a worshiper consistently adopt what would generally be considered a reverent demeanor, unless he had a well-established reputation for a very special kind of piety and occupied a seat along the Eastern wall of the synagogue (thus placing him close to the ark in which the Torah scrolls are kept), his deportment might well be the subject of intense criticism. Some resemblance to Jewish attitudes may perhaps be found among Catholics. In Italy, for example, great informality has prevailed at times among the congregation in spite of the liturgical service. In a far different setting, there are also some similarities in lower-class American Protestant sects and denominations, although Jewish worship lacks the high fervor and intensity characteristic of the services conducted by such groups. Essentially, however, the *form* of Orthodox worship does seem to be almost unique in its lack of solemnity.

If we study Jewish attitudes in the third settlement, we find that Orthodox worship is increasingly being stigmatized as unspiritual and lacking in proper decorum. This point of view is, of course, a function of the adoption of middle-class American norms of convention and aesthetics. Therefore in addition to modifying the position of women, the Conservative group has stressed a further reform: the presentation of a religious service which is "Jewish" but at the same time in conformity with the outward characteristics of worship—on the level of decorum—as practiced by other groups of a similar class level. The strong feeling about the decorum problem is conveyed by the following excerpt which purports to summarize public reaction to one of the first Conservative services held in Milwaukee: "The synagogue was filled to capacity . . . all commended the dignity . . . that characterized the services and contrasted markedly with the disorder that they had come to associate with traditional forms of worship." [11]

How has decorum been introduced? It will be recalled that in Orthodoxy the important services are led by the cantor. Such functionaries specialize in the elaborate rendition, frequently with the aid of a choir, of selected portions of the liturgy. The cantor has little interest in the behavior of the congregation other than during the time of his solos. Before beginning such prayers, he may pause and wait until order has been restored. If the form of the service is to be revised, it must be conducted by someone who will supply real leadership. The rabbi is the obvious choice to discharge this responsibility; it is his counterpart in the Protestant church who conducts the service. Thus the Conservative spiritual leader has come to be charged with planning the service so that it will proceed without interruption. He must see to it that there are no long pauses conducive to conversation, that the service is sufficiently varied so that boredom does not ensue with the attendant shift of interest away from the pulpit, and that breaches of decorum among congregants are quickly spotted and promptly dealt with.[12] In contrast to his Orthodox colleague, the Conservative rabbi actually *conducts* public worship.

To accomplish his task, the rabbi is assisted by a corps of ushers. They help seat the congregation (this is essential during the High Holidays when pews are reserved), and endeavor to keep the conversation of worshipers to a minimum. Also, the ushers must be on the watch to prevent individuals from moving about, for the Conservative worshiper is expected to remain in his seat at least during the important portions of the service. Visiting by infants and children, a feature of the Orthodox service which tends to create disturbance, is also restricted; children are expected to participate in the special services arranged for their benefit. Visiting in the main sanctuary on the High Holidays is usually confined to an especially arranged intermission.

It is not easy for Orthodox-bred individuals to accept

these new forms of behavior all at once. While in recent years a certain degree of decorum could be assumed, during the 1920's when development of the Conservative pattern was in process, synagogue officials experienced real difficulty as they sought to enforce the new regulations. An official of a leading Cleveland synagogue, for example, stated at the time that:

A great effort is being made to impress upon the congregation the importance of decorum. In many of the conservative Synagogues of America the services are [still] disturbed by constant whispering on the part of the audience. . . . [Our ushers] give to every worshiper upon entering the following card: "Worship without decorum is unworthy of an intelligent congregation. Please refrain from all conversation. . . ." [13]

That officials are still not satisfied may be surmised from a more recent source:

Outweighing all these demands for appropriate appearance [of male worshipers] are, however, the demands for appropriate conduct at the service. . . . demands should be pressed at all seasons of the year and should be hammered home in particular at High Holiday time.[14]

3. "Commercialism" in the Synagogue

The synagogue practices referred to under the heading of "commercialism" include: (a) "Shenodering," a general term referring to the pledging of money for the opportunity of participating in the Torah service. (b) The holding of auctions during holiday and festival services for the purpose of "selling" certain particularly honorific privileges: by stimulating competitive instincts, large amounts may be pledged. (c) The Yom Kippur appeal: fund raising which takes place during *Kol Nidre,* a particularly holy service. Since attendance is at a maximum and the worshiper is presumably in a receptive frame of mind, generous donations may be forthcoming. While these practices are related to decorum inasmuch as an additional diversion is created, they require separate treatment.

In the *shtetl,* and in the areas of first and second settlement, there is little criticism of these practices. They are thought of as efficient devices for the raising of sums vitally needed to provide support for religious needs and communal charities. The distribution of the honors, and the amounts of the donations (announced publicly) become the subject of much interested comment.[15]

It will be recalled that in Judaism there is no sharp division between sacred and secular, and consequently little development of separate norms for each area. This system conflicts with the Christian—and American—one which distinguishes between the sacred and the profane, defines which situations belong to each category, and provides for differential behavior. The "unspiritual" practices of the daily market place are excluded from the sanctuary on Sunday. Most Protestant denominations prefer to employ a relatively inconspicuous technique to raise some of the funds which they require. This is the passing (in silence) of a collection plate preceded by only a minimum, if any, amount of stimulation from the pulpit. While auctions, raffles, bingo games, and similar devices are still used to help finance churches, particularly Catholic ones, these activities are not carried on inside the sanctuary. If held on church property, generally they take place in the community hall or in some adjacent building.

It is not surprising then that as Jews internalize new norms, they tend to view their traditional methods of raising funds with increasing disapproval. Customary techniques are *now* felt to be singularly inappropriate to the religious setting: ". . . there is no charitable expression in

the English language that can connote the desecration of
a Torah honor and the degradation of a House of Worship into a market place of vulgar vanities and rude commercialism." [16] Since the clientele of the Conservative
synagogue is on the whole prosperous, some of the devices
can be dispensed with easily. Membership dues come to
provide an increasingly large proportion of congregational
revenues.[17] Also, except for emergency needs, money for
communal charities is no longer raised during services.
Modification of the system is consequently taking place;
features of the Protestant technique of the silent appeal
are being adapted, although the ordinance which prohib-
its the carrying of money on the Sabbath and holidays
complicates the process. However, individuals who receive
honors are still generally expected to make a special contribution, but they are encouraged to do so in a "spiritual"
manner:

The principle of the "silent appeal" applies equally to the
system of Torah donations. Many congregations have done
away with the desecrating system of "airing" individual charitable impulses during the central part of the service—the
reading of the Torah. They insist on anonymity in giving and
thus cut the props from under all those displays of ill-starred
fund raising campaigns that are dynamiting the very founda-
tions of dignity in the synagogue. All announcements of
pledges are eliminated. . . . Everyone however who is called
to the Torah is handed an envelope which serves as a reminder
and a convenient means of forwarding his donation. . . .[18]

Those congregations which have dispensed, in part or
in toto, with the traditional method of raising funds are
proud that their actions are now consistent with American
norms: "We, in Congregation Rodfei Zedek, have set
an example to Chicago Jewry, of the possibility of elim-
inating from our services direct appeals for funds, and
embarrassing solicitations." [19] That the problem is still

considered to be a vexing one can be gathered from the
pointed remarks made by a lay synagogue official:

Conservative Judaism maintains dignity in Judaism. . . . After
all, why did we drift away from the so-called Orthodox point
of view? Because we recognize that . . . [it] is obsolete in
America. . . . We want to create a service that should be appli-
cable to our children and to the future generations. . . .
It is a very spiritual elevation when a man goes up to the
Torah and he doesn't have to be bothered [with auctions and
donations]. He should pay for it, he should pay for it even
more . . . [but a congregation] should not depend upon the
individual whims of the person who comes up to the Torah.
. . . a synagogue stands for dignity in Jewish life and let's
uphold that dignity. . . . As far as "shenodering" is concerned,
if it could be eliminated that stands for dignity. I was sorry to
hear [at this convention] also that in some congregations they
[still] have appeals on Kol Nidre night. Now, mind you, Kol
Nidre night, the most holy night in the year, all of a sudden
the rabbi gets up and makes an appeal . . . and immediately
[the Jew] feels, where is he? Is he in a theatre? Or is he in a
meeting place where the speaker is asking for an appeal for
some organization? [20]

Ostensibly most officials of Conservative congregations
share this sentiment. When polled on the question: "Are
you in favor of fund-raising during services?" only 29%
answered in the affirmative.[21] However, the system is too
useful to be dispensed with in its entirety. Most congregations still employ *Kol Nidre* appeals. Apparently this
occasion is a propitious one for fund-raising. Thus the
choice between proper normative observance and ever-
present institutional needs is frequently resolved in favor
of the latter, and institutional maintenance acts as a vested
interest blocking social change. It is regretted that the
rabbi's sermon must in fact be an appeal for funds, but
institutions whose overhead is large or who have pressing

needs for expansion see no other way of meeting their requirements:

Raising funds or standards on the High Holidays—that is the question. It is a dilemma that has plagued many congregational leaders who have awakened to the shame of commercialization of the holiest of divine services and who have to cope with the despairing problem of securing the ways and means for the upkeep of the congregation for the entire year. What a heart-breaking alternative! [22]

Congregations experiment with techniques which allow for retention of the system, but at the same time reduce somewhat the degree of normative violation:

. . . many synagogues, and especially large synagogue centers, [cannot] dispense with the Kol Nidre night appeals and . . . the sale of seats for the High Holidays in the immediate future. The problem confronting many synagogues is how to *spiritualize* and how to remove the obnoxious elements from the Kol Nidre appeal. . . . This is the Season of the year . . . when the Jew is imbued with the spirit of giving in order to maintain his house of worship. . . .[23]

It is worthwhile speculating that there are emotional factors present which block change in spite of the conscious will. The giving of charity, and particuarly *its influence in assuring the individual's continued good fortune,* is a prominent motif in the cultural system of the East European Jew.[23a] Certain deep-seated attitudes, we know, tend to continue in spite of considerable acculturation. Thus it may be that the worshiper is still eager (although, wishing to conform with the norms, he professes quite the opposite) to make a public demonstration on the holiest day of the year of his eagerness to render a material gift to his Lord. Although "commercialism" may be distasteful, it may be even more of a personal threat were he to be deprived of the opportunity of making an offer-

ing. By restricting his donations throughout the year, the
worshiper may *force* the scheduling of an appeal on *Kol
Nidre* night.

B.

THE PROGRAM OF WORSHIP

1. Traditional Services

In addition to form, the *program* of worship in the Conservative synagogue possesses some distinctive features in
comparison with Orthodoxy. All Conservative synagogues
conduct High Holiday services; their halls are filled to
capacity much like the Orthodox congregations in the
second settlement. While no special devices need to be
employed in order to fill the seats, it is significant that
not all of those who use synagogue facilities actually attend: it was found that only 74% of the fathers of children registered in the religious school conducted by a
Conservative synagogue in New York City participate in
public worship during the High Holidays.[24] But it is generally believed that the High Holidays have retained their
hold, and this is true in the sense that those who have
some measure of religious interest do attend the services.
The low ratio existing between the total number of seats
in synagogues and temples and the total Jewish population
results in the crowding of all available facilities.

With the exception of the High Holidays, however,
interest in the traditional program of services has declined.
Conditions vary according to the size and location of the
individual congregation, but on the whole the satisfaction felt about High Holiday attendance is missing when
the other services are considered. Frequently, it is *not* that
the year-round program of traditional services must be
cancelled because of lack of attendance. Rather, it is that

these services seem to appeal to a small group of comparatively uninfluential or peripheral individuals who represent only one age-grade in the congregation.

Conservative synagogues have not taken a complacent attitude toward this situation. In order to improve attendance, well-designed publicity is customarily sent out to members in advance of the services, and the worship program may be advertised in the public press.[25] Telephone squads are sometimes organized to call each home on the congregational roster and invite attendance. Also, the rabbi attempts to improve matters. He may see to it that duties usually handled by one person are divided among many, or that new activities are created in connection with the service—all on the theory that "use them or lose them." As an added feature, refreshments will be served. In many congregations guest rabbis and lecturers are invited to occupy the pulpit in the hope that a new face and a prominent reputation may attract additional worshipers.

Attendance at the traditional services is rarely increased by the employment of such promotional devices. The fact that at some of the services significant religious rites are performed helps to explain why the traditional worship program has been preserved. Such ceremonies, rather than the services themselves, apparently provide the motivation for the attendance of the majority. The *Bar Mitzvah* and Confirmation rituals serve to attract many relatives and family friends of the candidates; the *Yizkor* and the *Kaddish* prayers, said in memory of the dead, also draw worshipers.

To study these processes, we may start with the three daily services: the morning, afternoon, and evening prayers. According to information supplied by local officials in reply to the question "Do you have a daily service [in your congregation]?" only about half of the institutions still hold these services (see Table 1).†

Table 1

PERCENTAGE OF CONGREGATIONS
CONDUCTING DAILY SERVICES *

	MORNING SERVICE %	EVENING SERVICE ** %
Yes	54	45
No	46	54
No Answer	0	1
Total	100	100
Number of congregations	(200)	

* Source: United Synagogue, *Survey*, I, p. 3.
** "Evening" includes also the afternoon service since the two are recited as a single unit, or with only a short intermission between them.

It is acknowledged that when attendance is well above the required minimum, many of the worshipers have come only for the purpose of reciting the *Kaddish* prayer.[26] The regular attendants are a group of elders who were reared in the Orthodox atmosphere of the *shtetl*, and in the area of first settlement. Frequently these men were less pious before their retirement. Many of them—returning to the patterns of their youth—find the daily services to be an important means of reducing the "abyss of leisure" which they confront. Some might be worshiping in Orthodox synagogues but for the fact that they are living with, or near, their children who are active in the congregation.

Although most synagogues still conduct Sabbath serv-

---

† The holding of a daily service is still typical of the very large congregation but some of the medium-sized institutions have already been forced to discontinue it. The distribution by congregational size of the 200 institutions replying to the *Survey* was as follows:

Congregations with a membership of 100 families or less:	18%
" " " " " 101-200 " " "	25%
" " " " " 201-500 " " "	37%
" " " " " more than 500 families:	20%

ices on Saturday morning, attendance is small: 57% of
the institutions report less than 50 regular worshipers,
and 70% less than 100.[27] However, the *Bar Mitzvah* ceremony works toward the perpetuation of this service. In
very large congregations one or more candidates may be
available on each Sabbath, and attendance may therefore
reach impressive proportions. But like the daily service,
the hard core of Saturday worshipers consists of "old-
timers." Some congregations seek to improve conditions
by stimulating the participation of children or young people. It is thought that they may also help to bring their
parents back to the synagogue on Saturday morning. However, judging from the reaction to proposed reforms aimed
at increasing the number of regular worshipers, most
congregants remain apathetic.[28]

Attendance during festivals is also small. *Yizkor* on all
of the festivals, and Confirmation on *Shavuoth,* the late
spring holiday, do serve as reinforcement but ". . . in the
majority of cases the general 'Holiday consciousness' is on
the wane and is only feebly kept up by the memorial services provided by the Holiday calendar." [29] Furthermore:

. . . organized worship is breaking down; daily services have
practically disappeared in almost half of our congregations. . . .
Saturday morning services have mostly become a perfunctory
affair; Holiday Services on Passover, Sukkoth, and Shavuoth,
in terms of attendance, are negligible.[30]

Officials feel that steps must be taken to arrest this decline:

The task then is clear: a new approach must be sought and
new techniques must be developed . . . to give [*Shavuoth*]
status in the appreciation of the rank and file, and to "sell"
its values to our men, women, and children.[31]

To summarize, while the High Holidays have retained
their appeal, the remainder of the traditional program of

services does not fare well in the Conservative setting. This occurs despite the fact that the services may be publicized, that some have the advantage of being conducted in Westernized form, and that they are being reinforced by the celebration of various *rites de passage*. Judging from the age-levels of the worshipers, it appears that—barring the emergence of a religious revival of a certain type—decay will continue as surviving members of the old ghetto-bred generation diminish in number. This prediction would seem to hold true for the daily services in particular. Perhaps the women will come to play a more significant role at the festival and Sabbath services and thus help to keep them intact.

2. *Friday Night Services*

While Conservative-minded individuals apparently are not very frequent participants in the traditional program of worship except at High Holiday time, they do retain the value of "Jewishness." From a sociological perspective, it can be said that they still require some form of collective behavior which will serve as a focus for common strivings and help periodically to renew group loyalties. This can be accomplished by participation in ceremonies symbolizing common sentiments. Such participation must be based on the regnant attitudes of the community. For example, the type of Sabbath observance prescribed in the sacred system is noticeably absent in the area of third settlement. What *has* remained among a certain group is a feeling of nostalgia for the Sabbath of old and a rather vague desire to indulge in some form of behavior which will be expressive of the Sabbath spirit.

Thus a new service has come to be introduced. Saturday morning worship is being supplemented—and in many congregations has already been supplanted—by a service held on *Friday night.* Friday evening worship permits the individual to engage in prohibited activities on Saturday and yet at the same time participate in some type of Sabbath observance. Friday night worshipers need not feel very guilty about absenting themselves from the traditional Sabbath service. Furthermore, the new Friday night service is free of the rigor and legalistic approach to observance characteristic of Orthodoxy. It represents an accommodation to the new norms assimilated by the Conservative group.

We recall that in the second settlement a few members of the Orthodox group did attempt to institute some form of activity on Friday night which would compensate for diminished attendance on Saturday morning.* A lecture series devoted chiefly to Jewish topics was established, and congregational singing of Sabbath melodies, Jewish folk songs, and Zionist tunes was included in the program. Significantly, the rabbi did not participate. Prayer and worship activities were avoided either because this was felt to be too radical an innovation or as a move calculated to keep opposition to a minimum. While this program frequently became involved as an issue in the struggle for power within the synagogue, it was hard to attack it as being anti-Orthodox. It was, rather, *un*-Orthodox in form and content. Even the strongest proponents of the idea looked upon it as being only a supplement to the traditional program of religious services.

In contrast, the Friday night program in the Conservative synagogue is conducted in the form of a full worship service. It has largely replaced all other services in importance except those conducted on the High Holidays.[32] The trend toward Friday night is unmistakable, although it varies with the size of the congregation (see Table 2).

---

* See *infra,* p. 59.

In reply to the question "When does the main Sabbath service take place in your synagogue?" the answers of officials of medium-sized congregations (201-500 families) were distributed as follows: 57% replied "Friday evening," 14% "Saturday morning," and 27% considered both equally important. Smaller-sized congregations voted overwhelmingly for Friday night in contrast to the larger-sized institutions where the trend is toward considering both services equally important.

Table 2

TIME OF THE MAIN SABBATH SERVICE BY SIZE
OF CONGREGATION *

Congregations of

TIME OF SERVICE	100 FAMILIES OR LESS	101-200	201-500	OVER 500	SIZE NOT INDICATED
	%	%	%	%	%
Friday evening	84	69	57	36	51
Saturday morning	3	8	14	13	12
Both equally important	12	23	27	50	30
No answer	1	—	2	1	7
Total	100	100	100	100	100
Number of congregations (200)					

* Source: United Synagogue, *Survey*, I, p. 8.

Part of the reason for the popularity of Friday night is traceable to the fact that the time at which it is held is a convenient one for many potential worshipers. But the special characteristics of the Friday evening service are also important factors. First, it is notable that inactivity on the part of the worshiper is a dominant characteristic of this service. As we have pointed out, the congregation in the traditional type of Jewish worship is a very *activist* body. Furthermore, a detailed knowledge of the liturgy, as well as the ability to read Hebrew fluently, is essential for participation. The Friday night Conservative service, however, demands much less from the worshiper. He is only required to join in some responsive readings and in various other types of prayers, and to sing familiar hymns. Merely a minimum familiarity with the Hebrew language and liturgy is needed. This service, then, represents an adjustment to the declining knowledge of the prayer book and the language in which it is written. As with most middle-class worship, the action on the pulpit is central. In conformity with over-all trends in our culture, the individual is no longer an active participant, but is cast in the role of a spectator.[33]

The second central feature, one which fits in well with the general tenor of passivity, is that a sermon or address is almost invariably a part of these services. Furthermore it is a very *important* feature, for when asked about the "drawing-power" of the sermon, only 12% of the laity stated that it plays no role in influencing their attendance.[33a] Since sermon topics are widely advertised and are designed with an eye to attracting worshipers, the subject of these discourses is of special interest. (See Table 3.)

Table 3

SERMON TOPIC PREFERENCES *

SUBJECT	PREFERRED BY %
General problems of Jewry	76
Biblical interpretations	52
Religious observance	52
Ethical problems	44
Israel and Zionism	42
Political and social affairs	42
Psychological problems	29
Reviews of books and plays	20
Miscellaneous	3
No answer	2

Number of respondents (1145)

* Source: United Synagogue, *Survey*, I, p. 24.

It is highly significant that the favorite choice of congregants is for "Jewish problems": sermons on the situation of Jewry considered largely from the viewpoint of their ethnic-group status. As for sermons strictly in the field of religion, discourses about the Jewish sacred system—with the stress on what laws and rites retain significance in the modern world—are popular. It is notable that the preference is for discussions of the problem of *religious observance* rather than theological doctrine. Developments in Israel and general social issues are also of some interest. But the fact of greatest significance is that "ethical problems" (the subject of many church discourses) is fourth on the list—congregants do not regard it as constituting *the* central focus for attention. Those who judge the Friday evening service by the standards of non-ethnic religious groups are disappointed that ". . . a three-quarter majority desires to make the pulpit a forum for airing the general problems of the Jewish people . . ." [34] However, the preferences of the laity provide some confirmation of our hypothesis that the Conservative synagogue is in part a result of the desire of American Jews to continue with their ethnic group existence but to do so under the legitimation of religion.

Turning to other features, we find that the music at the Friday evening service is largely traditional in character. Although performed in conformity with the new aesthetic norms, the fundamental modes have remained relatively unchanged. This is so because only traditional harmonies and melodies succeed in arousing the religious sentiments of the worshiper. Those whose early experience was with Orthodoxy find that: "There is something about Hebrew music that just tugs at your heart strings whether you can interpret the Hebrew or not." [35] The popularity of the traditional music has led to the employ-

ment of cantors whenever possible: 53% of the congregations engage this type of functionary for their Friday evening services and more would do so if their budgets permitted.[36] The attitude of congregants has hampered the
growth of a further adaptation: the use of an organ. Only
24% of Conservative institutions employ the instrument
on Friday night, and consequently the organ is still typical only of Reform temples.[37]

The Friday night service is essentially a repetition of
the *Kabbalath Shabbath* prayers recited in the synagogue
at sundown before the Sabbath meal. For some years
congregations had used adaptations published privately
by various rabbis, but an official Conservative prayer book
for Friday night was issued in 1946.[38] The English translations of the Hebrew prayers is placed on facing pages
and the volume is arranged so that it is possible to shift
from one language to the other with ease. The printed
text is so organized as to lend itself to the presentation of
an orderly service under rabbinical leadership. Furthermore, the service is comparatively short. In 82% of the
congregations it runs between one and one-and-a-half
hours.[39] This includes the time devoted to the sermon.

There is one other feature of Friday evening worship
which is of crucial significance: after the service is concluded, a "social hour" is usually held.[40] Refreshments
are served and socializing may continue for quite some
time. Although attempts have been made to incorporate
a formal program (such as a discussion on topics of current interest) into the social hour, in most institutions
worshipers take a negative attitude toward such efforts.
They feel that there has already been enough content of
a serious nature by virtue of the rabbi's sermon.

Worship is thus not the only method of cementing
group loyalties at the Friday evening service. The con-

cluding portion of the proceedings is essentially organized along the lines of a voluntary association. The individual can meet his friends in pleasant surroundings, share with them in the partaking of food, and discuss family, clique, and group concerns. All of this takes place under the legitimation of religion. Synagogue leaders have recognized that both the worship and the *social* aspects contribute essential features to the Friday evening service:

The overwhelming majority of our congregations hold a late Friday night service. Moreover, it has developed, through the social hour usually following the service, into a most important instrument for the social intercourse of the congregational membership. By virtue of this dual function, it [the Friday night service] has become a yardstick for the effectiveness of a congregation and for its rabbinic or lay leadership.[41]

Another factor requires analysis before the character and function of the service can be fully understood. It will be recalled that the Orthodox synagogues of the second settlement were relatively isolated from the many Jewish activities which took place in the neighborhood. Of course there is a danger in comparing these results, obtained in the study of one community, with those derived from a nation-wide poll. Nevertheless, it seems safe to say that by way of contrast with Orthodoxy, the *Conservative* movement tends to recognize that Jews have elaborated a rich associational life outside of the synagogue, and that it is in the interests of institutional survival to deal with this development realistically. The largest and most popular congregations may be able to disregard the extra-synagogual affiliations of their members, but the majority of Conservative institutions must follow a different policy.[42] Periodically, they hold "special Sabbaths" at which they honor one or another of the popular Jewish organizations. The service becomes an added feature of the program of the organization, and the association consequently receives additional publicity and recognition. The synagogue in turn benefits by increased attendance and improved public relations. It has demonstrated that it is capable of integrating itself into the structure of the sub-community and that it welcomes all Jews, whether affiliated or unaffiliated. Understandably, those who believe that the synagogue is pre-eminent in Jewish life feel negative about this technique. They tend to look askance at the congregation's lack of independence and they minimize the benefits which can accrue as a result of this compromise:

A stand on basic principles will have to be taken. . . . These special Sabbaths, dedicated to various secular organizations are in some congregations crowding out the Sabbath altogether. . . .

These special Sabbaths may produce the deceptive up-lift of having a tinsel audience for some Friday nights, but in the last analysis they degrade the services. . . . The attendance value of these special efforts in minimal. The special public puts in a special appearance once a year and lets it go at that. But beyond these "practical" considerations is one principal point of compelling importance: the dignity of the pulpit must not be violated by a propounding of any organization's philosophy. . . . The pulpit is the place for the word of God. . . . If such Sabbaths are considered indispensable . . . then the time for proclaiming the philosophy and achievements of the organization is the Social Hour and the place is the Social Hall of the congregation.[43]

C.

THE CONTENT OF WORSHIP

1. Introduction: The Emphasis on Form

As we have seen, Conservatism has made decided changes in the form and program of worship. Now we must turn to a consideration of the relationship between program, form, and *content*. Preparatory to this, however, some special analysis of the *actual* changes in form is necessary. Because some services have changed more than others, we require a number of further details before the content problem can be clarified in all its ramifications.

The maximum amount of change should take place at those services which are not heavily weighted with tradition. But this general principle needs supplementation. The fact is that at those services in the Conservative synagogue to which few *Conservative* Jews come, little if any change has taken place from the mode prevailing in the Orthodox synagogue. This is the situation in respect to daily worship, and even the Saturday morning service remains largely traditional in form.[44] Many feel that these services are merely vestigial survivals from Orthodoxy. In the larger congregations the daily services are generally the responsibility of the sexton rather than the rabbi. In fact, many Conservative rabbis do not attend regularly for they also share the viewpoint of their congregants that daily worship is appropriate chiefly for mourners and "old-timers"—that the demands of modern living makes the schedule of three daily services obsolete. While in a number of places efforts have been made to increase attendance by making these services more Conservative, such reforms may prove to be dangerous. They can alienate the age-grade which now worships without attracting another group in its place. In summary, many congregations are able to carry on the full program of traditional religious services by the device of varying the form of their worship between Orthodoxy and Conservatism. Such flexibility has made Conservatism capable of satisfying disparate groups. Although some have objected by saying that "There is no logical explanation for having one Conservative Service one day and an Orthodox Service on the next," [45] on the whole the arrangement has been well received.

The most highly adapted services, fully Conservative in form, are those held on Friday night and at High Holiday time.* Notwithstanding changes in form, the *content* of these services remains highly traditional. *Thus, even where the shift in form has been a radical one, there has frequently been no important change in content.* This requires explanation. First, however, we must provide some further documentation proving that a disparity between form and content actually exists. For example, in speaking about the changes introduced by his movement, the spiritual leader of a large Eastern congregation mentions only changes in the area of form. He suggests no comparable changes in content:

Through a judicious choice of prayers; through responses both in Hebrew and in the vernacular; through congregational singing . . . through group participation at every level; through the introduction of readings, comments, explanations; through the shortened reading of the Torah [on the Sabbath], the triennial cycle, giving greater opportunity to interpret and less opportunity for the wandering of interest . . . we have done much to make the Sabbath, Festival, and High Holiday services exhilarating.[46]

Unlike rabbis, Conservative laymen seldom attempt to analyze their movement in print. For an expression of their opinion on this problem, we must rely chiefly on unpublished materials. The personal document quoted below was written by a successful professional man who had the usual Orthodox upbringing. Upon moving from a second

* The form of the festival services appears to be intermediate between the Friday night and High Holiday services, and the daily and Sabbath morning services.

to third settlement area, he joined a Conservative congregation. In this extract, he communicates something of the effects which the radical shifts in form had upon him. Significantly, he too fails to note any changes in content:

The biggest shock of all to me was the temple services on New Years and Yom Kippur. . . . I was born and bred in an orthodox shul with the accompanying multitudinous prayers, jams of people and children all joined together in a cacophonous symphony of loud and sometimes raucous appeals to the Almighty. Here it was so different. A large group of Jews, men and women, sitting quietly together for hours at a stretch, subdued prayers, no mass movements, no rustling and bustling, no weeping and wailing, no crying children, just the music of the choir and cantor being the only loud sounds heard. Truly it was a revelation to me. I looked around the congregation and saw a large number of younger people sitting intently and reverently reading their *Machzors* [holiday prayer books]. They supplied you with a talis and yarmelke [skull cap] at the door. No carrying packages. The *Machzor* was clear, concise and arranged in order so as to be easily followed when the rabbi announced the page numbers. I soon immersed myself in the prayers and responsive readings. I listened to the sermons and understood what it was all about. . . . After the services I sat for a few minutes and pondered. What was the score? Which of the sects in Judaism is getting to the ear of Heaven first?
    It is so different for me. Like another world. Religiosity in the sense that I have been accustomed to is strangely absent. It will take me quite a time to accustom myself to things. . . . It's a bit confusing but very pleasant.

During the earlier days of the movement, when Conservative individuals were still quite sensitive to Orthodox opinion, congregational spokesmen also made explicit the fact that while they had changed the form and program of worship, they had retained much of the traditional content. One local spokesman stated that:

The form of religious service in . . . [our] synagogue is conservative or modern orthodox, with sermons in English and responsive reading in English, hymns and prayers by cantor, choir and congregation both in Hebrew and English. *The traditional prayer book is used and the traditional ritual has been retained in all its essentials.* The family pew system has been adopted, and a social hour follows every Friday night service with a different member or organization in the center serving as hosts.[47]

2. *Forces Blocking Adaptations in Content*

What factors are responsible for the gap existing between the modernized procedures and the traditional prayers? The pervasiveness of the form-content dichotomy in Conservatism is apparently related to (1) the characteristics of the period during which the movement emerged, (2) the role played by its rabbinical leadership, and (3) the kind of public which Conservatism has attracted. Starting with the first of these factors, for comparative purposes it is worthwhile to study the forces behind the pioneer revision of the Jewish liturgy—the one made by the Reform group in Germany. The aim of this movement was to harmonize the content of the prayer book with the *Zeitgeist*. But below the surface another motivation was present: the desire of Jews to qualify for political rights and increased economic opportunity. It was feared that themes found in the liturgy might be used as arguments to block emancipation and integration.[48]

In contrast with Reform, the growth of Conservatism took place *after* Jewish political emancipation had been granted. Thus there were no practical considerations dictating radical changes in content, such as the deletion of references to Zion out of fear of being charged with dual loyalties. The need to effect ideological readjustment could not come from the "outside"—a potent source for change among minority groups generally. Thus the fact that Conservatism developed when Jewish emancipation was already a historical fact has had a profound effect in helping to insure the survival of traditional content.

If historical circumstance did not serve to generate pressures leading to change, it is conceivable that the impetus could have come from the rabbis. Constituting themselves into a bloc, perhaps *they* could have introduced revisions in content. While some students have overestimated the role of bureaucracies and pressure groups, such centers of influence and autonomy have at times been a strong factor in the decision-making process. In Conservatism, however, the influence of paid officials and of functionaries (the rabbis of local synagogues) on high policy has been minimal. Good reasons exist which account for their ineffectualness. Historically, Conservatism has been a movement led by *laymen* rather than by rabbis. In many of the synagogues built in the areas of third settlement, major changes were instituted by the laity themselves. This was done either with the consent of the rabbis, or as frequently happened since many of these congregations were new institutions, functionaries were engaged *after* the innovations had been conceived of, if not implemented.[49] Only those rabbis were considered who were known as approving of the reforms. Conservatism was not the type of movement established by a cohesive leadership group revolting against the *status quo;* the spiritual leaders, like the laity, were merely "disaffected" from Orthodoxy.

One additional consideration—the existence of extreme *congregationalism* among Jewry *—helps explain why rabbinical influence has been so small. This form of church

---

* See *infra,* pp. 40-42.

polity involves the maximization of lay control. With the exception of highly sectarian groups, the existence of a decentralized religious organization tends to lead to pliancy on the part of functionaries. On the other hand, centralized administration gives rise to bureaucracies. Since they become centers of autonomy, such bureaucracies are in a position to protect the structure against the pressure of the laity. Not only can the professionals lay claim to the keys to salvation under such conditions, but they may hold legal title to all church property. It is true, of course, that even in a decentralized religious organization some functionaries may develop into leaders of consequence. But their influence seems generally to be limited to a single congregation, or at best one community. Furthermore, their conceptions hardly survive their own lifetime. Decentralization, then, places crippling limitations on the possibilities of propagation and continuity of ideas on the part of functionaries.

The Conservative spiritual leader grasped that the main desire of his membership was for a modification of Orthodox forms so that Judaism would be adapted to new surroundings. Accordingly, most functionaries have limited themselves to the instituting of decorous services. Their personal predilections, whatever they may be, have seldom been reflected in the content of congregational worship. Frequently, congregants are unaware of the ideas of their spiritual leaders outside the area of form. Thus a member of a Minneapolis Conservative congregation, interviewed in connection with a study of his local community, stated that the rabbi *had* assisted in modifying forms but he did not mention any leadership outside this area:

I belong to the Conservative synagogue. Years ago all the men wore their own hats. There was no such thing as uniformity. I remember that I objected when the rabbi urged us to check our hats and wear skull caps. . . . Today I look back and wonder how I could possibly have objected.

There used to be a lot of talking while the services were being conducted. Today it's really quiet and orderly. People used to get up and walk out at any time but the rabbi made them stop that, and it's really so much better now. We have ushers and they watch you pretty carefully so there is no disturbance of any kind.[50]

We have been assuming that the ideology of the rabbis is strongly liberal, and that they are handicapped in effecting changes by virtue of the structure of the Jewish community. However, it should be pointed out that one portion of the Conservative rabbinate may be said to be apathetic to changes in content. These functionaries would not make any major revisions even if they had the power to do so. Another group—probably the majority, as we will see in Chapters VI and VII—desire changes and would institute them if the religious structure were constituted differently. Finally, there has been a small group of functionaries whose ideas have not only varied from their congregants', but who have gone so far as to attempt to implement their policies. Since the congregations have been traditional, these men—as opponents of the *status quo*—have sought to move their people leftward. Grouping themselves around Mordecai M. Kaplan, for many years a professor at the Jewish Theological Seminary of America and the founder of the "Reconstructionist Movement," * rabbis of this school of thought have generally met with stiff resistance. Kaplan himself has been no exception. At the Society for the Advancement of Judaism, a synagogue in New York City which he was instrumental

* See Chap. VII.

in establishing, this leader frequently attempted to institute changes in content as well as in form. While some ideas won acceptance, even his own congregation has demurred at times. To take a significant illustration, Kaplan felt at one point that the text of the famed *Kol Nidre* prayer recited on Yom Kippur had ". . . long ago lost all relevancy." [51] Accordingly, he kept the form of the prayer by retaining its familiar melody, but shifted the *content* by inserting one of the Psalms in place of the traditional words. He stated that: "We hope that the time will come when our members will demand a renovation of all liturgical texts whose meaning and relevancy have become obsolete." [52] This change apparently met with determined opposition, for when Kaplan's group later published a High Holiday prayer book, the traditional text was restored with only minor changes.[53]

It is significant to note the degree to which prayer books which incorporate radical changes in content have been accepted. Only six congregations have adopted the volumes published by the Reconstructionists for use on the High Holidays, and their *Sabbath Prayer Book* [54] is used by only five institutions.[55] For the High Holidays, most congregations still prefer an edition of the traditional text such as the "Adler Machzor," or an adaptation published by Morris Silverman.[56] Rabbi Silverman experimented widely in the field of Jewish liturgy and his volumes seem well adapted to the needs of the Conservative group: the prayers are arranged in such a way that they lend themselves to the holding of a decorous service while changes in content are kept to a minimum.

This leads us to a consideration of the position of the laity. We have mentioned that they are generally apathetic, or even opposed, to shifts in content. It is not difficult to trace the factors which help account for their attitude. Since Conservatism is a response to the process of embourgeoisement, it is the change to the *style of life* and worship characteristic of the new peer group which has been the chief concern. This holds true because ideologies and philosophical orientations change more slowly than less basic matters such as manners, dress, and aesthetic sensibilities. One Conservative rabbi who saw the emergence of the movement in a Midwestern community in the 1910's, himself noted somewhat caustically at the time that:

> The Orthodox element consists largely of immigrants in the process of establishing themselves economically in the new land of their adoption. To the Conservative class belong those who have acquired either through systematic education or through social or business intercourse, sufficient culture to disgust them with the conduct of the immigrant classes. . . . Their breaking away from the older elements is *not* due so much to a desire to improve the content of Jewish life as it is to establish organizations that should be similar in form to those of their wealthier fellow Jews or their Gentile friends.[57]

Perhaps shifts in content will occur in the future, but the movement is still so young that the interests of its recently-mobile adherents seems as yet chiefly limited to matters of form.

Implied above is the absence among the laity of many "intellectuals." Were such people attracted to the Conservative movement, it is possible that *they* would have opened the area of content to critical scrutiny.[58] While it is true as a rule that intellectuals have generally taken little part in religious affairs, this has not always been the case. The early German reform movement, for example, attracted a number of such individuals. For our purposes it is not necessary to set up criteria unambiguously differentiating "intellectuals" from "non-intellectuals," for the occupational distribution of the officers and board members of the congregations offers sufficient clues to the actual situation. In one study it was found that fully 55% of the leaders are business owners, executives, or managers. (See Table 4.) Doctors, lawyers, dentists, accountants, and some engineers together with a few social workers account for almost all of the 30% who are professionals. Academic

Table 4

OCCUPATIONS OF CONGREGATIONAL OFFICERS
AND BOARD MEMBERS *

	PERCENT	
Owners or Top Executives of Big Business	4	
Owners or Top Executives of Medium Business	22	
Owners or Top Executives of Small Business	24	55
Other Business Officers or Managers	5	
Professionals	30	
White-collar Workers	4	
Blue-collar Workers	1	
Retired	1	
Other	3	
No Answer	6	
Total	100	
Number of Respondents (1787)		

* Source: United Synagogue, *National Survey on Synagogue Leadership*, p. 5.

people, writers, researchers, and other types of intellectuals have generally been poorly represented in the movement even though many such people now send their children to a synagogue because of their desire to provide them with a Jewish education.

Although some rabbis (in the past mainly those from the Reconstructionist group) have stated that steps should be taken to correct the situation, many functionaries ignore the problem aware as they are that the movement has been able to prosper without the support of the intel-

lectual. The fact that many Jewish intellectuals preferred
to participate in radical movements rather than in synagogue affairs has served to produce some strong reactions,
among them the following one on the part of a leading
figure in the Conservative rabbinate:

One of the things that has irritated me from the time I was a
youngster . . . was to be told that the intellectuals are not
part of Jewish life. I remember when I was sixteen or seventeen if anybody wanted to hurt my dignity all he had to say is
that the smart boys are part of the Communist Party or So-
cialists. . . . Now, the intellectuals are not part of any kind
of life. They are individualists. Let us not insult ourselves by
saying that the intellectuals are not part of any religious movement in Jewish life.[59]

In summary, little demand for change in content has
come from the middle-class Jew who fashioned the Conservative synagogue long after Jewish emancipation had
been won. The Conservative movement has been led by
successful business and professional men whose efforts have
been devoted to "practical" matters; and intellectual fer-
ment has been missing from the Conservative synagogue.
Furthermore, the decentralized character of Jewish life
has served to limit the influence of the functionaries. Most
rabbis have confined themselves to the application of
changes in the form and program of worship calculated to
harmonize synagogue modes with newly-achieved status.

3. The Content Issue Reconsidered

While it is true that severe limitations have been imposed upon the professionals, that the laity have been
apathetic, and that the influence of intellectuals has been
absent, these factors do not constitute a complete explanation of our problem. First, the existence of the lag between
changed forms and traditional content is not fully appar-

ent to many lay people—because of certain peculiar conditions the gap is in fact frequently obscured. Second,
while revision is rare, additions to the liturgy have been
made. These additions are modern in emphasis, and are
not always consistent with tradition. Lastly, some changes
designed to modernize the old content itself have actually
been effected. Even though small in number, they are still
of some significance.

Students of Jewish theology are familiar with the fact
that the traditional liturgy includes many petitions calling for the rebuilding of the Temple in Jerusalem and for
the restoration there of the sacrificial cult, that it affirms
that Jews are God's chosen people and stresses that the
Torah has been supernaturally revealed. Some prayers are
intended to hurry the arrival of the Messiah who will be
of the Davidic line, and still other petitions call for a related event to take place: the resurrection of the dead.
Many of the prayers are also strongly ethnocentrically
oriented. Finally, while the Almighty is a merciful God
who is slow to anger and abundant in lovingkindness, the
Supreme Being is also a jealous and wrathful God who
exacts obedience from his children.

No study of the theological opinions of Conservative
Jewry has ever been made, but it is safe to say that relatively few present-day congregants share *all* of these orientations and ideas. While feelings of ethnocentrism tend
to remain strong, secularism has brought about the de-
valuation of much of the old type of supernaturalistic
viewpoint. This trend can be illustrated by quoting from
literature distributed by the Conservative movement. According to tradition, the Jew should observe the Sabbath
because it is God's will that he do so. In appealing for
a reinvigoration of the holiday, Conservatism, however,

speaks in terms of *social utility*—in this case the potential contribution of observance to better mental health. Only secondarily is it suggested that the Sabbath may have something more than therapeutic significance, and, furthermore, no Divine sanctions for non-observance are inferred. The performance of a religious obligation becomes essentially a technique for achieving personality adjustment:

> The Sabbath in Jewish tradition and history occupies a pre-eminent position. It has nurtured the intellect as well as the soul of the Jew; it has counterbalanced his disappointments; and it has afforded him a blessed opportunity for personality adjustment.
>
> The significance of the Sabbath is very relevant to the life of modern Jews. We continually carry with us the tension . . . of daily living, with disastrous consequences on our physiological and mental health. The Sabbath properly observed . . . offers us the opportunity . . . to preserve our psychological, physical, and spiritual equilibrium. Besides, Judaism is inconceivable without the Sabbath, its ritual, its observances, its leisure for study and meditation.[60]

This appeal represents, in the words of one sociologist, a reversal of the ". . . ends-means relation implied in the conception of religion as an ultimate value in experience." [61] *Given this degree of secularization, how can the traditional content remain so well preserved?*

A logical starting point for answering this question is the problem of language. The comprehension of the Hebrew prayers by the average Conservative layman is minimal: only 10% state that they can fully understand the text.[62] In a poll of lay synagogue officials and board members who were asked: "How well can you follow the Hebrew text of the service?" an even lower figure (8%) was obtained (see Table 5). Were the ideological content

Table 5

ABILITY TO READ AND UNDERSTAND
HEBREW PRAYERS *

	PERCENT
Cannot read the Hebrew prayers	13
Reads but cannot understand	51
Reads and understands quite a lot	27
Reads and can understand all	8 **
No answer	1
Total	100
Number of respondents (1787)	

* Source: United Synagogue, *National Survey on Synagogue Leadership*, p. 7.
** It should be explained that this situation is partly a result of the fact that in the traditional Jewish curriculum mechanical reading of the liturgy rather than its comprehension is stressed. The emphasis has been on *comprehension* of the (Hebrew) Biblical text and on the rapid *reading* of the prayers.

of the prayers wholly explicit, their character might well serve to alienate one or more groups of members. However, since a prayer book providing both the Hebrew text and an *English* translation is used in Conservative synagogues, mere ignorance of Hebrew should not serve to obscure the meaning. The translation should reveal the gap between present-day thinking and traditional Judaism. But in practice the actual character of the prayer is not always made apparent. Knowing that the *fundamental* attitude of their people is quite traditional, and themselves subject to cross pressures, the functionaries have elaborated adjustive techniques which serve to *moderate* the lags between form and content.

One of their important methods is that of supplementation: not deleting material from the traditional text but merely adding to it, frequently in the form of an appendix. Thus liturgy specialists like Rabbis Silverman, Kaplan, and Goldman collected, or themselves composed, supplementary materials.[63] The official Conservative *Sabbath and Festival Prayer Book* provides almost one hundred pages of such prayers and readings. In addition to the usual services, these prayers furnish inspirational material for services held on American holidays and patriotic occasions, celebrations which are not touched upon in the traditional text. The new prayers help to satisfy younger congregants who may be less fluent in their reading of Hebrew, or individuals who have a liberal religious outlook. The supplementary prayers are almost entirely in English and they do not allude to the sacrificial system, the subordination of woman, physical resurrection, and similar ideas.[64] *By holding a service at which the traditional text is used, by glossing over objectionable portions or having them read or chanted in Hebrew, and by stressing English readings whose content is definitely modern in emphasis,* it is possible to satisfy a wide audience.

Another characteristic of Conservatism, also essentially an adjustive technique, is that the prayers are *not* translated literally. The apathy or resistance toward making changes in the traditional texts on the part of the layman, as well as the ambivalence of the rabbis themselves, encourages scholars to render the prayers in a very free translation. Given the limited knowledge of Hebrew possessed by most laymen, the special character of the translations is hardly noticed. It is admitted by the rabbis that many of their "translations" are essentially paraphrases. The editor of the Conservative prayer book, for example, speaks of the employment of ". . . legitimate paraphrases in terms of the modern outlook." [65]

The taking of such liberties reflects an idea propounded by Kaplan. This is the technique of "reinterpretation." The concept is an old one, for it has been used in many of the historic religions. Reinterpretation involves the redefinition of traditional concepts and practices—they are approached as the functional equivalents of modern ideas.

In essence, after stating a religious concept in its original form, one goes on to ask: "What meaning does this have for us today?" The logic is to the effect that when we read prayer A (or perform rite B based on this text), we do not mean C (what was originally meant), but rather concept D is implied (what the text would have stated if it had been composed in modern times).[66] Thus the *sense* of the liturgy can be changed without disturbing the wording; there is no necessity, as in early Reform Judaism, for expurgation. The desire for "authentic" and genuinely "Jewish" prayers is satisfied, and the "reactionary" literal meaning is obscured. When expounded or translated, the liturgy turns out to be modern in emphasis. Robert Gordis, a leading Conservative rabbi, stated that:

There are other instances where our attitudes now vary from older concepts. In many cases, it is possible to reinterpret traditional phrases in order to express our own convictions. . . . Words may mean for us more than they originally meant. Thus the word "abodah" "religious worship" which our ancestors equated with the sacrificial system in the Temple may quite properly mean for us the entire system of public religious observance. . . . We are therefore not called upon to eliminate such phrases. . . .[67]

Similarly: ". . . the emphasis in the prayer book upon the Messiah need not mean for us the belief in a personal redeemer."[68] The prayer book is essentially poetry: "It must be approached with warm emotion and not in a mood of cold intellectuality."[69]

Kaplan attempted to call a halt when it became obvious that far-fetched analogies were being used and that reinterpretation was helping to buttress the *status quo:*

Some have attempted to obviate the need for change in the traditional prayers by reading into them meanings completely at variance with what they meant to those who framed them. This practice is fraught with danger . . . unless we eliminate from the traditional text statements of belief which are untenable and of desires which we do not or should not cherish, we mislead the simple and alienate the sophisticated.[70]

While conceding that reinterpretation still had a place, he contended that *revision* was essential. However, since reinterpretation has filled a real need in the Conservative movement, most rabbis have continued to rely upon it.

The lag problem was avoided on the official level for some years by neglecting to publish Conservative editions of the various prayer books. Except for a single authoritative volume produced in the 1920's,[71] all prayer books were published under individual rabbinical sponsorship. Finally the laity demanded official Conservative editions and thus the *Sabbath and Festival Prayer Book* was published. It is essentially an adaptation of the work of Rabbi Silverman.[72] In preparing the volume, the editors were faced with three cross-pressures. In Gordis' terminology, they ". . . evolved three principles": (a) continuity with tradition, (b) relevance to contemporary needs and ideals, and (c) intellectual integrity.[73] In facing up to the last principle, it was finally admitted that "There will naturally be instances, however, where reinterpretation is impossible, and [where] the traditional formulation cannot be made to serve our modern outlook." [74] With much trepidation, a few revisions in the Hebrew text were authorized:

Thus the endeavor to maintain the principles of the continuity of tradition, relevance to the modern age and intellectual integrity have led us to a deeper understanding of the prayer book. The results include more adequate rendering, legitimate paraphrases in terms of the modern outlook, a small number of changes and deletions in the traditional text, and a good deal of supplementary material drawn from our rich literature.[75]

These revisions did not satisfy the Reconstructionist group. They had lost interest in the effort when it became apparent that the majority of the editors were mainly interested in matters of form.

Some rabbis feared that there would be strong objections to the changes, but antagonism did not develop. The age-grade that was best acquainted with each detail of the classical texts, and most closely attached to them, are the "old-timers," who do not constitute the core membership of the congregations and whose opinions are not crucial. In speaking to fellow rabbis, one leading official said that:

As you know, our Prayer Book has certain changes in the text. . . . I was rather skeptical about those changes and thought they would cause revolutions in many of our congregations. I came to realize that Judaism is not so fragile and that it is not true that if you tamper here and there with tradition, suddenly you destroy the traditional framework. . . .
We cannot say that these changes have brought masses to the Synagogue and have solved the problem of teaching people how to pray. These changes were a result of our desire to be intellectually honest.[76]

Professionals feel gratified with the minor changes made in content, worshipers have hardly noticed them, and supplementation and reinterpretation continue as the chief adjustive devices.

How may we seek to explain the essential problem in this area—encountered by both layman and rabbi alike—which serves as the master-key to their behavior? The answer would seem to be that although ritual is only a symbolic means of achieving a desired result, it tends to become an *end* in itself. The worshiper feels that only by using the *correct* (i.e., traditional) formula can he establish contact with the Deity and consequently have ". . . an effect on the concrete and spiritual world." [77] The Hebrew prayers—like all religious petitions—have achieved a certain sacredness; they have come to possess very strong emotional associations. Given additionally Judaism's legalistic framework, Eastern background, and age-old traditions, the reasons for some of the rigidities which we have encountered become clear. Also, the affect with which the area is charged, and the efforts at readjustment—almost touched with pathos at times—becomes more understandable.

Those who are "advanced" in their thinking and thus have broken with the system pose a definite problem. Rabbi Simon Greenberg advised lay people that:

. . . when you have a prayer whose content is definitely and positively counter to your innermost ethical understanding, don't recite it. Does anybody compel you to say it? The Jewish prayer book has been more or less an anthology of prayers.[78]

Such a response would hardly seem to constitute an adequate answer. Perhaps in spite of the numerous inhibitory factors which we have detailed, this particular part of the worship problem in Conservatism is fated to be one of the most dynamic aspects of the movement as a whole.

V

Social Activities
and Jewish Education
in the Conservative Synagogue

A.

INTRODUCTION:
THE COMPROMISE WITH SECULARISM

SINCE the role of the Conservative synagogue as a *Beth Tefillah,* or house of prayer, has been analyzed, we may now consider its function as a *Beth Keneseth,* or house of assembly. First, a general trend among most modern religious groups, the *compromise with secularism,* requires assessment.

Students of social organization have recognized that religious institutions express both a *social* as well as a suprasocial interest: "The church . . . is distinguished from other associations by its suprasocial orientation. . . . But the church is at the same time a fellowship, a brotherhood of believers, a basis of social intercourse." [1] Neither the social nor the suprasocial orientation can be neglected, although one or the other will be more strongly emphasized depending on the particular culture. Observers generally agree that the *social* has been the main focus of attention in the United States.[2] Typically, American churches do not confine themselves to assisting their members in the search for cosmic security. Rather, their ramified activities demonstrate that they recognize the necessity of competing with the secular part of the social structure for attention and support. It is not unusual now, for example, to find religious institutions sponsoring community-wide programs of social and recreational activities. This is done with little regard to the "mystical unity" of the participants. By this compromise with secularism, the church is able to reinforce its claim to community support; it is, after all, doing much "good work."

The fact that the religious group is Protestant, Catholic. or Jewish, fundamentalist or modernist, ethnic or "nonethnic," may help determine the exact motivation and direction for their social activities.[3] It is safe to say, however, that the growth of social and recreational programs in most religious institutions represents a response growing out of the desire for *self-maintenance*. It is motivated by the proliferation of activities taking place outside the doors of the church. Some of these activities are incorporated into the church program, and as a consequence many of the enterprises now being carried on inside religious institutions grow out of secular values. As long as they are within what the church defines as worthwhile leisure-time pursuits, the program can be considered legitimate. Although the church and the participant may be differently motivated, both may gain from such innovations.[4]

We have already shown how—during a crucial period

in the development of the American Jewish community extending from World War I to the late 1920's—Orthodoxy failed to establish its own type of synagogue as a real basis of social intercourse. Before we study the response of Conservatism we must analyze how the Reform movement, as a precursor group, reacted to the "compromise with secularism" trend. It is clear from historical records that Reform did institute non-worship activities for the purpose of institutional reinforcement. A large number of the sisterhoods and youth groups of the older Reform synagogues were founded before the turn of the century. However, although many Reform synagogues built "temple centers" or "temple houses," with several notable exceptions these were not very active institutions. They were mainly used for meetings sponsored by the handful of synagogue affiliates.[5] The temples, like some of the older high-status churches, possessed venerable histories and assured places in the community. They hesitated to expand their activities and to gain too many new adherents. Although their members, like the mass of Jews, led a segregated social life, some of their leading supporters hoped that this would be a transitory phenomenon. They were suspicious of too much non-religious activity on synagogue premises. This would express, in the words of one rabbi who served this class, the "racial consciousness" of the group.[6]

Some of the Reform institutions which went so far as to actually initiate an intensive program of non-worship activities found that they were not happy with the results. For example, one leading spiritual leader of an upper-class Reform congregation in Cleveland, Dr. Abba Hillel Silver, expressed his disillusionment with the center program. He stated that it attracted "the unaffiliated" to his temple. The class level of these individuals, we may infer, was lower than that of most members of the congregation. Silver felt that ministering to these individuals was not the primary concern of himself or of his group. The social needs of the core members of the congregation were being adequately met by city and country clubs. Status differences in the congregation (West Europeans vs. East Europeans) made the formation of strong clique groups inevitable. Whereas these divisions were not too apparent during worship, they were underlined in the social program. Furthermore, Silver concluded, social activities create a diversion from the religious objectives of the institution.[7]

But since religious institutions must seek to maintain themselves in a predominantly secular society, compromises had to be made. The precise extent to which this was done varied with each institution. Long-established Reform temples maintained their usual programs as long as this was feasible. Many of the high-status congregations finally developed mass activities such as public forums which stressed programs whose content was non-sectarian in nature. Such activities were favored because they did not involve the formation of clique groups with attendant problems of status. Reform congregations founded in more recent decades, and consequently having a membership which could not claim top status, generally offered fewer objections to revisions of the synagogue program.

B.

SOCIAL ACTIVITIES
AND ETHNIC GROUP MAINTENANCE

One other concept in addition to the compromise with secularism is required before the problem under study will become entirely clear. This is the status of Jewry as an ethnic group and of the Jewish religious institution as an "ethnic church." As we shall see, Judaism's ethnic-church character is particularly important in connection with the attitude of Conservatism toward synagogue activities of a non-worship character.

Despite the persistences which we have pointed out,* the direction of movement in our society is toward the discarding of ethnic identification. As a consequence, the ethnic church must either transform itself into a non-ethnic institution—in most cases hardly a feasible plan—or it must seek to retard the assimilation of its members. The development of an abundant social life in the ethnic community which parallels and frequently offers greater gratification than is available in the larger society is a feasible device to arrest such tendencies. Its employment by the ethnic church may be described as a *survival technique in a conflict society*. The ethnic churches may state, as do non-ethnic institutions, that their youth groups are for the purpose of combating juvenile delinquency and providing a wholesome social environment—that adult clubs help to develop the personality of their members and are making worthwhile contributions to community life. But the ethnic church has a special interest in developing these good works. The encouragement of non-religious activities, in the form of ethnic associations, is vital to the continuation of its religious program. The non-ethnic type of institution has the specific problem of reconciling itself to, and finding a place in, an urban culture where secularism has challenged traditional values. The ethnic church faces this issue also, but secularism may seem to it to be only a reflection of other problems such as acculturation and assimilation. It must stake its future not only on the assumption by its members of a religious mission, but more significantly on their acceptance of the ethnic bur-

---

* See *infra*, pp. 32-33.

den. Especially as far as Jewry is concerned, in evaluating social and recreational activities we must take the special needs of the institution as an *ethnic* church into consideration, although the compromise-with-secularism factor must by no means be underrated.

We developed the idea earlier that in our society religion is a socially accepted way of perpetuating group differences.* It follows then that not only does the synagogue need the ethnicity of Jewry for its self-maintenance, but that many Jews feel that they require the synagogue if Jewish distinctiveness is to be preserved. Pressures toward reinforcement thus arise both from those interested in the institution itself (individuals who display deep religious feelings, or those who, by social or family position, may be strongly identified with a particular synagogue), as well as from those who may be classified as "ethnic survivalists." We have just seen how the desire for ethnic survivalism was diluted and obscured in "old line" Reform Judaism. We have also noted how Orthodoxy tended to limit the employment of the synagogue as a medium for survivalism —it continued to rely upon worship as its chief activity when the old rituals no longer fully expressed the collective life.[8] The special contribution of Conservatism has been its relatively uninhibited "exploitation" of the new type of synagogue—the kind which is a house of assembly as much or more than it is a house of prayer—for the purposes of group survival. The movement has been able to do so because it has not been strongly affected by cosmopolitanism as with Reform, or by institutional rigidity as with Orthodoxy.

The lay people who founded the Conservative movement lacked the intellectual tools with which to develop a systematic analysis of what they were about, as well as

* See *infra*, pp. 37-40.

the verbal skills needed to make their objectives explicit. For an expression of the sentiments which have motivated them, it is necessary to turn to the rabbis, and especially to Mordecai M. Kaplan. He was one of the earliest among his group to study the works of Durkheim, Cooley, and other social scientists with care. Integrating a functionalist approach with his pragmatic leanings, he was able to raise to a conceptual level the objectives of his colleagues—both lay and professional—when they founded Conservative "synagogue centers."

Kaplan advocated the establishment of local religious institutions which would have additional functions other than worship and the study of the sacred system. He reasoned that since the contemporary synagogue must serve as the bulwark against assimilation, this objective could only result if large numbers participated and if in so doing they gained a feeling of "social togetherness." Since he felt that constant association and participation in common activities would lead to greater group solidarity, Kaplan urged his rabbinical students not to content themselves only with improvements in ritual and decorum. Such reforms, while desirable, could hardly solve survival problems in a non-Jewish environment. New features would have to be added supplementing or replacing worship as a means of reducing *anomie*. Reforms would help achieve greater group solidarity and a sense of improved morale:

It therefore seemed to me that the only way to counteract the disintegrative influences within, as well as without, Jewish life was to create the *conditions* that would not only set in motion socially and psychologically constructive forces, but that would also make them forces for religion. What was needed . . . was to transform the synagogue into a . . . neighborhood Jewish center. Instead of the primary purpose of congregational organizations being worship, it should be social togetherness. . . .

The history of the Synagogue . . . is a striking illustration of the importance of creating new social agencies when new conditions arise that threaten the life of a people or of its religion. The integration of Jews into a non-Jewish civilization created such conditions. They, therefore, justify transforming the Synagogue into a new kind of social agent, to be known as a "Jewish center." The function of the Jewish center would have to be the all-inclusive one of developing around the leisure interests a sense of social solidarity through face-to-face association and friendship.[9]

The recreational activities which were to be carried on by the synagogue center, or "institutional synagogue" as it was sometimes called, would rally all Jews of the neighborhood whether they were religious or irreligious. It was hoped that once in the synagogue, individuals with only social interests would broaden their activities to include spiritual matters as well. However, the growth of religiosity was not to be the crucial test of the policy. Whatever be the purposes for which individuals might come together, the overriding consideration was that all would be meeting as Jews in a Jewish institution. Israel H. Levinthal, the rabbi of the Brooklyn Jewish Center—one of the pioneer institutional synagogues—has stated that:

If the Synagogue as a *Beth Hatefilah* has lost its hold upon the masses, some institution would have to be created that could and would attract the people so that the group consciousness of the Jew might be maintained. The name center seems to work this magic with thousands who would not be attracted to the place if we simply called it Synagogue or Temple. . . .

The center is a seven-day synagogue not a one-day synagogue. From early morning to late at night its doors should be open. It is true that many will come for other purposes than to meet God. But let them come. . . .[10]

Thus most Conservative synagogues have, from the start, carried on a much fuller program of social and recreational activities than has been true for most Orthodox or Reform institutions. This has been done both because of the need for organizational maintenance as in the non-ethnic church, as well as for the purpose of ethnic group preservation.[11] Conservative synagogues are supported for their religious functions as well as because of their sponsorship of activities which "help keep the Jews together." [12] While these categories of *institutional* and *ethnic* maintenance can be analyzed separately as we have done, except when there is special tension between the two functions they appear to the observer in the field as a single phenomenon.

C.

THE CONSERVATIVE SYNAGOGUE AS A "HOUSE OF ASSEMBLY"

The exact degree to which social and recreational activities are incorporated into the congregational program varies from synagogue to synagogue. Ideally, the synagogue center contains a swimming pool, gymnasium, library, clubrooms, public halls, and classrooms, in addition to facilities for worship. It provides professional club leaders who supervise groups for adults as well as for children, and it presents public lectures. It attempts to make some provision in the program for every age and interest level. Presumably all Jewish organizations are invited to use the facilities for their programs. Since the desire is to serve the needs of *all* the Jews of the neighborhood, only a moderate charge should be made for membership.[13]

Most institutions have not developed a schedule of activities of such wide interest. It would be impossible for the average synagogue to institute a center program of these proportions—three or four hundred members constitute an insufficient base for such an undertaking. Actually, however, problems of money and manpower are secondary. In essence, congregationalism is *incompatible* with the center concept, for under this form of polity the local religious group tends to form a *social unit*. As a result, while the institution does not really become an exclusive organization, the strain towards homogeniety in respect to class and status is strong. Only where the denomination is inclined toward episcopalianism * are the same local units patronized by *several* social classes. Under these conditions the congregation as a social unit becomes almost non-existent and the institution tends to take on the earmarks of a cathedral.[14] It may be said that the program of the typical Conservative synagogue has blended congregationalism—with its implicit social stratification and isolationism—with features of Kaplan's "center": the adapted synagogue which employs the techniques of the settlement house in a middle-class setting and drops the "uplift" and negatively Jewish features of such institutions.[15]

Most Conservative synagogues have been satisfied to leave elaborate leisure-time programming to the Jewish community center. Center and synagogue may feel mutually threatened at times,[16] but the Conservative movement has generally been more adept than Reform or Orthodoxy in meeting the challenge of the center by copying some of its techniques. Conflict is frequently avoided since the two institutions are often not located in the same neighborhood, and also because the class base of each of them varies somewhat. The Conservative synagogue generally prefers to keep its membership fee high.

* See *infra,* p. 40.

It carries on only as much of a center program as is necessitated by the desire of its own adherents, the need to attract new members, the competition of other congregations, and the strength of the center movement in the community.[17]

If we analyze the social program of the average synagogue, it becomes apparent that (as in Protestantism) it is the "sisterhood"—the organization composed of adult women—which is the strongest of all the auxiliaries. There are even synagogues in which the sisterhood roster is larger than the entire congregational membership. It is worthwhile to mention that the Conservative sisterhood differs somewhat from the ladies auxiliary of the second settlement Orthodox synagogue, and that it frequently has a more elaborate round of activities than is true for its Protestant counterpart. This occurs because the sisterhood incorporates features of the usual church auxiliary together with the type of program typical of the woman's club. Also, the sisterhood frequently has a voice in deciding synagogue policy. It should be noted that while within the congregation the position of the group is very secure, most sisterhoods must compete with the other popular Jewish women's organizations such as Hadassah. There is much overlapping in membership between sisterhoods and such groups.

The typical sisterhood holds meetings at regular intervals and in the period between such gatherings much committee activity takes place. Perusing synagogue bulletins, it is discovered that the meetings are chiefly held in the afternoon and "dessert," "donor," and "membership" luncheons are popular. Also, an annual luncheon is held each year at a well-known hotel. Speakers address the group on a variety of topics including current events, Jewish problems, and mental health. Outside of New York

City entertainers present synopses of the latest Broadway hits. Many sisterhoods hold fashion shows and produce their own musical revues. They raise money for their own institution, for community projects, and for the needs of the Conservative movement. Most of them run a gift shop where Israeli art objects, books and records of Jewish interest, ritual objects, and home decorations may be purchased. Some also sponsor short courses—frequently taught by the rabbi—on Bible, current Jewish problems, or the meaning of the holidays and festivals.

Generally speaking, the men's club is less successful than the sisterhood, and there are even some synagogues which do not have such a group. This organization is an innovation—it will be recalled that most second settlement congregations made no provision for sociability in terms of organizing a special voluntary association for adult males. Like its female counterpart, the men's club of the average Conservative synagogue competes for support with other organizations. In this case they are fraternal orders like the B'nai B'rith, groups such as the Zionist Organization of America, as well as the men's clubs of other synagogues and temples. The men's club raises money for worthy causes, although its activity in this field is minor compared with that of the sisterhood. Sports are a real focus of interest for the men's club, with bowling leading in popularity. The monthly meetings include discussions of current topics presented by the rabbi or an outside speaker, entertainment of various kinds, an occasional father-and-son affair, and talks by leading professional sportsmen. Frequently time is set aside for card games. Also, refreshments are served at the conclusion of the evening.

In recent years an additional adult group has become popular: the "young marrieds." In some congregations the organization is designated as the "couples club." Most of the members are the parents of young children. Frequently the program of the "couples club" expresses mainly the interests of its female members, even though most of the leading officers may be males. The women who participate generally consider themselves too youthful for the sisterhood. Some also have little leisure time during the afternoon hours when sisterhood meetings take place, and, unlike the other groups, the members of the "young marrieds" make a point of engaging in activities together with their spouses. On the whole the group is better educated than the sisterhood or men's club membership, and their programs are frequently somewhat more sophisticated in content. They discuss political, social, and Jewish problems, as well as the techniques of child-rearing. They do not emphasize fund-raising.

Another organization which overlaps the membership of all three groups is the parents' association. It tends to attract the mothers of Hebrew school students. Its leadership is frequently drawn from those who are older than the young marrieds but who are junior to the officers of the sisterhood. Some institutions have also founded "golden age" groups. This organization appeals to elderly parents of synagogue members, to those who are themselves members of the congregation, and to the unaffiliated individuals living in the neighborhood.

Most of the larger congregations sponsor young adult groups. These organizations include unmarried individuals of both sexes up to the age of thirty. Since the emphasis of the "20-30's" (as they are sometimes called) is on socializing, they hold many dances, parties, and "mixers." The proceeds of some of these affairs are donated to charitable causes. While most such organizations are run by a handful of active individuals, in metropolitan communities their gatherings may attract hundreds of young people.

Rabbis and congregational leaders have frequently expressed dissatisfaction with these young adult groups. They feel that the members of such organizations lack religious enthusiasm and show little interest in Jewish cultural activities. However, the crux of the problem would seem to be that many of the members of these groups are *not* children of synagogue members; their class position is frequently below the one from which the synagogue draws most of its clientele. While some of the male young adults may be aspiring professionals or businessmen, they have not yet established themselves firmly and their class position is still somewhat ambiguous. Unlike members of the other groups who have not joined the congregation, the young adults cannot be considered as prospects for synagogue membership. When they marry they will leave the group and will most probably make their home in another neighborhood or community. Although to a lesser extent than in Reform, the Conservative leadership wonders whether programming for such individuals is properly its concern. Ambivalence toward the "20-30's" illustrates the clash of institutionalism and ethnicity. Of course the officials recognize that the promotion of such groups makes a contribution to group survival inasmuch as their social program works toward reducing the threat of intermarriage. But at the same time they feel that the young adults are of little help in providing present or future support for their synagogue, for they believe that members tend to feel a minimum amount of loyalty to the sponsoring institution. Synagogue officials imagine that if individuals from unaffiliated families would drop out, the social status of the group would improve and consequently more children of their own members might participate. Thus they feel under obligation to sponsor such activities because of their ideological commitments as Conservative Jews, but their role as institutional leaders results in giving them a feeling of uneasiness about these groups.[18]

In summary, the successful congregation must have active affiliated organizations to serve as an inducement for synagogue affiliation. According to one Conservative source:

> Whereas the Holy Holiday services and the school can provide a strong reason for membership, they are not nearly sufficient to develop or maintain the necessary degree of loyalty. . . .
> One of these ties is too weak—existing for only three days—whereas the other is too temporary, continuing only for the period of the child's schooling. It is important therefore to expand the activities so that the member has many other bonds. . . . Forums, men's club activities, sisterhood activities, late Friday evening services, adult classes, social functions and youth organizations should be . . . made as attractive as possible so that our men and women will have many . . . contacts with our congregational orbit, and so that in the varied activities there will be greater likelihood for everyone to find some points of interest.[19]

Significantly, the Conservative synagogue bases itself on the family unit, and part of the variety of its program results from the desire to cater to the needs of various family members. One layman, an official of a Philadelphia synagogue, has explained that:

> The activities of [our] congregation and its affiliated groups became so expanded that every member in the family had some affiliation and rarely a day passed that someone in the family did not have something to do at the synagogue. With our affiliated organizations we established bonds beginning at the age of five and extending through old age. Temple Sinai became a veritable House of Assembly.[20]

According to Rabbi Greenberg:

With the introduction into the blueprint of our organizational structure of the congregational nursery and the kinder-
garten schools, and the United Synagogue Youth, we have
completed the framework within which a Jew may live his
spiritual and social life as a Jew within our movement, beginning with his earliest youth to the ripest old age.[21]

Related to this process of growing institutionalization
is the fact that the active congregant finds that much of
his social life takes place within the portals of the synagogue. His "outside" activities may well be with the
friends he has made there, and thus he is bound to the
congregation through social ties as well as suprasocial interests. Certainly the contrast between the traditional type
of Orthodox synagogue and the Conservative congregation is manifest:

One of the most important milestones in the return of so
many of our people to our temples was when we drew into the
orbit of the synagogue practically all of the many activities
of our people which had for so long been completely dis-
jointed and unassociated.[22]

In spite of the desire to draw the alienated back into
the fold, there are counterforces at work. We have noticed
that ethnic group preservation is an important element
accounting for institutional reorganization and the consequent introduction of Conservatism. However, at some
point congregationalism, as motivated by the need for
self-maintenance as well as by status drives, places a limitation on the synagogue program. The tendency of those
who are congregationally centered is to limit the area of
concern to synagogue members. For example, in an extem-
poraneous discussion at a national convention one lay
official explained that:

I believe [someone] mentioned something about permitting non-members to participate in the synagogue and thus create in them the interest of synagogue affiliation. I would like to say that in my experience it has been that the more you restrict participation . . . to your membership and not make it too loose an affiliation, the greater respect the non-members all have for the synagogue. . . . [We should] not encourage too much of this outside participation, because if a person wants to participate in a synagogue without contributing for that participation, I say that person has no self-respect.[23]

D.

THE CONSERVATIVE SYNAGOGUE AS A "HOUSE OF STUDY"

According to one authoritative report, during 1950 almost twice as many children were enrolled in Conservative schools than in those sponsored by Reform institutions. Therefore, since the number of schools directly sponsored by Orthodox institutions is relatively small, nearly *half* of all Sunday and Hebrew school pupils attending congregational (as distinguished from communal) Jewish schools are enrolled in classes sponsored by the Conservative group. (See Table 6.)

Table 6

RECORDED ENROLLMENT OF JEWISH SCHOOLS UNDER CONGREGATIONAL AND NON-CONGREGATIONAL AUSPICES IN 100 COMMUNITIES, 1950 *

AUSPICES	NUMBER	PERCENT
Conservative	44,598	45.3
Reform	24,666	25.0
Orthodox	11,453	11.6
Inter-congregational	758	0.7
Total Congregational	81,475	82.7
Non-Congregational	17,056	17.3
Total	98,531	100.0

* Source: *American Jewish Year Book*, LII (1951), 101.

It is significant to note that in the Conservative schools, children in the elementary grades comprise 89% of the total registration.[24] These students are classified on the basis of the number of days which they attend per week. Those who come only once are enrolled in the Sunday school; those attending two days (i.e., afternoons) or more are Hebrew school students. The majority (63%) are enrolled for only a single weekly session. (See Table 7.) Sig-

Table 7

ENROLLMENT IN CONSERVATIVE SCHOOLS IN 100 COMMUNITIES BY NUMBER OF DAYS OF ATTENDANCE PER WEEK, 1950 *

DAYS PER WEEK	NUMBER	PERCENT
Sunday	26,986	63.3
2-Day	1,508	3.5
3-Day	8,316	19.5
4-Day	4,197	9.8
5-Day	1,613	3.8
Total	42,620	100.0

* Source: American Jewish Year Book, LII (1951), 103.

nificantly, girls exceed boys by 8% in Sunday school classes; boys outnumber girls by 41% in the Hebrew schools.[25]

The rapid growth of the Conservative school indicates that it has been in adjustment with the wishes of the parents. As Kaplan noted in an earlier period, the flexibility of its dual system has served to attract individuals with different goals:

. . . most of the congregations have to maintain a double system of schooling in order to meet the wishes of the two classes of members that are usually to be found . . . namely, those whose slogan is "More Judaism," and those who ask for "Less Judaism." Most congregations, therefore, maintain both a Sunday school and a Hebrew school.[26]

In actuality there is very little difference between Reform
and Conservative Sunday schools. Since Reform pioneered
in the establishment of classes of this type (close to 90%
of their children attend only on Sunday morning), most
of the better textbooks and methods are Reform-spon-
sored. Such textbooks and methods are extensively employed in Conservative schools.

The Hebrew school course of study represents an
adaptation of the Talmud Torah curriculum, but one
which is much less intensive: Talmud Torah students attend five days out of seven, and their curriculum has generally called for approximately ten hours of instruction
per week. The curriculum used by the majority of Conservative Hebrew schools requires somewhere between
five and six hours of instruction and the majority of these
schools are at present three-day-a-week institutions: pupils
attend on two weekdays plus Sunday morning. The large
congregations attempt to keep Sunday and Hebrew school
students in separate classes on Sunday morning.[27]

Not only do the Conservative schools represent an adjustment to the desires of parents in terms of intensity
of instruction, but their content orientation is in keeping with the type of Jewishness practiced in the third
settlement. It will be recalled that with the general decline in observance and the lessened Jewishness of the
home, in this area it is the synagogue which becomes the
chief place where the religion is practiced. Spiritual values
are focused on one institution instead of permeating all
structures, and the strength of the congregation helps to
compensate for the erosion apparent in other areas. While
this trend is a general one among all American religious
groups, it is particularly noticeable in Judaism with its
many extra-synagogual rituals.

The program of the Conservative Jewish school reflects

this shift. The teacher tends to stress the prayers customarily used for public, rather than for private devotion, as well as those rituals needed in the home for only the most important festivals. Little emphasis is placed on the *personal* observance of the traditional code.[28] Mention of certain Jewish rituals which are no longer practiced by most congregants is avoided. The school does not concentrate on the pursuit of "pure" Jewish knowledge but rather emphasizes the mastery of certain skills which in later life may help the individual to fit into congregational life. Thus by the end of his Hebrew school course the graduate should be equipped to follow the Conservative religious service with some degree of understanding. It may be pointed out that this emphasis results partly from the religious services sponsored by the "junior congregations." These groups comprise chiefly the students of the Hebrew schools and they conduct their own services each Sabbath. While this is considered an extracurricular activity in some congregations, it receives a good deal of emphasis in most of the synagogues.[29]

Opinion about the effectiveness of the Conservative school is divided. The results of a poll answered by the parents of the students indicates that, for the most part, they are satisfied with the system.[30] However, because of the many non-linguistic students as well as the character of the curriculum offered for those who *do* study the Hebrew language, specialists frequently take a different view. One leading educator, Uriah Z. Engelman, has termed the congregational school the "Sodom Bed of Jewish Education."[31] Like many others, he has pointed out that Conservative schools are frequently small in size and thus are not efficient educational units. Furthermore, the schools are an instrumentality of the *congregation* and they may tend to stress institutional loyalty at the expense of Jewish communal solidarity.[32] In addition, the subject of financing has received critical scrutiny. Although the congregation benefits greatly from these educational activities, the major portion of its budget is customarily spent on other things. The school tends to become merely another service rendered by the congregation.

Many educators feel that it is difficult to supervise and coordinate this type of school. They point out that while the congregational school is ready to use some of the services offered by the local bureaus of Jewish education, it tends to resist outside control:

. . . the main weakness of the congregational school is the fact that, as an isolated unit, it operates outside of a school system. Only a school system with its coordinated procedures and collective motivation can bring effective results. The school's problems are always considered in the framework of the congregation rather than of the community.[33]

Also, the rabbi may be placed in charge of the school and he may not be prepared, educationally or temperamentally, to assume this task.[34]

Advocates of the congregational school point out that, regardless of the preferences of educators, their type of institution is becoming increasingly important. They believe that "Low standards are not inherent in the organic structure of the congregational school and should not be accepted as inevitable." [35] They charge that many graduates of communal schools such as Talmud Torahs have failed to affiliate with a synagogue during adulthood. In contrast, the congregational school brings the child into closer relationship with the synagogue and presumably increases the likelihood of affiliation. Its structure, they add, provides for contact between home, school, and synagogue. Lastly, the proponents of the congregational sys-

tem charge that communal Talmud Torahs over-empha-
sized Jewish nationalistic values. According to an official
Conservative publication:

Today the congregational school admittedly occupies a prominent and permanent place in the field of Jewish education.
This development has imposed a responsibility upon the congregations, a responsibility which in too many instances they
were not prepared to meet. Failing to formulate their own
curriculum in terms of their particular needs and attitudes,
they usually took over the curriculum of the Talmud Torah
without providing as adequately for its implementation. Congregational schools were usually small, independent units. . . .
Educational standards were lowered as reflected in an over-
emphasis on the Sunday school and in fewer hours of instruction in the weekday sessions, in poorly trained teachers, and
in inadequate supervision and facilities.
    Fortunately, this was not universally true. Some congrega-
tional schools succeeded in maintaining high standards. . . .
[The faults of the congregational school] may be traced to
remediable causes. The congregational school, moreover, has
potentialities for enriching the whole educational process, the
most important being the opportunity it provides to bring
the children into close relationship with the synagogue, its
affiliated organizations, and its many activities. Equally important is the closer bond with the child's home which a congregational school affords. The child is in the school, the
mother is in the Sisterhood, the father in the Men's Club, and
the sister or brother in the Young People's League. The rabbi,
too, is in a strategic position to help establish a harmonious
interchange of influence between home and school.[36]

This statement fails to emphasize the factor of self-inter-
est: since the school enables the synagogue to strengthen
its membership and financial structure, it provides a significant new focus for activity and thus is a great boon
to the institution. Additionally, while the congregation
provides a communal service by virtue of its sponsorship,
it soon becomes dependent on this activity and again the

stage is set for a potential clash between the need for institutional self-maintenance, and larger religious and ethnic values. In a particularly candid statement, one well-known rabbi has commented:

In too many of our communities . . . we have two sets of schools . . . primarily resulting from economic and social stratification. One is a system of private schooling, known as congregational schools, generally open only to those who can afford to pay relatively high fees or who can afford to be members of a congregation, and another system of Hebrew education supported by public funds intended frequently for children whose parents are unable to meet the financial demands of private schools. This cannot obtain in a well unified Jewish community which would attempt . . . [to] bring the blessings of Jewish religion to all. . . . It may mean that congregational schools will have to become community schools open to all children on the same basis . . . with the consequence that the reason which is now offered for membership in many congregations will disappear.[37]

The Conservative movement denotes its schools as being in the congregational category, but it has been sensitive to the charge that they are not community institutions. Officials take pains to point out that the schools serve all children regardless of the congregational affiliation of their parents. It is true that in some neighborhoods (particularly those which have many synagogues), this is actually so. However, there are congregations which actually limit enrollment to the children of members.[38] Others allow non-members to register their offspring, but the fees which they charge are adjusted so that it may not cost anything extra—frequently depending upon the number of children in the family—to join the synagogue. In fact it may actually be cheaper to do so. In some congregations a member receives free schooling for his children and in others he may be entitled to a substantial reduc-

tion in fees. Since additional members mean more interest
and ultimately larger support, there is a constant tempta-
tion to institute restrictions which will result in an increased synagogue roster:

> The School is a tremendously important factor in the at-
> traction of the parents to the congregation. . . .
> The old impelling force which drives the Jew to a place of
> worship on the High Holy Days is [also] still a very powerful
> factor . . . these two services . . . are the strongest practical
> arguments that we can possibly present to the members of
> our community for membership. . . . This realization, coupled
> with our lack of space, has led us to . . . limit these privileges
> to members. . . .
> The advantage of this procedure is immeasurable . . . it
> changes the status of "member" to so many who otherwise
> would consider themselves only customers of the congrega-
> tion. As a member he, in many cases, identifies himself more
> closely with the congregation and concerns himself with its
> problems and responsibilities.[39]

According to the rabbi of this particular synagogue:

> Too many of our Conservative congregations still permit
> non-members to avail themselves of the two most attractive
> services we offer. . . . Small wonder that they have a problem
> of reaching the unaffiliated!
> My own congregation and some others . . . have never had
> a membership problem because they refused to defeat their
> own ends by selling [their] most precious commodities on the
> open market. They have made synagogue membership a requi-
> site for sending children to their religious school and for
> synagogue worship on the Holy Days.
>
> This position . . . is as sound morally as it is financially.
> The congregation which lacks the . . . determination to adopt
> it, must reconcile itself to waging perennial membership cam-
> paigns.[40]

Significantly, congregationalism in the educational field
has more ramified effects than is true for social or worship

activities. While these last two concerns can generally be carried on effectively in small units, this is not always the case with education: "If Conservative congregations could put aside petty jealousies . . . and combine in those localities where it is possible to organize one large regional school, there would be a tremendous gain." [41] Louis Katzoff, himself a Conservative rabbi, has noted that ". . . ideological differences added to the desire on the part of congregations to build individual loyalties, have developed sectarianism and isolation, creating a condition which is not conducive to a combination of resources." [42]

It is of interest to study what occurs when a congregation agrees to relinquish its autonomy in the educational sphere. This has happened, particularly in smaller cities where the size and geographical dispersion of the Jewish population may force a modification of congregationalism. The rabbi of the single local Conservative synagogue in one such community complained that: "I don't have close contact with the Hebrew school kids and their parents." In spite of the communal system, he added that, "I have made intensive efforts to get to know the children of our synagogue." This spiritual leader recruited a group from among the families of his members, and children's services are being held each week under congregational, rather than communal, auspices. Special holiday parties are also organized for the children of Conservative synagogue members. Some of the classes of the community school are held on the premises of the Conservative congregation. In addition, since the communal school system does not have a synagogue of its own in which to perform the *Bar Mitzvah* and Confirmation ceremonies, these events are held under congregational auspices. Apparently the central bureau of Jewish education recognizes that it must keep the communal system sufficiently flexible so as to permit the congregation to inculcate its own special loyalties. In turn the spiritual leader has specified that at least in theory in the smaller community the plan ". . . has many advantages for the children getting more effective Hebrew instruction, and that consideration should govern." Enough options exist within present arrangements to assure institutional self-maintenance.[43]

E.

TRENDS IN CONSERVATIVE JEWISH EDUCATION

In recent years the modest goals of the congregational school, in contrast to the old Talmud Torah, have become increasingly clear. Those who feel the most guilty about having acceded to the Conservative pattern of Jewish education are the rabbis. Hence Gordis has admitted that:

. . . probably the most crucial [of our weaknesses] has been our widespread lack of success in Jewish education. Most Conservative congregations have been content to create a counterpart of the Reform Sunday school. . . .

The Hebrew School . . . has generally been the stepchild of our educational system instead of being the cornerstone. Instead of fighting the trend [toward the reduction of standards] we [rabbis] have all too often surrendered.[44]

As a consequence, the functionaries have spearheaded efforts to persuade their school boards to raise standards. Among the changes which have taken place in recent years are somewhat higher requirements for those wishing to qualify for *Bar Mitzvah*. In general boys must now register by their tenth birthday so that they will have the advantage of at least three years of Hebrew instruction.[45] To stimulate the enrollment of girls in Hebrew school, the *Bas*

Mitzvah ceremony—an innovation developed by Kaplan to serve as the counterpart of the male *Bar Mitzvah*—has been widely publicized. However, while 51% of the congregations have instituted the ritual, usually only a small group of families in these synagogues avail themselves of the ceremony.[46] There has been a tendency to prolong the course of study in Sunday school by delaying the age of Confirmation for one or two years, and a movement also has started to confine Sunday school registration only to children in the younger age brackets (all of the older children would have to attend Hebrew School). While this latter effort has succeeded in various places, the plan has been blocked in some communities by congregational officials who fear that it would involve a loss of membership to Reform. Personnel problems, financial limitations, and the lack of desire to give girls the same education accorded to boys have also played a part.

In addition to these efforts at intensification, synagogue leaders have sought to find a number of avenues which would not conflict with the ideas of those parents who are satisfied with present Hebrew and Sunday school programs. They have thus looked for opportunities which would enable them to give *supplementary* instruction. One example is the founding of congregational nursery schools. Programs of Jewish content have been introduced into most of these schools and thus the process of Jewish education can begin earlier than was customary before. However, it has been necessary to exercise care so that the school becomes a ". . . *Jewish* nursery school rather than a nursery school for Jewish children." [47] This has constituted a problem since the nursery school appeals to the parent on the basis of what it can contribute to the personality development of his child rather than in terms of its sectarian purposes. Another recent innovation of significance is the attempt to supplement weekday classes by further practice in Hebrew language, and in "Jewish living," at summer camps. Since large numbers of the children of synagogue members are sent to such camps in any case, it has not been difficult to induce a small percentage to enroll in the "Ramah Camps" of the Conservative movement.[48]

There is some sentiment at present among the Conservative rabbinate favoring the establishment of Jewish parochial, or "all-day" schools. While the day school movement has been intensively promoted in recent years by Orthodox elements, disillusionment with the results of the congregational system of Jewish education has served to arouse some interest in this type of program.[49] The rabbis see the day school as an educational instrument which could serve at least a minority of the present Hebrew school students.

Possibly there will be a small growth of these kinds of schools in Conservatism in the future. If so, it should be recognized that differences in motivation may well exist between the rabbis and the most active promoters of these schools, and those who will form the bulk of the clientele. This may occur since Jewish parochial schools in middle-class neighborhoods tend to take on the character of *private* schools. After observing such a school (one conducted under Orthodox auspices), a Jewish educator stated:

School A now has upwards of 500 students. I should estimate that at least one-third do not come from Orthodox homes. You will find that practically all Conservative rabbis in the area who have children over the age of five send them to the school. The obvious aim of the school is to give the children the most intensive type of Jewish education possible. The parent who is concerned with the wholesome attachment of his child to Jewish life has, in many cases, lost faith in the afternoon school.

Among other factors . . . is the desire to avoid the irritation involved in getting growing children to attend supplementary schools. The all-day school is a two-in-one proposition that settles the problem. The overcrowded conditions of the public school is another factor. People have been hearing a good deal about the child-centered school, individual attention, and enriched programs. Parents turn to the all-day school because there is the notion that children will get these advantages there.

Many others are sympathetic to the concept of the private school. The day school is the most convenient form for them. Lastly, a day school solves many problems. The child is away all morning and early afternoon and mothers do not have to prepare lunches. No small blessing this, in the lives of young mothers of means.[50]

We have thus far dealt only with Jewish education during the years of childhood and early adolescence. Actually, little systematic training above the primary and junior high school level is given in the Conservative congregation. Although efforts are being made to extend the curriculum, as yet the results have been meager. The author of one study concluded that: "In the main no formal classes are conducted for children between the ages of 15-18." [51] There is a widespread feeling among both parents and children that *Bar Mitzvah* and Confirmation are equivalent to graduation exercises. The average parent is not strongly concerned about extending the religious or Jewish cultural horizon of his teen-age youngster. The parent does, however, have anxieties in the area of Jewish identification. The problem of intermarriage is of particular concern. From the viewpoint of the parent, if the child will spend his leisure time in the company of fellow-Jews, the probability of an intermarriage taking place is lessened.

The teen-ager himself feels that he has a more or less adequate amount of knowledge for future participation in the Jewish community. Many do desire to spend a good deal of their leisure time with Jewish, in preference to non-Jewish, friends. They thus require some club or organization whose membership is Jewish. As a consequence both parent and adolescent are satisfied if the congregation provides a social club, like the United Synagogue Youth, for teen-agers. It is understandable then why high school departments in the Conservative synagogues have difficulty in organizing and maintaining adequate enrollments.[52]

Most Conservative congregations offer little formal instruction for adults. In the relatively few places where the traditional study circles still exist, they are attended by small numbers of elderly men who also form the nucleus for the daily services. The type of Sunday morning adult Bible class common in Protestantism is lacking,[53] and the traditional type of Jewish learning has not been adapted to present-day needs. Some attempts have been made to present a *new* kind of Jewish curriculum which would parallel the general type of adult education effort both in terms of content and method. This learning does not claim sacredness, but competes for attention with other leisure-time activities taking place both inside and outside the synagogue. The resulting program of classes is frequently sponsored by one or several of the synagogue affiliates. Recent efforts include the establishment of the National Academy for Adult Jewish Studies to stimulate and provide material for these classes, and the development of laymen's institutes—an adaptation of the retreat idea. Nonetheless, informal education through sermons, forum series, and lecture programs, remains the chief type of instruction for the adults.[54]

VI

The Conservative Rabbi

THERE was no heroic "charismatic" leader who inspired
the formation of Conservatism. Furthermore, the group
has not been led by a corps of theologically-inspired elite.
From our analysis it is apparent that Conservatism has
been chiefly a movement sponsored and directed by *lay*
people. At the same time, however, the rabbis or functionaries have been exceedingly important. Without their
leadership the upbuilding of the Conservative synagogue
could not have been effected. We have noticed, for example, the important role which they play during worship.
Their contribution to the educational program of the
Conservative synagogue has also been made manifest.
Furthermore, they serve as organizers, administrators, and
advisors of the synagogue affiliates. Thus the rabbis are
active in each of the three functional areas of congregational life: worship, study, and assembly.

Historical analysis bears out this point of rabbinical
indispensability. Where Conservative congregations lacked
a spiritual leader, the lay officials soon discovered that
they could not properly administer the affairs of their
institution, integrate its varied activities, and promote

the congregation both within the Jewish as well as the non-Jewish community. With the installation of a properly trained and correctly oriented rabbi, these problems were eased. Thus a Pittsburgh congregation reported in the early 1920's that: "With the coming of [the] Rabbi . . . the spiritual, cultural and educational activities of the congregation moved forward and the Community Center is a beehive of activity every hour of the day." [1]

Since Conservatism started out as a congregationally-based movement—it is in fact only now strengthening its national agencies and coordinating its resources—it would have been incapable until recently of setting up the requisite training facilities for professionals. Years might have elapsed until funds were raised, a curriculum established, students recruited and matriculated, and a roster of alumni built up. During this period the movement would have languished. One of the important reasons for the vitality of Conservatism has been that a pool of talent, more or less sufficient to meet the demands of the congregations, has always existed. (While the supply of spiritual leaders has been augmented by the alumni of various Reform- or Orthodox-oriented seminaries, the main group has been Conservative-trained.)

How was the recruitment problem solved? In brief, due to needs generated *outside* of Conservatism, and without much participation on the part of the Conservative public, a suitable rabbinical school was endowed. The original donors were not personally attracted to the practice of Judaism on the Conservative level. But by the time they had lost interest because of the fulfillment of their original objectives, the movement had developed sufficiently so that Conservative Jewry was able to take over the support of the training institution and handle the recruitment of personnel. In order to gain a full understanding of the movement, particularly in its ideological aspects, it is necessary to study these developments in some detail.[2]

A.

THE CREATION OF THE SEMINARY

The Jewish Theological Seminary of America (hereafter referred to as the Seminary) was founded in 1886 by the more traditional element in the American Jewish community to counteract the influence of the Hebrew Union College—the Reform rabbinical school which had been established in 1875.[3] Although the Seminary made progress at first, during most of the period from 1886 to 1901 (the era of the "Old Seminary"), little interest could be generated. The institution succeeded in graduating only twenty-one students and its faculty consisted of but three teachers none of whom had much more than a local reputation. At the turn of the century the school was in virtual bankruptcy. This was traceable to the fact that the German group was in the process of embracing Reform and the traditionally-inclined Sephardic Jews—being few in number—could not provide sufficient support for the institution. There was in fact no need for Seminary graduates: the Sephardim and the German Jews were not opening any new synagogues of a traditional character.[4]

Casting about for some way to keep the Seminary from closing, some of the directors perceived a need which was not being met by any existing body: supplying Americanized rabbis for the immigrant group. Instead of training functionaries for the synagogues peopled by those who had come here during the first and second waves of immigration, or by their descendants, the directors reasoned that the Seminary could become a center for training spiritual leaders who would minister to the last of the

Jewish groups arriving on these shores. On this basis a relatively large sum of money was raised. To understand the reasons for the success of the appeal, it should be recalled—as was explained in Chapter I—that Jewish immigration has stretched over three centuries, that the European background of the immigrants has been various, and that these plus other factors have contributed to wide differences in class and status.

Significantly, ties of ethnicity and religion may be tenuous or conflicted, but concern with the group can remain high. This is so because in the case of the Jews, individual status is frequently regulated by the process of *group ascription* even more than it is by individual achievement, time of arrival here, and other such personal factors. This mechanism of group ascription poses a special problem to members of the upper-class who have lost any very distinctive cultural or religious traits. Also, even the middle- and upper-class member who belongs to the segment of the minority community where alienation is not a large problem, may be fearful about new developments which might alter his status. While little can be done to affect general social forces of an adverse character, within the ethnic community itself steps may be taken which—it is imagined—will help arrest any decline in status.

To the older groups, the arrivals from Eastern Europe posed such a status threat. The German Jews in particular responded by founding institutions for the Americanization of the East European. These included social settlements, organizations working toward occupational redistribution, and agencies seeking to direct the geographical settlement of the immigrants. It was during this period that the Seminary received an adequate endowment: it was thought that the school would train functionaries who would have a beneficent influence on the immigrant. By thus helping to speed the adjustment of the East Europeans, the amount of anti-Semitism which the newcomers might inadvertently generate could be reduced.[5]

It is true that there were other motives besides the status-threat problem which helped impel all these efforts. But the Jewish situation is essentially different from that encountered among non-Jewish groups. Among the latter the appeal to assist the fellow ethnic is placed on the level of philanthropy, religious sentiment, or the demonstration of group solidarity. However, Americanization in the Jewish community has been essentially a control technique motivated by the dynamic of group relations—it has thus played a more important role in the shaping of communal policy than is true for other groups. It is notable that, unlike most immigrant-serving organizations, the agencies working among Jews have not required outside subsidy. On the contrary, their budgets have been entirely covered by individuals whose group identification is the same as that of the public which constitutes the clientele. This tendency has not been wholly a result of economic factors.

Early in the Seminary's history its president issued an appeal for support directed to wealthy individuals who had failed to donate sizeable amounts to the endowment fund. He suggested that the school would make the type of contribution to Americanization efforts which could not be duplicated by the Hebrew Union College. Consequently, it was reasoned, support of the Seminary was a non-partisan issue:

The gradual influx of our co-religionists . . . in former years developed no difficulties because they were as gradually assimilated socially, geographically and commercially. This sudden transplantation of a vast multitude congregating in certain sections of our large cities, constitutes an entirely different condition. Few of us realize how serious the problem is.

Whatever is to be done, must be done by those who are in thorough sympathy with those for whom it is done. By sympathy is not here meant simply a general fellow-feeling for the needs of these people; but besides this, a thorough knowledge of what those needs are; an acquaintance with the character, nature, and temperament of the people. . . .

It is in the light of these principles that we bespeak . . . [the] support which is necessary. . . . What nobler work than for some of our graduates . . . to go to these people and instill into their minds and hearts . . . culture, refinement and civilization. . . .

The equipment of such missionaries, the training of Rabbis who though fitted by culture and scholarship to occupy positions in the pulpits of the most cultivated congregations, shall also be able to successfully undertake such work among their humbler coreligionists, is indeed, an object that ought to . . . secure the support of the Jews, and of every Jewish congregation in the United States.[6]

A prominent Sephardic rabbi developed the same theme some years later:

The future of American Judaism will be powerfully affected by the Russian Jews. . . .

Who shall take him by his hand, or rather his children? Is there not grand work here for the graduates. . . . Our own safety, our own good name, require it.

We have to choose between striving for learning and culture, or allowing these communities to honor learning of but one kind in their own peculiar way, to maintain services which show little love for culture, and which repel—methods which fail in the second generation.

These congregations will be either the fame or the shame of American Judaism. They can make the American Judaism of the future equal to the golden age of Spanish Judaism . . . or they will, by uncouthness or by infidelity, or by lax ideas of moral right in business or social life, feed the prejudice against us. . . .

Our own interests require that they shall be supplied with ministers who shall be acceptable to them. . . .

Yet we need not the Seminary for the sake of supplying the spiritual wants of the Russian congregations only. We, indeed, require it for our own spiritual needs and for our own children's spiritual well-being.[7]

After 1901 the institution was reorganized and representatives of the founding group accepted a secondary position. A group of philanthropists composed of German-Jewish-descended bankers, merchants, and attorneys took control. Jacob H. Schiff, the most important American Jew of the time, became the crucial personality on the new board, which was headed for some years by Louis Marshall. Much of the administrative work was directed by Dr. Cyrus Adler. Support from the leading American Jewish families, such as the Guggenheims, the Lewisohns, and the Lehmans, was forthcoming.[8]

Although the members of the philanthropic group were affiliated with Reform, they agreed that no attempt should be made to change the traditional character of the Seminary.[9] The philanthropists recognized that Reform had little appeal to the immigrants. They felt that a modified Orthodoxy, stripped of ghetto characteristics, would be the type of Judaism most suitable for the East Europeans. The connection between the Seminary and Conservatism came about because the third settlement congregations of the type which we have described obtained their rabbis from this particular institution. Apparently Seminary policy was such that its graduates were better suited to act as their spiritual leaders than those who came from the various other rabbinical schools.

In the sections which follow we shall analyze the special problems of the teachers and administrators, the students and alumni, and the board members. We shall consider the character of the studies at the Seminary, as well as the "atmosphere" of the school.

B.

CHARACTERISTICS OF THE SEMINARY PROGRAM

Four essential characteristics of the Seminary's program are among the factors responsible for making their graduates acceptable to the congregations: (1) the Seminary's recognition of its role as a rabbinical training school, (2) its stress on the English language, (3) the compromise character of the religious observance which it has exacted from the student body, and (4) its cultivation of the "science of Judaism." In regard to the first of these factors, the Seminary is one of several modern rabbinical schools which represent a new type of Jewish institution. The *yeshiva*, the traditional academy of higher learning, is a school for the study of Jewish law. It is not a seminary in the usual sense of the term, for no special professional training is offered. Ideally only a small number of the students become religious specialists. The school is predominantly oriented to preparing the student for life, or what would be called in the present era the practice of Orthodox Judaism. The modern rabbinical school, however, *is* an institution for the training of professionals. Although the Seminary has added a variety of departments, it has remained predominantly an institution devoted to educating individuals who plan to become practicing rabbis.[10]

As a professional school, the institution has been under pressure to train *only* those persons who give promise of future success in the field. This policy violates the tradi-

tional norm which stresses the obligation to teach all who
are capable of learning regardless of the nature of their
vocational aspirations or personality traits. While Solomon Schechter, the revered scholar and teacher who served
as President from 1902 to 1915, showed his willingness to
dedicate the Seminary to the training of professionals, he
foresaw possible dangerous consequences. Apparently he
was not altogether happy with the policy:

. . . we live now in an age of specialization. Funerals and bur-
ials have been raised to the dignity of a fine art and praying
has become a close profession. The old Sacred Brotherhood
had thus to disappear, and their work mostly devolves now
upon the minister. But how shall we approach this part of
our instruction? . . . a man may show the most brilliant record in undergraduate days and yet be utterly wanting in tact,
delicacy . . . and similar qualities necessary for the office of
pastor. . . . I consider it not without danger to create a religious aristocracy which might soon claim the King . . . and
crowd the rest of us out from his Divine Presence. Such things
have happened in other communities and may also happen
to us when we create a separate class of *religieux*. . . .
. . . we [Jews] have lost our vigor and seem to be in need of
artificial support like other denominations. The support has
to be created . . . but . . . the experiment is risky.[11]

A seminary, as an institution which trains religious specialists, is charged with three separate tasks:

(a) The *transmission* of that body of knowledge which
teachers, administrators, board members, and alumni believe is required for the successful practice of the profession.

(b) The *indoctrination* of appropriate theological views.
The institution must seek to inculcate attitudes toward
the body of knowledge which it teaches.[12]

(c) The *adjustment* of the student to his future professional role. The aspirant must be taught to abide by

a code of ethics and procedures, and to relate himself in prescribed ways to his fellow practitioners and to his future clientele.

Although some attention has been paid to each of these areas, only an uneasy adjustment has been effected. The basic problem has been that the teachers (or *schoolmen*) have hesitated to break completely with tradition and to create a curriculum adjusted to the present occupational role of the rabbi. It is true that the doctor, the lawyer, the engineer, have all been trained in professional schools where a hiatus between training and later practice is common. Thus while problems in this area are not unique to Jewish theological institutions, they have been particularly serious there because of the rapidity of the acculturation process among the laity.

A leading requirement of the congregations was that their spiritual leaders possess an adequate knowledge of English. It is consequently important to note that Seminary graduates were prepared to carry on their professional duties in this language. Except for the Reform institution, during the early period the Seminary was the only school which educated its men along such lines. Schechter's attitude toward Yiddish was negative,[13] and although both teachers and students were in almost all cases fluent in Yiddish, English became the language of conversation and instruction. One faculty member was designated as the "Professor of English and Rhetoric." Students were encouraged to rid themselves of heavy accents and intonations. Schechter stressed that ". . . more than mere knowledge of English grammar and composition, students need to do reading [in English literature] which will give elegance to their style and refinement to their thoughts." [14]

Thus these future rabbis were well prepared for the language pattern of the area of third settlement.

The Seminary student was also suitable for a Conservative post by virtue of the compromise character of his personal religious observance. Like all theological schools, the religious regimen practiced at the institution has been more strict than the one observed by the laity. The professional is expected to be more rigorous in normative adherence than the non-professional of his denomination —by definition the religious virtuoso should exceed the spiritual amateur. Those leading the cloistered life, having all the facilities at their disposal which aid in greater observance, are expected to take advantage of their isolation. This may have dysfunctional consequences: if such exercises are strongly cultivated, those who are destined to serve congregations and hence to perform ministerial functions may have been rendered unfit for their task in the process of training—they become "too religious." But the Seminary student, although more observant than the average Conservative Jew, has not been required to follow a very strict regimen. Encouragement of piety in the form of observance of the *mitzvoth* (religious commandments) has been at a minimum. Candidates have been merely required to be Sabbath observers and to conform to the dietary laws.[15] To select only two examples out of the numerous positive and negative *mitzvoth* which have been disregarded, students have been free to dispense with *Shaatnez*—the law regulating the fiber content of clothing. The prohibition against the cutting of the beard is another case in point. It is a particularly important example since the beard is an especially striking deviation and the

congregations would not have accepted spiritual leaders
who adhered to this regulation.

Although individual students have varied in the extent
of their observance, and at certain periods greater zeal has
been in fashion than at other times, these rabbis have
been prepared—if only on the basis of their own derelictions—to tolerate the comparatively low degree of observance characteristic of Conservative Jewry.[16] Seminary
policy has resulted in men "religious" enough so that
vicariously their congregants can observe some of the basic
regulations of the sacred system such as Sabbath or
Kashruth (the laws relating to food) but not so strict as to
produce a spiritual leader whose observance would offend
the congregant, or one who would be prevented from
fulfilling his duties in the Jewish and non-Jewish communities. In essence, the pattern followed by the rabbi has
not reflected too unfavorably on the one characteristic of
the laity.

Turning to the last factor, the curriculum of the school
has been based upon the "science of Judaism" *(Wissenschaft des Judentums).*[17] Instead of Talmudic learning
constituting the entire curriculum as was true in the
yeshiva, the science of Judaism idea implies taking as subject matter the *entire* Jewish heritage. But even more significantly, it involves the investigation of Judaism according to scientific canons: studying it with the same type of
objectivity, learning, and technical devices employed in
the investigation of any other culture. This indeed constitutes a decided departure from traditional procedures.

While the typical Conservative layman has few interests
or concerns with this type of problem, the adoption of the
science of Judaism concept has had important effects for
him. It has helped to make his future Conservative rabbi

intellectually liberal. It has inculcated in the spiritual leader a spirit of relativism and thus dissuaded him from adopting dogmatic attitudes. Studying the panorama of Jewish history, the aspirant cannot but notice evolutionary trends and environmental influences. Consequently he tends toward acceptance of the dominant trends of his own historical period which he conceives as only another era in the epochal history of the Jew—one which will surely be supplanted eventually by yet another pattern of adjustment. If congregants are responding to historical forces beyond individual control, the Seminary-trained rabbi can hardly feel very strong antipathies toward them because of their derelictions.

It will be helpful to give several examples of how the science of Judaism concept has operated, and how it has served to throw some new light upon very old problems. The late Louis Ginzberg, acknowledged as the outstanding scholar of the institution, was one of the foremost authorities in the field of rabbinics. In explaining the differences between the Babylonian Talmud and the Palestinian Talmud, he did not attempt to resolve variations and contradictions between the two texts by using the traditional hermeneutical devices. Rather, he developed the idea that the differences were an expression of the contrasting cultures and economic systems found in the two areas.[18] Similarly, Louis Finkelstein, now Chancellor of the Seminary, made a detailed study of the forces behind the cleavage between the Pharisees and the Sadducees —the reasons for the growth of these two schools of rabbinic thought had perplexed numerous scholars. Like Ginzberg, Finkelstein also did not content himself with the traditional methods of resolving such problems; instead, he advanced a sociological analysis:

. . . the prophetic, Pharisaic, and rabbinical traditions were the products of a persistent cultural battle . . . between the submerged, unlanded groups, and their oppressors, the great landowners. Beginning in the primitive opposition of the semi-nomadic shepherd and the settled farmer, the struggle developed into a new alignment of the small peasant of the highland against the more prosperous farmer of the valleys. . . . From the province the conflict was transferred to the cities, where it expressed itself in the resistance of traders and artisans to the nobles and courtiers. Finally, it appeared in the sanctuary itself in the bitter rivalry between Levite and priest.[19]

Neither sect determined its views by such artificial and spurious principles as "literal" and "liberal" interpretation of Scripture. They were both ready to adhere to the letter of the Law or to depart from it as best suited the needs of their following. Indeed, they would have considered themselves false to the needs of their groups had they acted otherwise.[20]

While such ideas may seem commonplace to social scientists, coming from traditionally-minded rabbinical scholars, they indicate the existence of radical shifts in thought-processes. Until recently, the background of senior faculty members was essentially similar.[21] Most of them came from Eastern Europe and received the traditional type of Jewish education. If born in the United States or educated here, they were from Orthodox families and had the advantage of a similar type of preparation in Talmudic studies. Like thousands of other Jewish youths, they left the world of the *yeshiva* for the Western European or American university. The conceptions and tools of scientific scholarship were revealed to them, and continuing with their rabbinic studies in the light of new orientations and methods, the Seminary group attempted to blend traditional Judaism and modern culture. A former student, writing of Ginzberg, suggests the advantages

which his teacher derived from this process of cross-fertili-
zation:

Combining perhaps to a degree no scholar ever did "the thor-
rough Talmudic learning of the Eastern Talmudist and the
philologic-historical approach of the student of the *juedische
Wissenschaft,*" or to put it in the inimitable phrase of Dr.
Schechter, the method of the one and the madness of the
other, he was able to advance the study of the Halakah [Jewish
law] intrinsically as well as to shed light on many of its his-
torico-literary problems.[22]

However, a tendency to halt short of whole-hearted
acceptance of modernism is evident. For example, Finkelstein has not held consistently to the position which he
developed in his volumes on the Pharisees. On at least
one occasion he has reverted to the traditional position
which holds that Jews constitute a unique "priest people"
and hence are highly different from other groups. Aban-
doning sociological determinism, he has stated: "Among
all other peoples, social forces determine ideas. . . . There
is only one exception to this great rule, there is only one
people and one tradition in which ideas have made social
forces, and that is our tradition." [23] A different type of
example, but actually one along similar lines, is provided
by Ginzberg. Although honored by leading universities
because of his distinguished contributions to scholarship,
one of his students disclosed that he always yearned for
approval from the type of Orthodox Talmudic scholars
under whom he had studied as a youth—this notwithstanding the fact that he had long since abandoned their methods and doctrines.[24]

These instances of ambivalence result from the fact
that scientific methodology is radically different from the
traditional scholastic procedures of learned Jews. The new
orientation hence involves many disturbing implications
for those who have been trained in the classical mode—

even though ostensibly they have broken with the old system. While such problems have seemed less meaningful in recent years as (1) European-born and trained teachers and students have been fewer in number and (2) "crisis theology" has had a counterpart in Jewish circles, the reconciliation of contrasting cultural traditions has been a problem of real significance during most of the period under review. We shall now turn to a more detailed consideration of areas of strain and furthermore to an analysis of the type of adjustment patterns which have been developed.

C.

DISCONTINUITIES AND CONFLICTS: THE PROBLEM OF ROLE

For significant clues to areas of discontinuity and conflict, we must return to an examination of the role of the rabbi in the local congregation. It has already been pointed out that the Conservative functionary is crucial for the worship program. His importance in the educational and social activities has also been stressed. However, we have not as yet highlighted the fact that the rabbi—as the ranking professional on the synagogue staff—spearheads the *promotional* efforts of his congregation.[25] The Conservative synagogue seeks to combat indifference to Jewish values. Also, it is in competition with other congregations and with extra-synagogual Jewish activities. As a consequence, the functionary must serve as a resource person delivering suggestions which are intended to place his institution ahead of its rivals. Since new features and attractions are important, he must read the bulletins published by other synagogues, discuss his problems with other rabbis, and solicit ideas from his lay people.

As the promoter of the congregation, it is required of the rabbi that he be active in non-congregational affairs. It is he who is chiefly responsible for relating the congregation to two larger structures: the Jewish community and the non-Jewish community. Consequently the successful rabbi is expected to be active in the affairs of both. In so doing he helps to reinforce the prestige of the congregation and thus makes membership in his particular synagogue desirable. Also, as is mainly characteristic in the smaller communities, he must seek to raise the status of his ethnic group in the eyes of the larger community.

Institutional maintenance requires that a certain level of integration within the congregation itself be achieved. This is difficult in the modern synagogue where congregants have *varied* interests and viewpoints. Because of such heterogeneity, the rabbi is required to serve as a figure to whom all can rally. If he exercises a measure of impartiality, he may succeed in integrating highly disparate forces around his person. It is therefore important that the Conservative rabbi, like his Reform colleague (and even the more traditional type of functionary who serves the modernized "neo-Orthodox" congregation), be a friendly person who is able to relate easily to others.[26]

That the rabbi is a prime factor in achieving synagogual integration is further demonstrated when we realize that he seeks to establish for the congregant a special relationship with the institution—one which differs from that possessed by individuals who are numbered among the unaffiliated. The connection between the rabbi and the non-congregant tends to become essentially that of one "secondary group" member to another—the unaffiliated individual can hire the rabbi to render those services of a religious nature which he may require from time to

time. Such relationships are contractual and are termi-
nated upon performance of the ceremony. With the congregant, however, the bond is more primary, for the rabbi
is *his* rabbi, and the functionary may attend family affairs
and share in the congregant's joys and sorrows.[27] Although
the association between rabbi and congregant is in reality
what may be termed "synthetic primaryship" (especially
if we consider the turnover in congregational membership, as well as the constant stream of applications by functionaries for a change in their rabbinical posts), if adroitly
handled it is capable of providing much comfort to the
congregant and of integrating him closely into the institutional structure.

All of this is in contrast to the classical role of the
rabbi—that of arbiter and expert in the history, doctrines
and practices of the Jewish sacred system. However, notwithstanding the introduction of many new courses, much
of the Seminary curriculum is still centered about the
study of the Jewish legalistic tradition. Although Talmudic material is taught in a scientific manner, even
such modernized studies cannot be of much practical use
to the Conservative rabbi. The assumption for the concentration of courses on the sacred system is that individuals are interested in maximum observance—the rabbi
should be able to indicate what constitutes this observance
and to subsume novel situations under some traditional
legal category. When circumstances compel change, individuals will consult with rabbinical authority to legitimate deviations. But Conservative Jewry—as an acculturated group—understandably does not take the steps which
are required for the preservation of the integrity of the
system. According to one rabbi, the fact that he is a specialist in Jewish law is of little interest to his congregants:

I receive practically no inquiries about ritual or legal problems. Only on one holiday do people ask me a few questions—that's Passover. A death in the family may also provoke a query or two about the proper observance of the rites for the departed. People do ask me questions, but generally this takes place at a dinner party and they start out this way: "By the way, Rabbi, there is something that I've been meaning to ask you." Then they recite some ritualistic variation which they have observed or heard about, possibly from a parent or grandparent. Perhaps it is a Jewish adaptation of one or another East European peasant superstition. The question has no relevancy to the congregant's own religious observance but it is just a curiosity which he would like to have explained.[28]

The functionaries tend to be "over-trained" in one area and underprepared in others. It is true that the services in the Seminary synagogue serve as training for fulfilling the role of conductors of public worship, or *priests*. Training in homiletics is also given: students deliver addresses at the services and thus prepare themselves to serve as *preachers*.[29] While both of these roles are outside of the work functions of the traditional rabbi, a compromise has been effected and whether by formal or informal means, some training is being given in these two important areas. However, Conservative spiritual leaders must perform many other roles in addition to their duties as preacher-priest and rabbi, and while the aspirants may be given a brief course in "practical rabbinics," they are relatively unprepared for these further roles. First, they serve as *clerics*—as an arm of the state which has empowered them to perform certain rituals and requires them to record these ceremonies. While this role may not call for any preparation, many rabbis feel that in their capacity as *rectors*, or administrators, they require specialized training. Since they give counsel, guidance, and assistance to individuals in meeting the crises of life, the rabbis function as *pastors,* and in this role lack of orientation is felt to be even more serious. Also of significance is the fact that although they head their own families, the functionaries are in a sense members of many families. Assuming the headship of congregations, in a psychological sense they serve as *fathers.* Lastly, since the spiritual leaders are personages of some consequence in their communities and are given membership on various boards, semi-public bodies, and agencies in the field of social welfare, they act as *parsons.*[30]

It will be helpful if these developments are placed in historical perspective. Traditionally, the Jewish functionary has served as a "scholar-saint" [31] in a sacred society. He has been granted the authority to interpret, and ultimately to administer, a well-esteemed and highly intricate religious code. In the network of power relations, his place as a religious specialist who had to be reckoned with in the decision-making process was recognized. He was able to control some of the conditions relative to his role and function. But in the present-day Jewish community, as a result of the new system of shared values which has served as the background for our investigation, there is a radical readjustment in the role of the religious specialist. The crux of the change is the decay of the "rabbi" role. It is being relegated to an inferior position, and the roles of preacher, pastor, rector, and priest are coming to occupy the resulting void.

These changes modify the very "face" of the profession. The sanction of the rabbi is no longer required for the correct practice of Judaism. The authority previously possessed by the religious specialist has for all practical purposes been transferred to the laity.[32] The laity have always influenced what shall—and shall not—constitute Jewish law. Until the modern period, however, social change was always gradual, and revisions were arrived at in consultation with rabbinic authority. Thus the influence of the laity was obscured.

The Jewish spiritual leader has had comparatively little preparation which would serve to reconcile him to the transfer of authority. Since the process has been so sudden, it poses far-reaching problems for the religious specialist. It not only forces him to rearrange somewhat the rank order of his roles as well as to encompass some which traditionally do not belong to him, but actually he must change his self-image. Also, the skills learned by the aspirant at his rabbinical school now require more than the kind of supplementation which can be gained through the serving of a brief internship as in other professions. Rather, they tend to be almost completely obsolete.

For his former authority, the functionary can try to substitute the force of personality; he may also compensate by fulfilling his varied roles with thoroughness and skill. But even if he is a highly successful spiritual leader, the rabbinical role comes to occupy for the Jewish religious specialist a position rather akin to its place in the role constellation of the Protestant minister.[33] It is true that the importance accorded to the functionary because of his role as preacher, pastor, rector, and parson may serve to reinforce professional status and to improve damaged self-esteem. But it can never fully compensate for the deprivation felt by those who come from an East European background and who thus may have internalized some of the traditional attitudes with respect to their roles.[34] Having no alternative, the Conservative functionaries have *had* to accede to these changes.[35] However, if we review the large amount of material written or spoken by rabbis primarily for circulation among their colleagues, it becomes apparent from the content that what is involved essentially is a quest for *legitimation* on the part of those who are failing to exercise the traditional rabbinical role.

Significantly, congregants are unaware of this whole problem—as laymen they are hardly in a position to appreciate the difficulties encountered by their spiritual leaders in the readjustment process. They, of course, lack any of the role conflicts suffered by the functionaries. Being relatively ignorant of problems in the area of systematic theology, they cannot appreciate the intellectual dilemmas encountered by those whose profession entails the manipulation of such categories.

D.

DISCONTINUITIES AND CONFLICTS: THE PROBLEM OF INDOCTRINATION

We have thus far studied the type of knowledge which is transmitted to the rabbi, as well as the contrast between the work for which he is prepared and his actual occupational role. We come next to the problem of indoctrination. Perhaps of all three areas (*transmission* of knowledge, *indoctrination* of theological views, and *adjustment* to professional role), this one has created the most vexing problem. The essential issue can be stated succinctly: since the teacher himself has been ambivalent and could not arrive at an exact formulation of his religious ideology, he has been unable to carry out the indoctrination procedure. At most he has been able to convey some rather general perspectives to his students. His outlook—that of the science of Judaism—is essentially a *method,* not a philosophical system. The inability of the Seminary, as a theological school, to present its students with a coherent religious ideology has given rise to four different techniques which serve as adjustive devices compensating for the resulting vacuum. We label them "objectivism," "scholarship," "eclecticism," and "compartmentalism."

The teacher who operates with the first of these devices tends to avoid his role as a theologian and religious thinker by taking as his function that of the expert. Like the secular teacher, he contends that the student is free to make up his own mind on the basis of the evidence presented. One rabbi, looking back on his student days, concluded that:

The Seminary . . . apart from exacting from its students conformity to certain traditional norms of religious behavior did not seek to indoctrinate them with any single outlook on Jewish life and left to them the responsibility for formulating their own philosophy of Judaism on the basis of their own thought and experience.[36]

Another position has been that of avoiding discussions of current problems and instead stressing the *past*. This we label "scholarship" because the instructor claims that as yet he cannot answer the questions which bedevil his students; all of the evidence is not in, the archives are unopened, the trends are still unclear. In setting up the curriculum of the Seminary, the tendency has been for courses to be weighted with materials pertaining to the Jewish culture of ancient and medieval days. Frequently a knowledge of the modern period has been left to the individual reading of the student.[37] Although a great admirer of his teacher, Goldman, for example, noted how Ginzberg—who had apparently never solved for himself the problem of modernism vs. tradition—tended to avoid discussion of contemporary problems:

. . . Ginzberg has taught that Jewish law has been produced by evolution and to those who have maintained that this view was out of harmony with his resistance to change, he has replied that the latter has always come about spontaneously and unconsciously and in any event required the sanction of authority. What in the present day anarchy of Jewish observance we are to recognize as spontaneous and what we are to reject as willful, or how we are to call the necessary authority into existence, he has not made clear.[38]

Schechter may be regarded as typical of those taking the position of eclecticism. The eclectic is one who is highly individualistic in his formulations. He is bothered by competing philosophical positions, each of which—although highly polarized—seems to him to contain a degree of truth. Since he tries to synthesize opposing philosophies and frequently fails in his objective because of problems inherent in the nature of the task, one cannot be quite sure just what he believes. Much depends on which particular statement is emphasized out of the bulk of his work. Thus when Bentwich attempted to reconstruct Schechter's position on certain important religious problems, he was forced to conclude that:

. . . [Schechter] maintained a critical attitude towards the Bible but also a belief in divine revelation . . . he rebelled against the rival of revelation in the shape of history. In fact, he had not a logical system or a philosophy of Judaism, but an immense and romantic love of it.[39]

The position of "compartmentalism" involves keeping scientific work separate from other concerns and attitudes. One is untraditional in thought and in method of investigation but nonetheless follows the Orthodox pattern of personal behavior. The teacher cannot be criticized for personal violations of the precepts of the religious code. Deviations, confined to the philosophical level, appear in scholarly publications which can be understood only by the chosen few.[40]

Kaplan has been the only individual among the teachers of the Conservative rabbinate to eschew these devices. Unlike the others, he was not inclined to antiquarianism. On the contrary, he has devoted his main scholarly efforts to building a new philosophical system for the modern Jew. Many students who were eager for a more definite orientation on the problem of combining the modern with the traditional were strongly impressed with his ideas:

Having come from the usual Jewish home of Orthodox outlook, I held the accepted views of the Bible, as other Jewish youths in a similar environment. I was also sorely perplexed and ofttimes much confused about the Holy Scriptures. So long as I live I shall recall the excitement of those evenings of Bible study with Dr. Kaplan when . . . a new Bible, indeed a new and thrilling world, was revealed to me.[41]

[Kaplan] has presented to us not a worn-out system . . . to whose deeper meanings our hearts do not respond. Rather has he given us a philosophy responsive to the yearnings . . . of our modern thought-life. . . . we watched this masterful teacher at work, always seeking to provide a principle of integration for the diverse facts, conflicting values and religious and moral ideas of the modern Jew.

This, then, is the sort of teaching which has . . . given us . . . a new belief in the future of the Jew . . . and a new mood about the creation and preservation of Jewish loyalties and ideals in the Diaspora.[42]

Most members of the faculty and administration disapproved of Kaplan's efforts. They were bothered by his attempts to make *explicit* the way in which the norms of East and West, of tradition and modernism, were clashing. Also, his suggestions for revisions in ceremony and liturgy

met with disfavor. His dismissal was discussed, but no
action was taken. Allowing Kaplan to continue with his
teaching had the effect on him of reinforcing his loyalty
to the Seminary and of reducing the threat of his leading
a secessionist movement.[43] At various periods in the history of the institution positions on the faculty had to be
left vacant for long stretches of time. These included the
chairs of Bible and theology. It was difficult to find men
who combined sound scholarship, a viewpoint that con-
formed to the one held by the majority of teachers, and
who would also employ the various adjustive devices
noted previously. No younger men were appointed to
carry on in the Kaplan tradition.[44]

It may be said that the failure of the Seminary to institute a process of indoctrination has contributed to a
heightened sense of frustration on the part of the Conservative functionary: he has not had a substantial set of
ideological principles to which he could look for guidance.
At the same time, however, it must be emphasized that
this deficiency—like other similar ones—has worked toward institutional stability. Lacking exact principles, the
Seminary-trained rabbi has been flexible and thus able to
adjust to congregations which, although denominating
themselves as Conservative, yet display a certain variety.
We noted, for example, that some employ an organ during worship. Others, however, feeling that this is "un-
Jewish" and contrary to the traditional law, prohibit the
use of a musical instrument. Since his teachers did not
provide guidance on such problems, the rabbi is tempted
to accept the direction of the laity. While congregations
welcome such attitudes on the part of their functionaries,
the absence of authoritative procedures (and hence guides
for action) constitutes a potential threat to rabbinical
morale.

E.

DISCONTINUITIES AND CONFLICTS:
SCHOOLMEN vs. PRACTITIONERS

One of the important factors influencing the adjustment of the novice to his future professional role is the
nature of his training. In many professional schools the
teachers are not practitioners, or even ex-practitioners.
Because of their isolation, they are not subject to the demands made upon those who are "out in the field." The
curriculum which they fashion may not always stress practical studies, or it may not even include a consideration
of the latest methods. In most cases the proclivities of the
schoolmen—in whatever direction they may be—are moderated by the strong influences exercised by the practitioners on the professional school. Practitioners are usually well represented on evaluation committees, boards of
trustees, and other institutional policy-making bodies.
This occurs because they generally have behind them
strong professional associations and they can also claim
to represent the public interest. Successful alumni are in
a position to provide sizeable endowments or to influence
grant-giving organizations. Even though the schoolmen,
tending to constitute themselves into centers of semi-
autonomy, might not be overly concerned with the future
adjustment of the aspirant (they may be more interested
in inculcating pure rather than applied knowledge), the
practitioner exercises his influence to keep the scales in
balance.

In regard to the Seminary, this basic process has been
more or less absent. The interaction between student and
teacher (and hence between alumnus and teacher) has
differed from that which is found in non-Jewish theolog-

ical schools, not to speak of the average type of professional training institution. Seminary students and alumni tend to *defer* to their mentors to an unusual degree. In this instance, practitioners are very hesitant about interfering with schoolmen. How has this come about? Why the deviation from general patterns?

Attitudes in this area can be traced back to age-old Jewish culture patterns. According to the traditional system, the association between master and pupil has a quality of *sacredness* about it. The student is highly dependent upon his mentor, for it is the teacher who raises him from the dishonor of ignorance and makes him a knowledgable member of society. In the final analysis the association between teacher and student bears a strong resemblance to the parent-child relationship. All of this of course derives from the high value placed upon learning. While most Jews have by now moderated such attitudes or have channelized them into secular fields, as might be expected, rabbinical aspirants have tended to retain the traditional viewpoint longer than others.

The teachers whom the Conservative rabbinical student encountered at the Seminary not only approached Jewish subjects in conformity with the standards of higher learning, but their technical mastery of the corpus of Jewish law and literature was equal or superior to the level found in the *yeshiva*. Questions to which former Orthodox teachers had no satisfactory answers hardly puzzled these instructors. In relating what Ginzberg's courses meant to him as a student who had received his preliminary schooling in institutions of the traditional kind, Goldman had this to say:

. . . he has given the lie to the cry of legalism, and if he has not silenced the detractors of Pharisaic Judaism . . . he has certainly caused them to reel. With . . . an abundance of erudition he has demonstrated once and for all that the law had not been static but evolving . . . and that differences of opinion among the Rabbis were not formalistic, a kind of show of skill in pedantry, but concerned living issues. Employing by way of illustration the disagreements between the Hillelites and Shammaites, the matrix of nearly all Talmudic controversy, he consigns to oblivion . . . an infinite number of conjectures . . . regarding these schools. It is strange that men should have for generations repeated their words and debated their meaning, without wondering why it was that these two schools should have been so persistently . . . contradictory of each other. No one thought of inquiring into the motives and factors that had divided them. It was left to Professor Ginzberg to enlighten us. The Hillelites and the Shammaites, he revealed, were not recluse pedants engaged in a battle of words but the representatives of different economic and social strata clashing over the interests of their respective groups. What a revelation that was. . . .[45]

Under these conditions the fledgling rabbi has tended to transfer adoration—which normatively he was required to give to the learned class but which he could no longer accord to Orthodox instructors—to the Seminary teachers.[46] In a relatively secularized atmosphere, the student attempted to recreate a relationship more appropriate to the sacred environment from which he sprang, and from which he had become alienated both on philosophical grounds as well as because of his aspirations to serve a *middle-class* Conservative congregation instead of a more humble Orthodox synagogue.

The existence of such deference, being inappropriate in a secular order, has had ramified consequences. Since the practitioner is hesitant about demanding a revision of the curriculum and thus is actually best prepared for a role which becomes only a minor professional function, much of his activity is consequently improvised and learned while "on the job." Those who are somewhat rigid or who lack imagination fail to find much satisfaction in their work situation. There exists some rather generalized resentment as a result of the Seminary's failure to train for all of the roles which are exercised and hence to truly prepare the novice for the adjustment he will be required to make.

Given his Orthodox background, however, the practitioner may wish to perpetuate the fiction that he is actually exercising the rabbinical role to some degree. He may do so when in the company of his colleagues. Since attendance at rabbinical conventions is confined to functionaries, long and heated debates may be held there on various problems of Talmudic law. In addition the rabbi can develop support for the Seminary and strive to make it a "bulwark of Torah"—that is, help solidify its financial structure so that the institution can withstand external pressures and carry out a type of program which he would not attempt in his local synagogue. By strengthening the Seminary, the practitioner creates a center of rabbinical learning—one where the older values can be conserved in spite of the impact of the environment. While the rabbi cannot but feel somewhat alienated from the local Conservative synagogue (it is after all the province of the layman), the Seminary can give him a sense of expansiveness, *for here a type of "rabbinical culture" is being preserved safe from the influence of the uninitiated.*

These remarks require documentation as well as some further clarification. According to tradition, the rabbi should devote himself to a constant *enrichment* of his knowledge of the legal code. However, as we have seen, he has inadequate motivation for so doing either on the basis of status rewards (the laity do not much revere

Talmudic learning) or the demands of his institutionalized role. New functions also impose upon him a very
heavy load of duties. The rabbi consequently foregoes
continued systematic Talmudic study since he lacks both
leisure and motivation.

Except for the few functionaries who are especially
attracted to this type of learning, the majority are content
to have a knowledge of the legalistic tradition remain part
of their professional preparation.[47] It is true that now and
then a movement starts in the Conservative rabbinate to
revive interest in Talmudic studies. For example, on the
occasion of Ginzberg's seventieth birthday the functionaries—in order to please their teacher—attempted a systematic effort along these lines. It was said that:

> . . . the assiduous manner in which it [the Talmudic study
> plan] was carried out, as well as the very large number of men
> who participated in it, reveals to us that study is close to our
> hearts—no matter how preoccupied we are with congrega-
> tional, communal, national or world affairs. It indicates, more
> than anything else I know of, that we consider a knowledge of
> our Talmudic lore as basic to an intelligent and effective
> leadership for the present and to sound planning for the fu-
> ture. This is an important fact.
> . . . I urge that we make the *Siyyum Hashass* [celebration of
> the completion of a study of the whole set of Talmudic trac-
> tates] an integral part of our annual conventions and that
> we make it an occasion of honoring annually one of our Jewish
> scholars.[48]

The effort was short-lived. The rabbis had no time to
complete the required Talmudic assignments.[49]

All of this encourages the formation of guilt feelings
on the part of the functionary. This guilt can be reduced
by projecting the rabbinical role onto the Seminary
teacher. If the congregational rabbi himself no longer

studies the classical sources intensively, at least he may assist those at the Seminary who do. He may raise money in their behalf, or more significantly, he may accord them honor and homage. However, in spite of this, inasmuch as functionaries gradually lose interest in rabbinical learning, they cannot but help earn the disapproval of the schoolmen. Their deference does not result in making the attitude of the scholars any more sympathetic. On the contrary, the schoolmen tend to take advantage of the great prestige accorded to the scholar in the traditional Jewish system and to denigrate the rabbis. They are able to play upon the guilt which the rabbi feels as the result of his new role constellation, and his acceptance of the shift of authority. They imply that the functionaries are not *really* rabbis; it is only the Seminary teacher who is still a true spiritual leader. In addressing the Rabbinical Assembly—the union of Conservative rabbis—one prominent Midwestern spiritual leader stated that:

I need not tell you how untypical is the attitude of the professors toward American Jewish life . . . and I am sorry to say, towards the graduates of the Seminary. How much of a gap there is between the way in which we approach our problems and speak as if we possess authority, and the kind of feeling that prevails among the revered scholars who were and are our teachers.[50]

Another important rabbi has commented that:

The very fact that we ourselves may want to follow a certain pattern and as one of the rabbis expressed it . . . certain members of our faculty, our parents [sic!], have put us in shackles and in bonds, and in irons, so that we cannot move . . . is humiliating to us . . . [they] laugh at us as ignoramuses . . . [and imply] that we have been graduated as social workers and not as Rabbis for humanity.[51]

F.

DISCONTINUITIES AND CONFLICTS: THE ATTITUDE OF THE BOARD

The board of the Seminary has shown little concern with these problems. Representing another social stratum and motivated by different needs, they have lacked knowledge or interest in the type of discontinuities and conflicts which we have analyzed.[52] However, the differences of opinion which arose in the course of time between the faculty and administration, and the board are instructive, and they do serve to document our contention regarding the place of Americanization efforts in the development of Conservative Judaism. For example, the location of a new Seminary department, the Teachers Institute, provoked a good deal of dissension. At the time of the reorganization, Schiff had purchased ground and erected a building for the Seminary in the Morningside Heights district of Manhattan. The neighborhood was not a Jewish one nor was the location very convenient, but placing the building adjacent to the site of Columbia University was apparently a meaningful act to the donors.[53]

In 1909 Schiff presented a gift for the establishment of a teachers' training department. He insisted that it too be housed on Morningside Heights. It was pointed out that attendance in this department would be on a part-time basis only, and hence it was necessary to choose a more central location which would be closer to the home neighborhoods of the prospective students (chiefly the lower East Side and certain sections of Brooklyn), as well as to various Hebrew schools and Talmud Torahs. Schiff and others insisted, ostensibly because of the greater efficiency of a centralized administration, that students travel to the

Heights. Apparently they felt that establishing the school in a highly Jewish neighborhood would impede the Americanization of the student body and hence vitiate institutional purposes. The atmosphere of Morningside Heights, however, would be conducive to the proper kind of acculturation. After an impasse was reached and the establishment of the department imperiled, a compromise was arranged.[54]

Another point of contention was the Zionist issue. Since the board was heavily weighted with members of the German-Jewish upper class, it was opposed to this movement. The faculty and the students, East European Jews with an entirely different class origin, had strong Zionist inclinations. Schechter was under pressure to declare himself on Zionism; he finally delivered what amounted to an endorsement of the movement. While he indicated that in his opinion the leaders of Zionism lacked sufficient spirituality, he did make it clear that he felt that the movement was proving to be a positive force in the Jewish community. Specifically, it was attracting many individuals who had become alienated from the group—Zionism was thus proving helpful in the battle against assimilation. The differences between Schechter and Schiff on this issue were aired in the public press. In the exchange, Schiff stated that he was not only opposed to Zionism because of theoretical objections, but also on practical grounds: he feared that the movement would impede the progress of Americanization.[55]

The donors had many other community interests aside from the Seminary, and the institution never succeeded in occupying first rank among the various philanthropic endeavors. Schiff himself tended in time to give an increasing amount of attention to hospitals and social agencies.[56] This trend was strengthened by the inability of the Seminary, from the viewpoint of the donors, to exercise greater influence in the East European community. It became clear in time that, regardless of the Seminary, the Orthodox group would go ahead and build their own set of institutions. The split between Orthodoxy and Conservatism was not welcomed by the donors—they did not understand the necessity for any divisions in what they could only regard as a homogeneous group.[57]

Another point of criticism was that several Seminary-trained rabbis had accepted calls from Reform congregations—graduates were thus failing to minister to the immigrants and their children.[58] Actually, placement during the early years posed difficult problems. Seminary graduates were appropriate only for middle-class congregations. As we noticed, large numbers of such pulpits were not available before World War I. Thus until evolving class structure and acculturative processes produced the right type of congregations, opportunities were limited. But the donors were not inclined to reason that the tempo of Americanization (and hence the founding of suitable congregations) was chiefly geared to the ebb and flow of social and economic forces, and could not be substantially affected by the maneuverings of special groups within the minority community.

That there were differences in objectives between faculty and administration and the board became increasingly clear after 1910. During what may be termed his period of disillusionment (from about 1912 to his death in 1915), Schechter stated: "It is absolutely impossible that the Institution should flourish and succeed in its ultimate aims on support coming from those who are not in complete sympathy with it." [59] His realization of how he was being used to accomplish the purposes of the donors came as a rude awakening:

I must take it out of their minds that I came into this country for the purpose of converting the downtown [lower East Side] Jew to a more refined species of religion.[60]

. . . no consideration . . . would ever have induced me . . . [to assume the post] had I known that the Seminary was largely meant for a particular section of the community, forming a sort of higher Talmud Torah, having the purpose of reconciling the most unruly element in Jewry and giving it a little religious refinement. It is true that I never heard such a sentiment expressed by the Board but the growing indifference on the part of several of the Trustees . . . makes me believe that I am not quite wrong in my judgment . . .[61]

By the 1930's, some assimilation had taken place among the members of the old upper-class families. This, coupled with the Depression as well as the declining importance of the Americanization problem, resulted in decreased support.[62] A new appeal was made to the philanthropic group on the basis of the actual and potential contribution of the institution to the betterment of interfaith relations.[63] However, the donors were already contributing to other organizations which specialized in work of this kind, and little additional support was enlisted. Under the administration of Louis Finkelstein, an appeal for funds was made chiefly to Conservative Jewry. This was done largely through the graduates of the Seminary and it met with much success. Actually an expanded interfaith program at the Seminary has become an important means of gaining additional support from Conservative Jews as well as from outside sources.[64]

The board is still not wholly Conservative in composition—the institution is administered by a cohesive body of schoolmen who have succeeded in striking a balance between themselves and the laity and functionaries. The unified nature of the administrative group has resulted in much growth in the institution. There is little control on the part of the non-administrators of the Seminary's ideological direction. It is generally considered as the center of the right-wing forces in the Conservative movement.

G.

THE PROBLEM OF RECRUITMENT

What shall be the future sources of professional recruitment for the Conservative movement? In the past the bulk of the religious specialists have come from Orthodoxy. This has resulted in much homogeneity as between rabbi and congregant, for the background of the typical synagogue member was also Orthodox and his class origin was similar to that of the spiritual leader. The rabbi's mobility, in terms of leaving lower-class and lower-middle-class Orthodoxy and entering Conservatism, was paralleled by the layman's own experience in having joined the movement when he achieved solid middle-class rank and moved to the area of third settlement. Actually, much of the rapport which has existed between rabbi and congregant can be traced to this common factor.

Now that Conservatism has achieved a relatively high degree of institutionalization, the professionals—as those who have most at stake in institutional maintenance—face the problem of replacement. Shall their successors, like themselves, be recruited from Orthodoxy, thereby preserving class mobility? Or shall an attempt be made to recruit future rabbis from Conservative families? In recent years there has been a tendency to favor the second alternative. The explanation given for this is that:

We rely virtually exclusively on the students that are prepared . . . in other institutions. The Orthodox group leads this Seminary and every other Seminary. Unless we start preparing our own leadership, the time will come when we will not have that leadership.[65]

There has *not* been any serious lag in the number of recruits coming from Orthodox homes. The utilization of Conservative Jewry as a recruitment source points to efforts on the part of the present functionaries to raise their professional status and to strengthen their institutions by providing specialists whose class background will parallel that of their congregants. Limitations on the recruitment of candidates who possess lower-class backgrounds, as well as deviant opinions and objectionable personal habits (as sometimes occurs with ex-Orthodox aspirants), serves professional purposes although at the same time it increases institutionalization and rigidity.

Two problems are involved in this type of recruitment. The first is the question of status. The second is the educational problem. Functionaries are aware that most Conservative parents rank other professions far ahead of the rabbinate and thus would discourage their sons from choosing such a career.[66] The spiritual leaders can do nothing immediate about the status problem, but they can seek to improve Jewish education so that at least a few of their young people will have sufficient preparation to consider entering the rabbinate if they have any inclination along these lines. Since it is generally necessary to have continuous preparation in Jewish subjects if one is to qualify for the Conservative rabbinate or even for Hebrew school teaching, the lack of a substantial number of Conservative children who continue their education on the secondary school level *ipso facto* limits the number of possible candidates. Most Conservative congregations, we noticed, do not have satisfactory departments of secondary education.

There is no lack of such facilities in medium- and large-sized communities, for communal Hebrew high schools exist in most cities.[67] These institutions generally have excellent standards and are open to graduates of Hebrew schools and Talmud Torahs. But the potential of these schools in terms of possible professional recruitment is low. Only a small number of Conservative children attend them.[68] When they do enroll, Conservative students frequently experience difficulty, for their background is less rich than that possessed by Talmud Torah graduates. Moreover, those who succeed in effecting a satisfactory adjustment are frequently alienated somewhat from Conservatism. They tend to be attracted by Zionist or other youth groups outside of the synagogue structure. The cosmopolitan influences present in these schools may loosen the hold of rabbi and parent over the child in terms of the Conservative approach to Judaism.

As a result of the desire to restrict further recruitment from Orthodoxy and to enroll a professional group from among the Conservative constituency, the "Leadership Training Fellowship" has been founded. According to the plan, interested students of high school age need not go outside of the Conservative movement for their secondary Jewish education. Rather, they meet in the form of small study groups in their own congregations. If the rabbi does not have the time to teach the group himself (the ideal arrangement), he is required to meet with them regularly. Extensive use is made of club techniques, and even those adolescents who still receive their Hebrew education outside of the congregation are provided with an organization which features many of the elements of the intensive type of Jewish youth group. While the acceptance of any large number of Leadership Training Fellowship graduates for professional training would force the lowering of the Seminary's scholastic level (particularly in the area of Talmudic studies), the drive toward greater institutionalization may be able to offset the influence of those who would seek to preserve present standards. Furthermore, it is possible that some of the Reconstructionist-minded rabbis hope that L.T.F. graduates will help provide a liberally-minded student body.

The scheme has not been in operation long enough to provide much in the way of conclusions about its value. It is noteworthy that the function of the group in terms of professional recruitment is seldom stressed on the local level, where the emphasis is chiefly on the provision for an improved Jewish education. It is recognized by many rabbis that even if a low percentage of the members finally decide not to join the ranks of the professionals because of the status problem and other factors, at least a well educated and loyal cadre of Conservative lay leaders will have been created.

VII

The Question of Ideology

AS WAS noted at the start of our analysis, the determination of the exact ideological position of Conservatism has constituted a problem both for those outside as well as inside of the movement.* It is thus not surprising that attempts by previous investigators to arrive at very precise formulations have been unsuccessful. If descriptions were of a general character, they tended to portray more of a tendency than an ideology; if formulations were exact, they could be refuted on the basis that some group within the movement was being excluded. The confusion has been compounded since no organizational publications are regarded by Conservative Jewry as authoritative, no convention resolutions exist which define Conservatism with any precision, and no promotional materials have been issued which present the Conservative program. How then can the ideological problem be clarified?

The basic error of most investigators would seem to be that of treating the rabbis and the laymen as a unit. We have seen that in fact these two groups represent different

---

* See *infra*, p. 15. In the light of our purposes, it seems desirable to disregard the distinctions between "ideology" and "theology." We therefore will use these terms synonymously until Section "B."

worlds, the problems which each one confronts being special to its own sociological position. Since *laymen* rather
than rabbis were the real founders of Conservatism, a logical starting point in studying the problem of ideology is
a consideration of the attitudes of the laity.

A.

THE APPROACH OF THE LAITY

In contrast to subjects such as attendance at worship,
form of service, Jewish education, youth work, and synagogue administration, the material available in Conservative sources about the attitudes of the laity in the area of
religious ideology is relatively scanty. Significantly, the
two surveys conducted by the United Synagogue (the national union of Conservative congregations) do not touch
directly upon this problem. Occasionally, material found
in convention proceedings is enlightening. But for our
basic orientation we shall draw chiefly upon some of the
data gathered in a recent study of Jewish identification.[1]

The interviewing site for this research was a community
located on the Eastern seaboard (we shall call it "Eastville") whose Jewish population totals some 10,000 persons. The study design called for lengthy interviews dealing with the practices, beliefs and attitudes of Jews in
many areas related to their minority-group identification.
Interviews were held with young people aged 13-20, and
with either one of their parents. Most questions were
open-ended. The transmission of values from one generation to the other was a special focus of this research. Because of our particular purpose, we are somewhat more
interested in the attitudes of the Eastville parents than
we are in those of Eastville's young people.[2]

In the course of the interview, the adult respondents

were asked whether they considered themselves Reform, Conservative, or Orthodox Jews. Some 43% felt that they were Conservative (approximately the same percentage of adolescents described their parents as Conservative). These respondents were then asked: *"What do you mean when you say you are Conservative?"* *

The first significant fact is that only 4% of the adults answering the question: "What do you mean when you say you are Conservative?" reply in terms of *personal background* ("I was raised in a Conservative home"). This result is not surprising, however, for as we have pointed out, Conservatism is a recent development. The figure of 4% is strongly influenced by the fact that most of the parental respondents are between ages 40-49. But even a random sampling of the membership of the Eastville congregation would not change this figure substantially. While more of the younger members would come from a Conservative background, their influence could be offset by the members who are over fifty, who would originate almost entirely from an Orthodox environment.

This leads us to a consideration of an important finding about the Conservative Jews of Eastville. A total of 90% of them answer the question in terms of their *practices, personal behavior,* or *ideals.* ** On inspection these answers

---

* Since some who identify themselves as Conservative do not actually belong to Eastville's Conservative synagogue, our analysis is chiefly confined to the replies of those adults who *have* made such an affiliation. This is done on the assumption that their attitudes are more representative of Conservative opinion than are those of non-affiliated individuals.

** In addition a total of 34% of the respondents answer in terms of *synagogue affiliation*—they consider themselves Conservative because they belong to a Conservative congregation. Thus some individuals volunteer both "affiliation" as well as "personal practices, behavior, and ideals" in explanation of their Conservatism. The "affiliation" answer offers little material for analysis and interpretation; reference made to membership in the local Conservative synagogue is frequently deleted in the answers reproduced below.

appear to be highly varied, but it would seem that qualitative analysis could yield significant results.* Indeed,
after being studied intensively and grouped into meaningful categories, it became apparent that a *common* thread
does in fact run through all of the responses in this category.

From other data in the Eastville study we learn that all
the Conservative respondents come from the East European cultural milieu: in the main they are the offspring
of immigrant parents who were Orthodox Jews. Furthermore, the answers of Conservative respondents to various
queries designed to test Jewish identification indicate that
they ardently desire the *survival of Jewry as a recognizable
entity in American society.* This fits in with our analytical scheme, for the "desire for survival" factor was posited
in Chapter I as basic to an understanding of trends in
present-day Jewish communal life, and especially to the
growth of the Conservative movement.[3] Furthermore, the
Orthodox background of present-day Conservative Jewry
has constituted one of the central foci of our investigation.
An answer given by one of the Eastville respondents includes mention of both of these two important factors:

("What do you mean when you say you are Conservative?")

I've been brought up in a very religious home and . . . have
grown away from many of the customs. But I still have a
strong Jewish feeling.

Why does the Conservative Jew think of himself as
"Conservative"? Like the individual quoted above who
has "grown away" from the customs, the Conservative Jew

---

* While a rigorous coding type of procedure could have been attempted, a looser qualitative handling of the data is satisfactory for our
purposes.

no longer observes various rituals which he considers incumbent upon one who would regard himself as Orthodox. *Kashruth,* the system of food taboos, is seen by respondents as being the foremost criterion of differentiation between themselves and Orthodox Jewry. Although some respondents are ambiguous, quite a number of them feel that Conservatism permits its adherents wide latitude in the observance of *kashruth.* On the other hand, the Conservative Jew also conceives of himself as "Conservative" because he is not completely permissive—he still observes some of the dietary restrictions.*

The dominant pattern, already suggested in Chapter III, is the retention of at least some degree of *kashruth* in the home. However, the Conservative Jew—to use the popular expression—"eats out." That is, he consumes non-kosher food in public restaurants or at the home of friends. Just as the extent of observance differs from one Conservative household to another, the degree of compromise involved in "eating out" similarly varies. When dining, some may partake only of the permitted foods (ritualistically considered, these are of course non-kosher since they are prepared with non-kosher utensils, or are served on dishes which have previously contained non-kosher food). But then there are also those who do eat foods of the prohibited type, such as pork or shellfish. These distinctions, however, are not of the first importance. The really significant facts are that (1) the *isolating* function of the dietary laws no longer operates as far as most of Conservative Jewry is concerned; (2) nevertheless, the role of *kashruth* as an axis of *Jewishness* is still manifest. The follow-

---

* In Chapters I-III we stressed the legalistic, rigid, and Eastern nature of traditional Judaism; *kashruth* is of course one area which is highly legalistic, rigid, and departs widely from Western practice. However, its importance in the American Jewish community as a mark of differentiation is a matter which is worthy of some further analysis.

ing three respondents supply important evidence about the role of dietary laws in defining Conservatism:

("What do you mean when you say you are Conservative?")

What a question! Well, I keep a kosher home as far as possible, and I light [Sabbath] candles. But when I go out I eat all sorts of things I don't have at home. To me that's Conservative.

. . . I practice Orthodox habits in my home, that is, I have strictly an Orthodox kitchen, but we do eat out, and when you eat out you know you can't be sure of *kashruth*.

. . . I enjoy [eating] everything out that I don't have in my house, which is strictly Orthodox.

Data from the Eastville study would support the contention that there *are* Conservative Jews who have abandoned many (although in most cases not all) of the dietary laws both *inside* as well as outside of the home. But significantly, such individuals have guilt feelings. It appears that they concede that ideally they should be more observant. The ambivalence of the following respondent, for example, is clear:

("What do you mean when you say you are Conservative?")

We are not as strict as the rabbi would like us to be, but we keep all the festivals, the holidays. We always have a big *seder* and we don't have any bread during Passover. During the war I decided not to buy kosher meat any more because it was very difficult with the ration points. So we gave up keeping a kosher house. I had the worst feeling changing from kosher meat and it took me an awfully long time to get used to it. Even now I have guilty feelings about it, especially when the rabbi uses this as the chief topic of his sermon. But in many ways we do keep the Jewish customs nevertheless, and I could never buy pork or serve butter with meat at meals.

Just as this respondent stresses her observance of the holidays—taking pains to point out that her family always has a large *seder* on Passover—the individual quoted below suggests that regardless of lack of strictness about kitchen utensils, her children have been given a good Jewish education:

("Would you describe yourself as Reform, Conservative, or Orthodox?")

Conservative. . . . We use kosher foods, although I'm not too fussy about the dishes. We keep *milchig* [milk] and *fleischig* [meat] separate, but you know how some people are: If they make a mistake and mix it once, then they throw the dish away. I don't believe in that, but I buy kosher meats and we observe the holidays. . . . Our children are given a good Jewish education; I have two boys and a girl, and they all went to Hebrew school. The girl went to Hebrew school till the doctor told her she had to stop; the print was affecting her eyes and gave her headaches. But the boys got a very good education in Hebrew.

The defensiveness of another respondent, who also does not keep a kosher home, is plain:

("Would you describe yourself as Reform, Conservative, or Orthodox?")

Sort of in between—not Orthodox and not Reform. Let's say like the [people at the Conservative synagogue] . . . Well, I don't keep a kosher home but I am a 100% Jew at heart. I don't run to synagogue, but I wouldn't do anything to harm the Jewish people.

There is another deviation of Conservative Jewry which makes them feel "Conservative." This is their violation of the Sabbath:

("What do you mean when you say you are Conservative?")

I believe in the Jewish beliefs, but I am not a hundred percent religious. I ride on Saturday and strike matches and if you were really Orthodox you wouldn't do that.

However, *kashruth* is seen as the chief area of violation of the Orthodox norms.

It is notable that in none of the remarks of the respondents who have been quoted thus far is there any mention of a disagreement with the *theology* of Orthodoxy. From further reading of the Eastville interviews it becomes apparent that almost all the respondents feel that it is some aspect of their personal behavior which is in conflict with one or another of the *mitzvoth* of the Jewish sacred system. These, rather than any doctrinal deviations, result in their considering themselves "Conservative."

While some individuals describe themselves as Conservative because of their alienation from Orthodox practices, others define themselves from the opposite direction —they point out that they are Conservative because they are not *Reform.* Here again theology is not involved. Rather, certain Reform practices are distasteful to the Conservative Jew. Reform is "un-Jewish"—it is a form of Judaism which is too highly adapted. Significantly, however, the Conservative Jew describes Reform as "cold," "churchlike," or "going too far," rather than as being subversive or heretical.

From the Conservative standpoint the most jarring innovation is that in the Reform temple males do not cover their heads during worship. Another irritation is that most of the Reform prayers are recited in English rather than in Hebrew. Among various other deviations which strike the Conservative Jew as being objectionable is the fact that Reform sanctions traveling on holidays. While the Conservative Jew commonly travels on the Sabbath and the festivals, except in suburban areas where distances are prohibitive, he usually makes a point of walking to synagogue on the High Holidays. The parking of automobiles around a Jewish house of worship on *Rosh Hashonoh* and *Yom Kippur* strikes the Conservative Jew as being in very questionable taste.* The remarks of the following four respondents illustrate some of these points:

("What do you mean when you say you are Conservative?")

I believe [that] . . . there should be a certain amount of old and new customs. I don't like to walk into the synagogue feeling I'm in a church and take my hat off, and everything in English.

. . . [I'm] not Orthodox like my parents used to be, and I still like to wear a hat when I go to shul. Even the Pope wears a hat, you never see him without it.

It's hard to explain but I can't go over as far as the Reformed —not that I have anything against them. We've gone to them, but have gone back to the Conservative.

I wouldn't say I was religious—and I wouldn't say I was Reformed—because if I was Orthodox, I would have to follow all the laws which I don't—and Reform I don't like. I don't believe in going into temple and then coming out and riding. That's something I wouldn't do on our High Holidays.

This last respondent provides us with the master key to the feelings of the laity. Essentially, they believe that their movement is a "halfway house" between Reform and Orthodoxy. It is a type of Judaism which, while not orthodox, derives from traditional sources; while not completely reformed, it is sufficiently advanced so as to be "modern":

---

* Of course, respondents also feel that Reform Jews are overly neglectful of the *kashruth* laws. This point, however, is not touched upon in the quotations reproduced here.

("What do you mean when you say you are Conservative?")

Well, sort of not Orthodox but more Orthodox than Reform.

Well, I'm not 100% Orthodox, and of course I'm not Reformed—I'm just in between.

Now—I guess you'd call it the middle of the road, as far as being as strict as the Orthodox, yet not quite Reformed as the Reformed.

. . . I don't like the old-fashioned type, or the Reform. I'm between the two of them.

Well, we believe in everything Jewish and yet we are not too strict.

In line with this viewpoint of Conservatism as constituting a "halfway house," some respondents answer by mentioning a special aspect of their movement which they find attractive. They thereby imply (or sometimes actually state) their differences with Orthodoxy or Reform. Again, no approaches of a philosophical nature are apparent. Rather, adherents generally stress the agreeableness of the Conservative service. They like the fact that men and women sit together, that English translations of some of the prayers are used, and that some of the services are shorter than those conducted in the Orthodox synagogue:

("What do you mean when you say you are Conservative?")

I still buy Kosher meat. I don't know, I guess I believe in their form of worship—don't believe in Reform.

Well, I agree with the ideas. It's not . . . [like] the [Orthodox] synagogue on [X Street], where they speak [pray] entirely in Hebrew, and I don't understand what they are talking about. At . . . [our congregation] I can follow the service.

Well, the type of services we have, like most of the Orthodox people have a separation of men and women; the Conservative doesn't. The services are primarily more understandable for the younger generation. [Also] when I go to shul I like to sit with my husband and not be boxed away from him. I like the service, I understand the text. They conduct it in Hebrew and English, and I can read it in English and understand it more. If I had to do it in Hebrew I would just be unable, and I wouldn't know what they were talking about. I went to Hebrew school as a girl, but the way they taught you in those days, you never knew what you were learning.

I believe in the Conservative type of services rather than the strictly Orthodox. Actually Conservative means conserving, conserving of time, from the way services are conducted. That's from my experience in Orthodox synagogues.

A few individuals do attempt a somewhat more theoretical approach to Conservatism, but they can get no further than describing their movement with glittering generalities. According to them it is "progressive," or "modern." In actuality they cannot suggest any theological principles which would differentiate Conservatism from its two predecessor movements:

("What do you mean when you say you are Conservative?")

Orthodoxy is stagnant . . . whereas Conservative is progressive . . . at least I rationalize it that way.

Well, I believe I practice and keep the religion to a more modern way. I'm not fanatic, yet there are many ways I wouldn't think of not doing that the Reform have done away with. . . . I have gone into the Reform once in a while and feel strange.

What about the opinions of the offspring of Conservative parents? Presumably such young people have not experienced the process of alienation from Orthodoxy; they have also not been faced with the possibility of joining Reform. Unlike their parents, they have been educated in Conservative Sunday and Hebrew schools; a system of

Conservative thought might conceivably have been transmitted to them by their teachers.

It is notable, however, that young people give much the same type of responses as do their parents. While ample evidence exists pointing to the fact that in Eastville the Conservative school and synagogue *has* succeeded in inculcating institutional loyalties, there is no indication of the transmission of any substantial religious ideology. To both parent and child Conservatism is a happy medium between Reform and Orthodoxy which involves observing *some* of the customs:

("What do you mean when you say they [your parents] are Conservative?")

They believe in some customs and they don't believe in others.

Well—they aren't as religious as the Orthodox, and they're not as Reform as the Reformed—a happy medium between the two.

They don't go all out like the Orthodox, but they don't let everything go by like the Reformed.

Gosh, these are some questions! Well, let's see now. Well, I feel that they certainly don't observe all the Jewish traditions to the utmost, and therefore aren't Orthodox. . . . I guess you would say they are midway between nothing and something. I don't know how else to put it. I never thought before to define it.

The areas of violations volunteered by young people are the same as those advanced by adults: dietary laws and Sabbath. However, young people appear to mention the problem of Sabbath somewhat more frequently than do their parents:

("What do you mean when you say they [your parents] are Conservative?")

We don't go all the way with religious rituals down to the bottom. We keep the main customs. For example we work on

Shabbas. We think religion has its place; we don't go all the way into Reform, either.

Well, we don't go to extremes like turning out the lights for Friday and Saturday. I do homework on the Sabbath. We follow it just strict enough to be Conservative.

Well, I would say the Conservative approach fits them best—that is, looking at it from a point of view of the actual program of Conservatism. . . . We don't observe the Sabbath completely, and then too we eat out, eating meat meals outside, I mean.

They don't go to the extreme, say sometimes on Saturday you're not supposed to do any work, well, we would put out the lights and not think of that as work, and when we go out and eat, we wouldn't hesitate to order a bacon, lettuce and tomato sandwich.

Only a handful of young people have a wider perspective. The following respondent, for example, is highly atypical inasmuch as she suggests—in part—a *theological* approach. She has been away at school for some years—it is worthwhile speculating whether or not she would have given this type of answer had she remained at home and thus continued to observe the dietary laws:

("What do you think you will be when you are married and have your own family?")

Conservative. Well, I've—while I have some emotional attachment according to my upbringing, [but] being away at school so much, I've gotten away from *kashruth*. I would like to think of myself as still adhering to *kashruth* when I'm married, but I'm not sure that once being away from it that I would go back to it. In addition to that, on the plane of theology, I accept the theory of Conservatism or Reconstructionism of divine inspiration rather than divine revelation.

It was pointed out earlier that the Conservative movement has been created by the establishment of a certain type of synagogue by groups of East European Jews whose

class level and degree of acculturation made both Orthodoxy and Reform unacceptable.[4] The type of answers
given to the question "What do you mean when you say
you are Conservative?" by Eastville parents, as well as to
a related query asked of young people, reinforces the view
that in this community at least, the basis of group integration in Conservatism has *not* been an explicit ideology.
Rather, alienation from the Orthodoxy in which the inno-
vators and their followers were reared, and the unacceptable character of some of the practices common to Reform,
have served as the propelling forces. Furthermore, the
nature of the replies given by Eastville respondents indicates that they have not been indoctrinated with a common set of theological principles. The basis of integration
is loyalty to a given institution, a similar background, a
given class level, a more or less similar type of social
adjustment, as well as a *common amount and kind of
acculturation*. The Conservative Jews of Eastville see
themselves and their synagogue in terms of some middle
road between Orthodoxy and Reform which incorporates
the best features of both systems.[5] As it has been expressed
idiomatically, Conservative Judaism is a "50-50 proposition." [6]

B.

IDEOLOGICAL CLARIFICATION:
FORCES PRO AND CON

How do Conservative Jews feel about the fact that integration has been achieved on the basis of a common
level of acculturation and adjustment rather than by the
promulgation of an ideology? Is there a demand for a distinctive Conservative religious system? Do individuals feel

the need for guidance in matters of theological creed or religious code?

These are difficult questions to answer. They could only be considered authoritatively if given separate monographic treatment. In lieu of this, it seems safe to suggest that most of the laity at present feel that ideology is not a matter of really great concern. The paramount problem is to preserve—in spite of environmental pressures—something of the Jewish heritage. The general feeling is that this can be accomplished by expanding the Conservative movement—the main problem is to interest people in the synagogue. Also, some local congregational leaders feel that not only are their fellow laymen apathetic to ideological clarification, but that such discussions are dangerous since they might help promote dissension. An excerpt from the minutes of a United Synagogue board meeting provides some instructive material in this regard. The following discussion took place:

Mr. Rothschild: . . . the people when they come into a synagogue do not philosophize, and the important thing is to get them interested in synagogue life.
Mr. Sachs: I feel like Mr. Rothschild. . . . I was the president of a synagogue for many years . . . very few laymen have ever approached me to discuss the philosophy of the Conservative movement; they have simply joined because they have lived there; they wanted their children to go to school.
We have to take a definite stand. This is the Conservative movement; if you are a rightist you belong to the Orthodox; if you are a leftist you belong to the Reform. This is our philosophy; this is our tradition; these are our rituals. . . .[7]

It is undeniable, however, that there *are* individual Conservative Jews, even "pillars of the synagogue," who are troubled by what they regard as inconsistencies. However, their self-examination seems to be confined to problems of dietary violations rather than extending into the general area of religious ideology. The following two Eastville respondents illustrate this tendency:

("Would you describe yourself as Reform, Conservative, or Orthodox?")

I would describe myself as Conservative with Orthodox leanings in some respects and with liberal leanings in other respects. But the Conservative movement is sort of fluid anyhow, that is, as I know it. ["What do you mean when you say you are Conservative?"] I think my leanings toward Orthodoxy would probably emanate from a sentimental disposition more than from conviction—my father and mother were Orthodox, and I had a lot of respect for them, and I sort of hesitate to break certain traditions which I know they wanted me to follow—so in many cases I follow them symbolically, rather than to the letter. Even under the Conservative movement you are expected to carry out the laws of *kashruth*—I carry it out at home to a modified degree. I try not to bring food into the house which is non-kosher, but I don't hesitate to eat anything when not at home. I don't justify exactly what I'm doing myself.

("Is there anything about the Jewish religion or culture that you don't like?")

I don't like the hypocrisy lately of our Conservative movement. I really shouldn't say this, but it's true—people would be shocked if they knew I felt this way. . . . I feel that we are doing things on the outside that our children are taught not to do, at the synagogue and in the Sunday school. And as a pillar of the Conservative synagogue, both my husband and I feel confused as to what is wrong and what is right. . . . Maybe we're Reformed and don't know it, because we certainly don't lean towards Orthodoxy. Still, when we go to a Reform synagogue we feel that it's too cold.

A nationally known lay leader, while stating matters somewhat differently than these two individuals, also has

stressed the need for working out some consistent pattern
of observance:

> No amount of talk will dissipate the fact that there is con-
> fusion throughout our movement. Some people insist on say-
> ing "don't bring it up in public—time will help out." Well,
> the Conservative movement is about fifty years old. Some of
> us are getting pretty well along in life, and we want a scheme
> for living today.[8]

It is significant that in spite of the diffuse character of
such statements, ideological clarification does intrude itself now and then as a problem in Conservatism. What
are the forces which encourage, or inhibit, this tendency?
Trends in social stratification among Jews, the development of denominational rivalry, the present status of
Zionism, the influence of the Seminary group, and the
ambivalence of the laity and functionaries are among the
relevant factors which require discussion.

The nature of the evolving class structure of American
Jewry has served to encourage discussion of ideological
issues. Although our data on stratification is imprecise,
the underlying trend is clear: *There is a growing stabilization of the class position of most Jews at the middle level.*
The Jewish working class appears to be vanishing from all
but the largest communities—the phenomenon of an American Jewish working class may turn out to be characteristic of only the immigrant era.[9] On the top social level,
some degree of assimilation has taken place, particularly
among older American Jewish families. Jewish membership in the upper class has also been limited by low birth-
rates, the fact that Jews have not been able to gain access
to desirable positions in some of the key industries or
even to penetrate the top levels in certain professions, and

the fact that Jews have not retained their position in certain fields of endeavor once the businesses lost their speculative character. The diminishing importance of private banking as an element in American enterprise is another factor of importance in determining patterns of Jewish stratification. It would seem that the class distribution of American Jewry is coming to appear as diamond-shaped instead of in the form of a pyramid. Of course this phenomenon is not limited to the Jewish community, but it appears to be occurring with particular rapidity there.

When the group had been highly stratified, class and status served as the devices regulating religious affiliation. Since a sufficient pool of individuals existed in each level, the "denominations" could limit themselves to working among their special publics. Now, however, all must attract some middle-class adherents. The officials of each of the movements constitute power groups which seek to influence their group either to raise or to lower the class level to which it will appeal. In short, Reform, Conservatism and Orthodoxy must now compete against each other for affiliation and support.[10]

The pressure for ideological elaboration in Conservatism originates both from the direction of the laymen as well as from the officials. The latter are charged with expanding their movement and thus they seek to find some religious message or ritual which will be distinctive to their group—something which may be claimed as uniquely Conservative. Thoughtful laymen, on the other hand, start to wonder about what their movement stands for as they observe individuals of a similar class and status in Orthodoxy or Reform. Both laymen and officials begin to feel a need for ideological differentiation which will function in compensation for lack of class and status distinctiveness.

It is somewhat surprising to note that during the 1920's

a prominent Conservative rabbi was already concerned about the effect which growing homogeneity would have upon the ideological void in Conservatism. The "drift toward the middle," lately noted by students of Jewish life, apparently was already then beginning to emerge as a significant factor:

> In the past we were vague about our program. . . . Our role was essentially . . . to guard against the dangers of unmodified Reform, while accepting the principle of progress via interpretation. Now, however, Reform is becoming more Conservative. As Reform Judaism becomes more Conservative . . . it will leave to Conservative Judaism less and less to hold on to as its position.
>
> On the other hand there is the orthodox party which has become aggressive in recent years, and is first learning the lessons of organization. They have sloughed off their foreign mannerisms, Yiddish, learned organization and publicity. . . . Indeed, there are some among us who are puzzled to understand wherein we conservatives, so-called, differ from this revamped orthodoxy which permits decorum in the service and English in the sermon. . . .[11]

Thus the increased traditionalism of Reform, and the Americanization of Orthodoxy, tends to make the type of relationship existing between the three movements previously, less meaningful. According to one leading Conservative rabbi:

> No apology or defense is necessary therefore for the negations which were implicit in our position from the outset, although our positive formulations were by comparison pale and feeble. We spoke of the process of development. . . . We stressed the integrity of the Jewish motive in refutation of those who favored an easy and convenient capitulation to the environment. In the same breath we spoke of the flexibility and fluidity of our social heritage as Jews. . . .
>
> . . . we must face the truth that we have been halting between fear and danger; fear of the Orthodox and danger of Reform. . . . The time has come for our emergence from the valley of

indecision. For one thing, there is a growing grass-root demand for . . . clarification of our position. There is a growing impatience on the part of our people. . . .[12]

A desire for ideological elaboration occurs at the time when social distance is diminishing; resulting denominational rivalry tends to encourage *separatism* in each group. There is an attempt to demonstrate that the Conservative movement, for example, can by itself provide for all of the needs of its congregants. One well-known rabbi speaks of the ". . . stigma that has afflicted our movement all these years, where in our most traditional congregations we had and still have Reform textbooks." [13] It is notable that no objection to the *content* of the textbooks has been made, and indeed in most cases the Reform volumes are hardly sectarian in nature. The problem is rather that the Conservative movement has not made the necessary texts available under its *own* imprint.

In the 1940's it was observed with increasing frequency that while local synagogues—and to a somewhat lesser extent the Seminary—were strong institutions, the United Synagogue had remained largely a paper organization. The degree of solidarity and intercongregational cooperation attained by Reform served to demonstrate what could be accomplished by efficient organization:

. . . our movement . . . has suffered from two major defects in the past. . . . In the first place we have been very weak in regard to the philosophy in our movement. . . . We have been strong in action but weak in theory. Maybe that is the American way. It can be carried too far.

The second weakness of our movement has lain in the United Synagogue, in our national organization. We have been a peculiar kind of chain, for each link was stronger than the chain as a whole. Our congregations were beehives of activity . . . while the national organization . . . went begging for support.[14]

What we need is an integrated movement. Not a loose confederacy of 500 independent congregations headed by a Seminary, Rabbinical Assembly, and a United Synagogue which are at times working at cross purposes, whose allegiance to one and another is not always definite and to whom the allegiance in turn of the 500 Synagogues is largely perfunctory.[15]

When a new director of the United Synagogue (Rabbi Albert I. Gordon) was installed in the 1940's, one of the key points in his program was that it was unrealistic—even dishonest—to attempt to establish a strong national organization without first clarifying the Conservative ideology:

There is much to be desired both from the point of view of the loyalties we elicit and the sense of discipline we have a right to expect. . . .

I believe, therefore, that it is of tremendous importance that the Conservative congregations . . . undertake the arduous but all-rewarding task of formulating the program of Conservative Judaism . . . it is the most important task that confronts us. We must cease to be regarded as "middle-of-the-roaders" by our lay people and must instead evolve and develop a positive approach to Jewish life. . . .

We must help to overcome the confusion of thought with reference to the nature of Conservative Judaism. . . . I plead for the good-will of my colleagues and all those who guide the destiny of the . . . Seminary.[16]

Another development which has served to increase interest in ideological clarification is the present position of Zionism. Both laymen and professionals within Conservatism have been very loyal to this cause; the Conservative rabbinate in particular has provided much of the leadership for general (as distinguished from labor and religious) Zionism in the United States.[17] Sentiment among Conservative Jews was so strong that in the 1940's plans were formulated by the Zionist Organization of America to make use of the synagogue machinery in bolstering Zionist strength. The organization contemplated stressing

congregational enrollment rather than individual enrollment as before.[18] Under this new arrangement members
of a congregation were to be affiliated with a Zionist group
unless they specifically indicated a contrary desire: Zionist
dues would be billed together with congregational fees,
the synagogue membership would comprise a local Zionist
district, and Zionist activities would be incorporated into
the congregational program. Zionist leaders believed that
the plan would have its greatest impact upon Conservative
congregations. However, after some initial success, the
scheme died in most places for lack of support. Rabbis
and laymen, although staunch Zionists (and hence strongly
interested in the cause of ethnic group maintenance), indicated that the program did not belong in the synagogue
inasmuch as it would conflict with efforts directed toward
institutional maintenance. They preferred to support the
cause outside of the synagogue.

Regardless of this inability to coordinate Zionist and
congregational activities, Jewish nationalism did serve to
fill the ideological void created by the absence of a specifically Conservative system of ideas. A special variety of
Zionist thought known as "cultural Zionism" was popular
in Conservative circles.[19] It served to help rationalize the
continuance of residence in America by stressing the
worthwhileness of Jewish work in the Diaspora, and it
also indicated an appealing program of activity.

Recent developments have been responsible for modifying the picture. The loss of direction of Zionist activity
in America traceable to the establishment of the State of
Israel, the concentration of efforts in the area of fund-
raising, and the lack of fruitful cultural interchange between Israel and American Jewry, have all served to
highlight the weakness of the Conservative position.[20] Conservative rabbis in particular have become increasingly

critical of the general Zionist movement and of developments in Israel.[21] The great enthusiasm which had formerly characterized the rabbinate has helped to set in motion a reaction now that the "heroic" period of Zionism is over—there is consequently a searching for some more "religious" ideology. To the extent that functionaries in the Conservative movement are religionists in the general sense, there has been a tendency to discover tensions between Jewish nationalism and religion, and to emphasize those aspects of Judaism which are characteristic of a "normal" (i.e., non-ethnic) religion. It is also possible that the role of the Conservative rabbi as a "race leader" may have been modified by the fulfillment of Zionist aims.[22]

It is not surprising that the Seminary group has given little encouragement to efforts looking toward theological clarification. Should a Conservative ideology develop and a cohesive movement emerge, lay people would take over control of the Seminary and administrators and teachers would lose their semi-independent status.[23] In addition to the power factor, the Seminary group—being relatively secluded, concerned mainly with scholarship of the classical type, and observing Judaism according to Orthodox requirements—experiences few of the pressures which play upon laymen.[24] Therefore they not only have discouraged the growth of a Conservative ideology, but have also sometimes even avoided the use of the word "Conservative." Although the reality of the divisions in Jewish religious life are conceded on an organizational level, the Seminary group has wished to give their school the widest possible appeal. Consequently a rabbi and a layman have both commented that:

The Seminary which regards us as its children, when it comes to the question of helping the Seminary . . . very often refuses

to permit us to recognize it as our mother. . . . The very fact
that in the Seminary the word "Conservative" doesn't appear
in the literature, is, I think, humiliating. . . .[25]

For years we [the laymen] have thought of ourselves as a
group of people forming a movement that we call the Conservative movement. . . . In recent years there seems to have
developed in certain places a tendency to shy away from calling ourselves a definite movement. There seems to have developed a tendency among some of our leaders to place emphasis
in what we prefer to call nonsectarianism. The claim is made
that fundamentally there are no Orthodox, no Reform, and
no Conservative Jews—just Jews. If we will only follow the
formula of observance handed down by our ancestors all will
be well.[26]

In 1946, the United Synagogue established a "Committee on the Philosophy of Conservative Judaism." This was
done partly, at least, under the inspiration of its director,
Rabbi Gordon, who represented those advocating a strong
and cohesive Conservative movement on the national
scene.[27] After a comparatively short administration during
which he did much to revitalize the organization, Gordon
resigned his post. The Committee did not hold any meetings under the administration of Rabbi Simon Greenberg,
his successor. Greenberg represented neither the layman
nor the practicing rabbi (although he had served as the
spiritual leader of a prominent synagogue for a considerable time), but rather the schoolmen—he is the Vice-
Chancellor of the Seminary. To date, the United Synagogue has not pursued an independent course, nor has it
given voice to all shades of lay and rabbinical opinion.[28]

C.

THE PROBLEM OF THE RABBI

Unlike laymen, rabbis *do* require a set of legitimations.
While the sensitive congregant may feel a vague desire for

a consistent approach to religious observance, it is really the functionary who needs a defensible system of ideas— one which will justify his decisions and guide him in daily work. Not only must rabbis deal with lay people, but individuals outside of the Conservative movement—chiefly other religious specialists—frequently ask them challenging questions. Furthermore, the self-image possessed by the Conservative rabbi involves an assumption of the *intellectual* role; unlike the laity, the rabbis see themselves as thinkers. Understandably, then, ideological poverty constitutes a real problem for them.

The late Milton Steinberg, for example, was one of the most highly thought-of and forthright members of the Conservative rabbinate. The tone of his reply, in answer to the question "What is Conservative Judaism?", is significant:

In practice it is kind of middle-of-the-roadism . . . between Orthodoxy and Reform. This in a nutshell is the program. As to the theory, it is regrettably difficult to put it precisely. Truth to tell, Conservatism has still not formulated the philosophy on which it stands.[29]

Solomon Goldman, employing much more colorful language, also emphasized the indefiniteness of Conservatism. He held that the lay people were responsible for this regrettable situation. His sarcasm only thinly veiled the hurt he felt as a result of the ideological void:

. . . [in Conservatism] one can never be quite certain that he is speaking for anybody but himself. Conservative Judaism has nowhere been defined. . . . One searches . . . for even a trace of an attempt to deal with fundamentals. . . . These essential considerations seem either to have been overlooked because of the pressure of more "practical" affairs, or to have been studiously avoided because of excessive politeness. . . .
   The very name "Conservative Judaism" adds to the confusion. "Conservative" groups are commonly those which oppose

"progressive" groups, and in opposition to the Reform movement we already have Orthodoxy. . . .

But few Conservative Jews will agree that there is no difference between them and the Orthodox Jews. Rather they
will hasten to explain that they believe in the worth of progressive modern ideals; that they adopt the name "Conservative" only because they believe in conserving the permanent
spiritual and cultural values in Judaism. . . . At this the cap-
tious intellectual might denounce them as guilty of mere
sophistry. An intellectual . . . might ask to be told . . . how
much of the "heritage" they want to retain and what they
are planning to throw overboard. But these intellectuals never
"join" anyway, and the "Conservative" is too practical to
waste his time reading their "stuff." . . . As for the rank and
file members of the congregations, they buy their pews and
are easily satisfied with parties, services and sermons.[30]

Whoever is held responsible, the problem remains. Although publicly the rabbi may put a brave face on matters, his discomfort finds expression in the privacy of
rabbinical meetings:

> There are a multitude of problems with regard to marriage
> and divorce, with regard to the dietary laws, which none of
> our rabbis is able to solve on an individual basis. We are
> literally dooming our men to ineffectiveness and to frustra-
> tion by not providing them with the authority of our col-
> lective decision on all the basic issues which face them. . . . We
> are constantly being asked, "Where do you stand?" and by
> our answers reveal that we are not standing at all but doing
> some adroit side-stepping.[31]

Not all statements are as frank as this one, however. At
times, the rabbi—seeing no way out—may try to explain
the problem away:

It is joint and common action [rather than a philosophy]
that continues to be the bond that unites us. If it is difficult
to define Conservative Judaism, it is also difficult to define
democracy or freedom, or peace, or religion, or Judaism.[32]

One of the statements made by Greenberg is along the same line:

Much is frequently heard concerning the amorphous character of Conservative Judaism, the absence of a clearly formulated definition. . . . Conservative Judaism is writing its own definition of itself not in a debating society, nor in the mind of some philosopher, nor even in the resolutions adopted by committees or conventions. It is "defining" itself, as does every living, vital movement, through the institutions it is creating. . . . It will thus continue to define and redefine itself.[33]

The question now occurs as to why the rabbis have not worked more assiduously on solving the ideological question in Conservatism. We find that first there is the emotional problem: clarification of creedal and codal matters would involve a break with the schoolmen. It is apparent from material presented in the previous chapter that due to the nature of the traditional Jewish relationship between teacher and student, the majority of rabbis have not been prepared to act independently of their mentors. Next, there is an institutional problem: the layman acts independently of his spiritual leader. While some of the laity may look to their rabbis for guidance, significantly there is no sentiment in favor of shifting the balance of power. Could the rabbis overcome their feelings of dependence on the schoolmen and succeed in clarifying the Conservative position, when seeking to apply it they might well be faced with the intransigence of the laity. Speaking before a national convention, a congregational official probably reflected the opinion of his fellows when he said:

I take my rabbi's spiritual advice. . . . I will listen to his teaching for my personal edification; but when it comes to determine the religious character of my congregation . . . I reserve the right to ask my rabbi to implement the general feeling of myself and those other members of the congregation

who with me express them even though they might run
counter to what my rabbi personally feels.[34]

Furthermore, the rabbis know that although there has
been no deep religious revival, Conservative synagogues
are prosperous and affiliation is at an all-time high. Under
the circumstances, they are tempted to concede the wis-
dom of the policy of fluidity—the facts of institutional
growth do seem to bear out its practicality. Commenting
on the exceptionally large number of non-Seminary graduates applying for admission to the Rabbinical Assembly
(thereby giving evidence of a belief that as professionals
their careers would be more secure with the Conservative
movement than with Orthodoxy or Reform), one rabbi
stated:

This is the most dramatic evidence of all of the trend in
American Judaism. Whether we think we have a program
and platform or not, we do constitute a discernible if not a
definable pattern of Jewish religious life which is appealing
increasingly to congregations. . . .[35]

Thus the apathy of many laymen about these matters,
combined with the success of the Conservative congregation in attracting members, hardly serves to encourage
the rabbi to engage in the quest for ideological clarification.

Before the rabbis could present a program or platform,
they would have to achieve unanimity among themselves.
Just as laymen vary in the extent of their personal religious observance, so do the functionaries differ in their
opinions about theological matters. Their ideas are in fact
scattered on a continuum running from naturalism to
supernaturalism. It is difficult to say with exactness at
present just where the majority stand, for the one study
done on this problem is outdated.[35a] But the fact that

variation exists is hardly in doubt. While the rabbis debate these matters in privacy of their meetings, they are wary of exposing their lack of agreement. If their variability were brought to the surface and exposed to the laity, the whole problem might be even more troubling. For example, Julian Freeman of Indianapolis, the prominent layman who has been exceptionally interested in ideology (he is one of the few who has made much of an inquiry about these matters), has stated that:

> What further complicates the matter is that ten different Conservative rabbis will have ten different ideas of Conservative Judaism. I speak from personal experience when I tell you that in interviewing approximately ten Conservative rabbis who were candidates for our pulpit, each and every one of them had a different slant on Conservative Judaism.[36]

However, even if the rabbis could work out a consistent position, some difficulties would still remain. In arriving at any theological stand, the functionaries would at least have to *consider* the claim of tradition. Their creedal affirmations—whatever they might be—would not be of much interest to the laity. Rather it would be their ideas about the *mitzvoth,* or their codal recommendations, which would be of central concern. Significantly, while the rabbi might be able to reinterpret, and thereby to lighten the "yoke of the Law," he could hardly find sanction for the radical derelictions of many of the laymen.

The functionaries are in fact aware that any legal revisions which they might make about ritualistic matters would be so remote from the present state of religious observance as to prove embarrassing for both groups. Being pulled one way by the actual practices of lay people —with whom they must reckon—and in the opposite direction by the demands of the traditional code—whose requirements they must also consider—they have for the

most part solved their dilemma by inaction. Regardless
of their liberalism, however, in official pronouncements
they have generally upheld the traditional standpoint.
According to Steinberg:

. . . the leaders and official agencies of Conservatism have
failed to live up to their preachments. Affirming tradition *and*
progress, they have in half a century failed to commend a
single departure, no matter how slight, from old patterns.
For all practical purposes they might as well have been Orthodox.[37]

The lay people determine personal behavior and congregational policy, while the rabbis serve as the spokesmen for the Conservative movement. This of course results
in anomalies. For example, one of the more traditionally-
minded Conservative rabbis, exhorting the members of
his synagogue to increase their ritualistic observance,
pointed out that Conservatism had not sanctioned deviations from the traditional code. He received the following reaction:

. . . in the eyes of the layman, Conservative Judaism stands for
the right to be *mchallel Shabbat* [a Sabbath desecrator] and
to eat *treyfot* [non-kosher food]. . . . When I tell them that
Conservative Judaism believes in *Shmirat Shabbat* [observance
of the Sabbath] and in *kashruth,* they think that I am talking
out of my hat. . . .[38]

One perceptive layman, noting the character of rabbinical
pronouncements, has stated that ". . . according to the
present-day program of Conservative Judaism, there are
almost no Conservative Jews—only Conservative rabbis." [39]
Freeman, too, warned the rabbis that:

A religion in a purely democratic nation reflects the attitudes
and the true beliefs of the people themselves. The Rabbinate,
in the final sense, unless it wants to develop into a sect or
priesthood, can only mirror or reflect the attitudes of the multitude, and if they are going to concern themselves with a

pattern of living, it must be a pattern of living for the laymen.[40]

Similarly, Rabbi Israel M. Goldman told his colleagues that something would have to be done to bring theory and practice into closer harmony:

The general impression among lay people is that Conservative Judaism, to use the vernacular, is a "fifty-fifty" proposition. Can we afford to let that stand as the descriptive phrase of our movement? Recently a leader of the Reform Rabbinate spoke of our movement in these words: "Conservatism is Orthodox in theory and Reform in practice. . . ." Are we content to let that remain as the definition of our principles and practices? [41]

D.

THE "IDEOLOGY" OF CONSERVATISM

The points that we have made thus far can be summarized as follows: (1) Conservatism represents a common pattern of acculturation—a kind of social adjustment—which has been arrived at by lay people. It is seen by them as a "halfway house" between Reform and Orthodoxy. It possesses no ideological system in the usual sense of the term. (2) The lack of ideology does not constitute a serious problem for most laymen, but it has harassed many rabbis. (3) There has been a somewhat greater interest in recent years in ideological problems. This is traceable to the operation of social forces, and to organizational trends in the Jewish community. (4) The resistances and obstacles to ideological clarification are formidable. (5) The rabbis have been very hesitant about officially sanctioning any departures from Jewish tradition.

We pointed out earlier that the rabbi not only aspires to the role of intellectual, but that he is challenged by others to present the viewpoint of his movement. What body of conceptions, then, *does* he advance as constituting the principles of Conservatism?

According to Robert Gordis, the leading Conservative rabbi whose writings we have quoted previously, Conservatism is a movement traceable to 19th century Germany where Zacharias Frankel, a well-known rabbi of liberal tendencies and head of an important seminary, dissented from Reform and took as his position "positive-historical Judaism." The same reaction occurred in America where Solomon Schechter helped give form to the movement. Under him, the Seminary became ". . . the spiritual fountain-head of a new alignment in American Jewry—Conservative Judaism." [42] Other thinkers who have contributed to Conservatism are Achad Haam (Hebraist, Jewish philosopher, and the father of "cultural Zionism"), Mordecai M. Kaplan, and Louis Ginzberg. Due to the contributions of these men and others, Conservative Judaism has a definite program.[43] It represents a distinctive interpretation of Jewish tradition which takes into account the demands of contemporary American life.[44]

What did Frankel understand by "positive-historical Judaism?" According to Gordis:

. . . Frankel believed . . . that traditional Judaism through the ages was not static and unchanged, but, on the contrary, the product of historical development. This complex of values, practices and ideals, however, was not to be lightly surrendered, for the sake of convenience, conformity or material advantage, masquerading as love of progress. A positive attitude of reverence and understanding toward traditional Judaism was essential. Changes would and should occur, but they should be part of a gradual, organic growth.[45]

Most Conservative rabbis would agree with the formulation of "positive-historical Judaism" (the word "positive" is frequently omitted) which Steinberg arrived at:

. . . [the] nearest approach [of Conservatism] to an ideology is the phrase "historical Judaism," a key idiom of its original founders. This would seem to mean two things. First, Judaism is a *historical* phenomenon, that is to say, it is possessed of a rich and valuable past. . . . It means that Jews ought to preserve their heritage and, so far as they can, as it was transmitted to them. "Historical Judaism" has another significance. Judaism, it implies, is a phenomenon *in* history, a growing evolving organism . . . it must change in conformity with a changing world.[46]

What is the approach of the "Historical School" toward the problem of revelation? According to Kaplan the followers of the Historical School believe in divine revelation not as an historical event ". . . but [rather] as a theological concept." [47] However, as is indicated by the interview data from Eastville, the central problem to many Jews is one of code rather than creed. Because Judaism has been an ethnic, legalistic, Eastern-derived religion with strong tendencies toward rigidity, it is understandable why so many individuals have come to feel that it is not so much what you believe in as what you *do*. Thus the thinkers of the Historical School have had—above all— to formulate a rationale for observance. Circumstances have required them to give priority to the problem of what sanction for the *mitzvoth* can be substituted once revelation is discarded: If God does not command us to observe, who or what does? The solution to this problem has been the concept of "Catholic Israel"—an idea with which Schechter is identified. According to this conception, neither reason nor revelation is the basis for observance, but rather "the conscience of Catholic Israel" —i.e., the religious practice currently in vogue.

Since the majority of the Jewish group, or Catholic Israel, observed the *mitzvoth* at the time when Schechter and others elaborated this idea, following group patterns meant conforming to tradition. One could observe Jewish law on the basis that he was merely adhering to the customs and ceremonies of his people rather than because of any belief in a system of supernaturally sanctioned legislation. It was also stressed that observance of the rituals contributed to group integration and survival. Schechter explained the concept as follows:

It is not the mere revealed Bible that is of first importance to the Jew, but the Bible as it repeats itself in history, in other words, as it is interpreted by Tradition. . . . Since then the interpretation of Scripture or the Secondary Meaning is mainly a product of changing historical influences, it follows that the center of authority is actually removed from the Bible and placed in some *living body,* which, by reason of its being in touch with the ideal aspirations and the religious needs of the age, is best able to determine the nature of the Secondary Meaning. This living body, however, is not represented by any section of the nation, or any corporate priesthood . . . but by the collective conscience of Catholic Israel as embodied in the Universal Synagogue.[48]

Another consequence of this conception of Tradition is that it is neither Scripture nor primitive Judaism, but general custom which forms the real rule of practice. . . . Liberty was always given to the great teachers of every generation to make modifications and innovations in harmony with the spirit of existing institutions. . . . The norm as well as the sanction of Judaism is the practice actually in vogue. Its consecration is the consecration of general use—or, in other words, of Catholic Israel.[49]

E.

THE SHORTCOMINGS
OF THE CONSERVATIVE "IDEOLOGY"

According to Steinberg:

The confusion and lack of character that mark Conservatism derive in part from the fact that it has been content to let the slogan, "historical Judaism," do service for a philosophy. They stem however in considerable degree from a neglect of even that slight ideology.[50]

This statement, taken together with the various quotations from leaders of Conservative rabbinical opinion reproduced previously, indicates that the principles of Frankel, Schechter, *et al.,* are not satisfactory conceptions. If they were capable of development, why have the rabbis resisted the cultivation of what Steinberg terms "even that slight ideology"? It would seem safe to say that the neglect stems in part from the fact that the viewpoint of the Historical School presents such insuperable difficulties as to discourage attempts at theological clarification.

Only two publications have appeared which purport to explain the ideology of Conservatism. One, edited by Rabbi Theodore Friedman, consists of excerpts from the writings of Seminary presidents such as Adler and Finkelstein, of schoolmen and rabbis such as Friedlaender, Kaplan, Israel Levinthal, and Robert Gordis, as well as from other figures.[51] This volume was issued in mimeographed form—no printed edition of the collection has been produced. The other item, written by Gordis, is hardly larger than a good-sized pamphlet.[52] In it the author reviews the theories of various rabbis and scholars whose ideas are assumed, in sum, to constitute the ideology of Conservatism. However, the various conceptions can hardly be fitted together into one logical whole, and Gordis attempts to adjust matters by glossing over some of the contradictions and pointing up the areas of agreement. The comment which he made about Friedman's collection is relevant to his own work:

Our failure to evolve a philosophy has led to several unhappy consequences. Conservative Judaism has been accused of seeking to straddle the issues by making a principle of unclarity. Some of our most articulate voices have sought,

therefore, to evolve a new philosophy and program of action.
. . . Characteristically, when the National Academy for Adult
Jewish Studies wished to publish a manual on Conservative
Judaism, it could only issue a collection of papers concerning
which it confesses that "the points of view expressed are often
at variance with one another." [53]

The most glaring shortcoming of the ideology of the
Historical School is the concept of Catholic Israel. It had
been propounded by Jewish thinkers who wished to combat the innovations introduced by the Reform movement.
The Conservative school accused the Reform group of
breaking Jewish unity, of being secessionists. Since most
of Jewry at the time was observant, the Reformers could
be accused of not following the practices of Catholic Israel.
At present, however, most Jews are not very observant—it
is the traditional Jews who are the deviants. If one wishes
to adhere to the practices of Catholic Israel at present, he
should be free to desecrate the Sabbath and violate the
dietary laws!

The rabbis are, of course, hardly interested in aiding
and abetting further violations of the *mitzvoth*. Consequently, because of its complete inadequacy, Gordis is
forced to make a radical readjustment in the Catholic
Israel idea.[54] He thus respecifies its meaning: according
to him Catholic Israel includes only those who have remained loyal to various Jewish traditions, as well as individuals who are "sensitive" to their lack of observance
and to the problem of tradition in general.[55] The new
concept is of course a contradiction in terms—Gordis ad-
mits that it excludes the majority of Jews.[56] As critics have
pointed out, only a handful of Conservative Jewry, other
than the rabbis, qualify for membership in Catholic
Israel.

As if this were not enough, there is an additional problem which has troubled the Conservative rabbinate for some years. As we know, the viewpoint of the Historical School has been that Judaism is a phenomenon in history, it is the religious system of the Jews, it has gone through many different stages, and social change will necessitate further redefinitions of Judaism. However, *historical inevitability is hardly a guide to present-day dilemmas.* Specifically, how is Jewish law to be adjusted to contemporary needs? Furthermore, whose needs should be considered in the readjustment process?

Schechter had thought that only three changes were necessary in order to reconcile traditional Judaism with the American scene: the delivery of an English sermon, the introduction of order and decorum in the synagogue, and the use of modern methods, particularly in regard to Jewish pedagogy.[57] Apparently he believed that if any additional changes were needed, they could be legitimated by proper use of the classical type of rabbinical interpretation of the sacred system. His was the general viewpoint of Conservative leaders at the time—it was thought that the rigor of the legal system would be dissipated by the use of the *liberal* interpretation.[58]

All of this has proven to be completely unworkable. The rigidity of the legal system, and the persistence of the Orthodox group, has served to block efforts directed toward change. For example, the Rabbinical Assembly has tried repeatedly to effect some readjustment in one of the most obvious abuses of the Jewish legal code: the situation of the *agunah.** Louis Epstein, a learned Con-

---

* This is a wife whose husband has either abandoned her, or who is presumed dead although the body of the deceased has not been located nor is there any testimony from an individual who witnessed his death. In both cases the woman is legally barred from remarriage.

servative rabbi, devised a method of relief which was presumably within the established canons of Jewish law. His formula provided for the possibility of a *Bet Din* (rabbinical court) granting a divorce in the absence of the husband. After years of discussion and negotiation, it became clear that his proposal was unacceptable to the Orthodox rabbinate—the project was shelved.[59]

It was further hoped that through the Conservative rabbinical committees for the interpretation of Jewish law, authoritative answers would be provided to those in need of guidance about the application of the sacred system to present-day conditions. An effort was made to apply the most liberal construction possible within the established canons, but again these attempts were unsuccessful. Even the most radical answer was so much more strict than the current practices of lay people (and in cases which concerned synagogue policy, of the practices of the rabbis as well), that official opinions were unrealistic and unenforceable. Moreover, the committees received relatively few inquiries, for most congregants had broken with the concept of Judaism as a legalistic system and hence were uninterested in authoritative rabbinical interpretation. The rare layman who took the trouble to read one or another of the rabbinical decisions found that ". . . [when one reads] about some of the disputations in rabbinical circles . . . one wonders if our rabbis are in touch with reality." [60]

The rabbis who served on such committees were chiefly rightist-oriented. Most of the liberals had resigned from these bodies out of frustration. Even the rightists recognized how unrealistic it was to expect their colleagues to follow the decisions. In one case, for example, they advised a rabbi to do what he thought best regardless of their declared opinion, for they were aware that functionaries possessed no means for securing compliance.[61]

Men like Ginzberg, who were not in congregational work, tended to dismiss the validity of the changes instituted by the laymen.[62]

Matters reached an impasse by the early 1940's, and a new approach finally emerged. Essentially what it involved was that in some instances legal decisions would be rendered outside of the boundaries of what would constitute a liberal interpretation of Jewish law. This, then, was to be interpretation plus *legislation*. On this basis a new group was formed which represented all shades of rabbinical thinking. The reconstituted Law Committee was to render a majority opinion, but dissenters could write a minority report. Rabbis were free to follow either opinion, or neither one. All decisions were to be rendered in the classical form known as *responsa:*

> The decisions and opinions of the Law Committee can therefore only be taken as the collective . . . judgments within the Rabbinical Assembly, judgments arrived at after due consideration of all the viewpoints represented in our movement. These judgments or *responsa* are channels marking the main current . . . of our thinking. We take them as studied directions rather than directives. . . .
>
> Since no sanctions are to be imposed, and members are free to follow the majority or minority opinion, there is no need for a vote by the Convention on the specific questions considered by the Committee. . . .
>
> While we do not apply sanctions against members who refuse to accept even a unanimous decision of the Law Committee, such a unanimous decision is considered the *official opinion* of the Rabbinical Assembly and may be quoted as such.[63]

Thus, covertly the rabbis now recognize that they are not making decisions or writing *responsa,* but merely taking a poll of their membership. Since, however, they still retain something of the traditional image, they reserve the right to cultivate the legalistic system and to operate as if they still possessed authority. Recognizing where decisions might lead, by not requiring any organizational discipline the rabbis take steps to protect themselves from the possible result of their disputations. Conservative spiritual leaders may point to the *responsa* of the Law Committee as expressing the special approach of their movement.[64]

No large-scale campaign has been attempted in order to spread knowledge of rabbinical decisions among the laity. For example, the "National Sabbath Observance Effort" was started soon after the Law Committee, on a split decision, had indicated that it was permissible to modify Sabbath observance in regard to the laws governing travel and the use of electricity.[65] These decisions were described by members of the Rabbinical Assembly as of epochal significance. While the Rabbinical Assembly was a co-sponsor of the Sabbath revitalization program, in the voluminous promotional materials which were produced for the guidance of the laity no indication was made about the decisions which the rabbis had arrived at after years of highly charged discussion. But all of these results are not unexpected. Because of its obvious shortcomings and contrived nature, the Conservative "ideology" hardly serves as a guide to present-day dilemmas. It does not endow the functionaries with confidence in their decisons.

F.

IS THE CONSERVATIVE MOVEMENT SPLITTING?

Rabbinical conventions and publications are rife with heated discussions, proposals, and counter-proposals. The leftists (grouped around Dr. Kaplan and the Reconstructionist movement) and the rightists (centered around the Seminary) engage in heated debates. The point at issue revolves around how much liberty should be taken in officially sanctioning the modification of traditional practices, a problem which is related to larger theological considerations.[66] Significantly, these disagreements have not resulted in any internal split in Conservatism, and they give no promise of doing so even though some rabbis have threatened a schism. The base of the movement is the local congregation to which the superstructure—in the form of the national bodies—is very loosely related. Unless splits in the superstructure are paralleled by similar divisions in the base, the various wings among members of the Rabbinical Assembly can be tolerated at little cost to the strength and unity of the movement as a whole.

Appropriately, there are few if any leftists, centrists, and rightists of the rabbinical type in the congregations themselves. As we have pointed out, variations, both inter- and intra-congregational, do exist. Synagogues in some parts of the country are more traditional than in other sections. Synagogues in the same geographical area will differ somewhat in ritual depending on the size of the Jewish community, the average age of the congregants, the type of Reform synagogues in the district, and various other special factors. These variations are chiefly of local significance: the congregations are not aligned nationally in any right, left, or center wings. The laymen view differences in religious behavior and synagogual procedure as matters of preference rather than of principle. As was noted earlier, the variations among congregants are not consistent philosophical positions, but rather represent the discontinuities which emerged when the unity of the sacred system was broken:

. . . there are some among us who see nothing to Conservative Judaism but the fact that men and women sit together and the rabbi preaches in English. On the other extreme, [some] . . . come to the synagogue merely to answer their needs for social contacts. With a Congregation that runs . . . [from] extreme left we have had some tragically funny incidents of "Jewish Americana". . . . We have the case of many members, who, during the period of intermission on Yom Kippur rush to a corner drugstore for a drink and a sandwich, but flare into justifiable indignation when the use of the organ is mentioned. We have a smaller group who see no contradiction in coming to the Synagogue but three times a year and insisting upon the fact that the Cantor face the Ark.[67]

The rabbis themselves realize that the vehemence of their discussions is out of proportion to the amount of practical results which such controversies may have:

While we are discussing the trivialities and the minutiae, the very props of our Jewish life are disregarded, violated, and broken. Not 5 in 100 of our members are Sabbath observers; not 5 in 100 observe the Dietary Laws . . . and not even 1 in 100 cares about our decisions, or, for that matter, the legalistic decisions of any group. We buzz and we flutter . . . and the answer is nothingness.[68]

Since these controversies have no real consequences, they can therefore be all the more intense. The pressures which rabbis socialized in a traditional environment experience in the lay-controlled synagogue where congregants take a casual attitude toward the sacred system, makes for a high degree of frustration. Resulting aggressions, made respectable since they are formulated as part of ideological systems, can be acted out against colleagues without fear of reprisal: ". . . we take out on each other for the suppressed grievances which we dare not show to our congregations and our boards." [69]

Much of what passes for ideological discussion in Conservatism represents then the ruminations of the rabbis—it has no true ideological content. It symbolizes rather the discrepancy between the self-image of the spiritual leader and his actual occupational role. By confining the practice of the classical functions to occasional professional meetings and to the pages of technical journals, the rabbi may act out his traditional role without threatening the power structure of Jewish religious life or the norms of Conservative Jewry. The pondering of ritual problems, the consultation through the literature with the great rabbinical minds of the past, and the writing of scholarly opinions based on precedent, must be viewed essentially as adjustive techniques helping to mediate the crisis produced by clashes in role-playing.

In summary, although a few attempts have been made by the rabbis to develop a distinctive Conservative ideology and to obtain consensus, such endeavors have met with only very limited success. They have hardly been able to describe what is actually in existence in the Conservative movement, or to relate present realities to theoretical principles. The functionaries have not succeeded in spreading the few ideas which they have evolved among the laity. The concepts which they have presented are largely improvised. They express the needs and training of the religious specialists rather than of the mass of Conservative Jewry. The "ideology" has not as yet reached the stage of justifying—with any degree of sophistication—various institutional imperatives, although this is its present aim.

G.

RECONSTRUCTIONISM

We have, by design, postponed the discussion of Reconstructionism until this point. Inasmuch as Reconstructionism made what is essentially an abortive attempt to capture the Conservative movement (or at least the minds of the Conservative rabbinate), it constitutes properly a postscript to our discussion of ideological problems. Since thorough analysis of all the formulations and reformulations advanced by Dr. Kaplan as the founder and theoretician of Reconstructionism can hardly be attempted here, it is perhaps best to let him speak for himself. In discussing rightist, centrist, and leftist (or Reconstructionist) tendencies in Conservatism, Kaplan described his ideas as follows:

The two main principles of the Leftists are the following: a) To be a Jew means to be involved not only in a set of beliefs and practices usually identified as religion, but in the civilization or culture of a people, with all that such involvement implies. b) The Jewish religion in which the values of that civilization are utilized as a means of individual and collective salvation, though indebted for its unique character to the divine intuitions of its lawgivers, prophets and sages, has been subject to the laws and limitations of the human mind and spirit.

The principle that Judaism is to be reckoned with as a civilization . . . does not imply any idea or ideal that conflicts with traditional teaching. It is more than anything else a formula for the social strategy best suited to advance Jewish life. Instead of having Jewish life centered around the synagogue, Judaism viewed as a civilization calls for a distribution of authority and influence among the various organizations that carry on Jewish activities. Though the synagogue, by reason of its being the chief vehicle for the articulation of the meaning of Judaism, should normally be the chief mouthpiece of the Jewish people, both inwardly and in relation to the outer world, it should not aspire to be more than *primus inter pares*. This conception of the place of the synagogue in Jewish life should logically be acceptable, regardless of one's theological views concerning Judaism. But it is viewed by the Rightist and Centrist groups as a concession to secularism, for no other reason than that it regards the Jewish people as subject to the same laws of social groupings as are all other peoples.

The main differentia of the Leftist group, however, derives mainly from the principle that the Jewish religion has been subject to the laws and limitations of the human mind and spirit. That principle calls for a humanist conception of the origin, development and application of Jewish religion. It is not merely as a theoretic outlook, however, that this conception is stressed, but as suggesting the proper method of approach to all phases of Jewish teaching and preaching, from the most elementary to the most advanced stages of educational activity. It prescribes complete freedom of thought and inquiry, not merely as permissive but as imperative, no matter how deeply rooted the beliefs or traditions.[70]

It is significant to note that since Reconstructionists tend to look upon Jewish law in terms of being group patterns rather than as supernaturally inspired legislation, they have not been strongly troubled with the dilemmas in this area that have plagued some of their more traditionally minded fellows.

In *Judaism as a Civilization,* a volume which although published in 1934 is already regarded by some as a classic, Kaplan indicated both a theological approach as well as a larger ideological framework. Although we cannot deal with the main implications which his point of view suggests in terms of Jewish communal policy, the difference between his conception of God and the traditional supernaturalistic view was at once manifest.

Soon after the publication of *Judaism as a Civilization,* Kaplan and his co-workers started the publication of a magazine, *The Reconstructionist.* Later, the Jewish Reconstructionist Foundation was formed, and this agency has acted as sponsor of the movement. A number of chapters consisting of lay members have been formed in various cities; a Reconstructionist Rabbinical Fellowship is also functioning. In spite of these developments, Kaplan and his colleagues have never been able to decide whether they were actually a movement, or whether they constitute what they have termed a "school of thought." As Kaplan himself has confessed, part of the ambivalence of this group is traceable to his own personality. He has always wavered between scholarly endeavor and agitational work.[71]

Since no large-scale propaganda effort has been attempted, it is difficult to know exactly what are the reactions of most laymen to Reconstructionism. It is conceivable that—for example—many would be in agreement with some of Kaplan's ideas about Jewish communal policy. We do know that less than 20% of the rabbis are in *complete* sympathy with the views of Reconstructionism.[72] This is apparently traceable more to reservations about theological matters than to disagreement with the implications of Kaplan's views regarding Judaism as constituting a "civilization."

For insight into rabbinical attitudes, we again turn to Rabbi Milton Steinberg. Steinberg was not only a devoted friend of Kaplan's, but he took an active part in Reconstructionism. In his last years, however, he was increasingly critical of the group's theological approach. In a series of lectures delivered in 1950, he advanced some of the objections which have troubled quite a few of his less articulate colleagues:

[According to the Reconstructionist conception of God] . . . All we know, from experience, is that there are things in life which give us courage, love, joy—which enable us to live with a sense of meaning. These, for all practical purposes, are God.

Do you want to speculate whether God is an entity or being? That [according to Reconstructionism] is your privilege. Do you want to speculate on God's influence in the universe? That [according to Reconstructionism] is your privilege. [But]

When you say that God is the sum total of those forces which help us live and live better, there you have the real and meaningful aspect of Divine Nature.

Here is one of the points I have never been able to follow. To me it makes a great deal of difference whether God is an entity, a being in Himself, or whether He is an aspect of reality. In the second place I can't solve this question: When you say that God is the sum total of those forces which make for the enhancement of life, who is adding up the sum?

To me, Kaplan, whether he is doing what he is doing in the best of good faith or not, must have a different kind of mental structure than my own. He seems to me to be missing the main point. . . .

The second great reservation I have about Kaplan's theology is that the actuality of God becomes questionable. [Here Steinberg discussed *Als Ob* philosophy: "There are lots of things which probably aren't so, but we ought to live as if they were true. They are useful fictions."] Now it seems to me that the Kaplan theology isn't at that point, but it can readily slide to that point.[73]

Steinberg's last reservation was his feeling that the goal of Reconstructionist thinking did not coincide with the purpose of religion—the "desire to illuminate the nature of things." Finally, he criticized Reconstructionism for its hesitancy to make a "leap into faith." Thus, it would seem that in an age of theological conservatism the instrumentalism of Kaplan would not be popular. While his general views have been influential in setting the sights of American Jewish communal policy, it appears that his theological point of view has not been able to satisfy many members of the Conservative rabbinate.

VIII

Retrospect and Prospect

WE HAVE demonstrated that because of factors special to the Jewish tradition, and aggravated by a very high rate of social mobility, certain needs were so accentuated in the Jewish community as to require a greater degree of adjustment on the part of Orthodoxy than it was able to make. Distinguished by a pervasive interest in group survival, individuals who shared a similar class position, degree of acculturation, and a common background in the Judaism of Eastern Europe, established the first "Conservative" synagogues chiefly during the second and third decades of the century. These institutions brought into harmony newly achieved status with patterns of Jewish worship. Also, they added novel—and very effective—functions to the traditional synagogue program. The making of this type of adjustment was aided by the desire to continue group survival under the legitimation of religion. The growth of the Conservative synagogue characteristically took place in areas where older ethnic groups (or "old Americans") resided, where the initial ratio of Jews to non-Jews was small, and where the bulk of residents was middle-class.

The chief feature of Conservative worship is the emphasis on a revision of certain Orthodox forms, such as the kind of seating arrangement, the degree of decorum, and the appropriateness of secular concerns in a sacred setting. Revisions in all of these areas demonstrate the impact on Judaism—as an Eastern-derived and highly traditional type of sacred system—of the mores of Western culture (particularly the standards of middle-class Protestantism) and the force of secularism. Furthermore, it is of significance that in the Conservative service the language of prayer is both English as well as Hebrew.

In addition to revisions in the forms of worship, a further adjustment has been made in the program of services. Disinterest in the traditional services (with the exception of the High Holidays) has been partially compensated for by the inauguration of a new time for, and type of, divine convocation: the late Friday evening service. A mixture of general religious motivations and special ethnic needs has resulted in a unique type of worship in terms of the traditional Jewish norms.

The program of the typical Conservative synagogue includes a range of activity which offers the membership various gratifications—in addition to those derivable from an institution where the individual is given the possibility of satisfying strictly "religious" needs—of the type which resembles those available through participation in the voluntary association. All of this helps to reinforce Jewish ethnic-group solidarity, but although ethnic-group preservation represents an important motive for the development of Conservatism, this value tends to conflict at times with the need for institutional maintenance and the drive toward "congregationalism." This is well demonstrated by the educational program which the congregations sponsor for children. Presented as a community service, the Sunday and Hebrew schools of Conservatism have proved to be popular institutions which have been utilized to reinforce the social and religious program. They give promise of serving as sources of recruitment for future adherents.

The peculiar origin of the movement is at least part of the reason why the local institutions are so much stronger than the national agencies. While the strength of the congregations is slowly being transmitted to the over-all denominational bodies, the process has been complicated by the existence of three interest groups in the movement: the laity, the rabbis, and the schoolmen. The last-named group, whose prominence represents an incongruity in terms of the usual type of middle-class religious denomination, have retained their hold both because of personality factors as well as cultural features like the special place of scholarship in the Jewish tradition. Finally, the past role of Americanization efforts in Jewish community life has also been of significance in determining the character of the movement.

As we have noted, the Conservative rabbi occupies a middle ground between the layman and the scholar. He frequently has difficulty in resolving the conflict to which he is exposed. The rabbinate as a group represents a somewhat wide range of opinion, but in the lay-controlled synagogue their variability is of relatively small significance. The Conservative movement has not succeeded in building a substantial ideological or theological superstructure, and this lack is felt most keenly by the rabbis. The absence of the required conditions for ideological clarification, and the desire to avoid the strife which this process would entail, indicates that progress along these lines will be slow.

So much for an overview of our analysis of Conservatism. It will be worthwhile now to consider the *signifi-cance* of the movement. Our view is that when future historians chronicle the evolution of Judaism in America, they will find that Conservatism constitutes a crucial part of their story. The example of Reform will help to clarify this point. The greatest contribution of the German Reform movement may be said to be its function as the provider of a cushion for the disintegrative effects of emancipation. It helped to indicate a *modus vivendi* between assimilation and a no-longer acceptable Orthodoxy. In the same tradition, American Conservatism has cushioned the effects of the dissolution of Judaism as an integrated and highly traditional sacred system. It too has offered a *modus vivendi* for the alienated. True, its public has been different from that of German-Jewish Reform, and the conditions under which it has developed have also been radically different. Thus, while both movements have taken divergent paths, they do express the same need. In summary, the signal contribution of Conservatism would seem to be that of offering an acceptable pattern of adjustment to the American environment for many East European-derived Jews.

In the course of our study we have focused upon problems, discontinuities, dilemmas, and compromises. This is understandable since such areas offer the analyst fruitful leads in understanding the phenomenon under investigation. The shortcomings of this procedure, however, are several. Firstly, the social science analyst may seem—unwittingly on his part—to be assuming an attitude of superiority toward his material. Secondly, the normal routine and tempo of the institution may be obscured by the concentration on areas of stress. Lastly, the contributions which the movement has made to the functioning of the Jewish group, as well as to that of the larger society, can remain unclear unless special pains are taken to highlight them. In reference to the last point, suffice it to say that in a sense our analysis appears to validate the claims of Conservative enthusiasts who feel that their movement has "saved" a generation of Jews. Surely a group to which Reform had been unable to appeal, and upon which Orthodoxy had lost its hold, have been "brought back." A group has returned to the fold which would have remained outside of the synagogue, and perhaps would not have been strongly influenced by any other tendency in Jewish life.

The ingenuity and resourcefulness of Conservative Jewry, which has enabled the group to overcome some very serious difficulties, has not escaped the careful reader. In addition to its general contributions to Jewish life, it is furthermore apparent that some young people have been prepared by their elders to carry on with Conservatism. Such results have not always been attained by some of the other groups in the Jewish community. If there are unsatisfactory aspects, at the very least it will be granted that the movement has made a notable contribution to survivalism and that it provides a significant institutional framework for a possible revivified Judaism.

These contributions have not always been conceded. We have avoided an analysis of the criticisms of Conservatism on the part of Reform and Orthodox Jews, although certain of their attitudes toward the movement are implicit in some of our material. We have also abstained from giving systematic attention to the opinions of Jewish secularists and intellectuals. But it does not require much ingenuity to imagine how many react to the contrivances of the Conservative movement; any compromise movement constitutes an easy target for critical and sophisticated minds. It is apparent, however, that such individuals run a dual

risk. They may first overlook the contributions of Conservatism, and then they may fail to realize that they themselves have not succeeded in effecting what can be regarded
as an adequate pattern of adjustment. While the adjustments that various types of intellectuals and secularists
have made may be personally acceptable to them, the question of how satisfactory they are in terms of their transmis-
sive power to the next generation remains *the* crucial
issue.

If participation in an ethnically typed structure can continue to give people a sense of belongingness and thereby
remains an important means of reducing *anomie,* and if
ethnicity is not too strongly disvalued by the larger community, there is no reason why the vitality of Conservatism
should not continue for quite some time. Should American
social structure retain its present degree of stability, and
racial, ethnic, and religious separatism remain at current
levels, it is unlikely that Conservatism will be confronted
with any large-scale defections. A threat to Conservatism
could come from two directions: a religious revival or a
further growth of secularism. On the face of it, the first
alternative would seem to constitute a constructive rather
than a destructive force. It may be said that its first effects
might well be positive. However, since Conservatism's
"denominational" approach is so appropriate to the present level of observance and to the type of spirituality
which characterizes a considerable segment of American
Jewry, it would not appeal strongly to those who are attracted to sectarian movements. The rather modest demands which the movement makes upon its adherents—as
well as its compromise character—would make it difficult
for Conservatism to integrate into its structure individuals
with compelling religious urges. But the chance that this

possibility will occur seems remote. To most people the second alternative (a possible diminution of religion) seems a more likely occurrence. If general religious institutions suffer any further loss of influence, this tendency would be reflected in the Jewish community. However, expert observers feel that the trend toward a secularization of values has been arrested and that religious institutions will find, in the future, a "reservoir of good-will" which will enable them to survive at least at their present level of influence.

There will remain the problem of institutional rigidity. Already some students of Jewish life feel that Reform, Conservatism, and Orthodoxy have outlived their usefulness—that they are divisive forces in the Jewish community. Although it is conceded that these divisions have been expressive of deep social or ideological fissures, some state that growing homogeneity offers the possibility for the emergence of a distinctive "American Judaism" which will replace the traditional groupings. These prognosticators state that this development will usher in a great new period of Jewish life. They state that progress is being hampered by religious separatism. Whatever the merits of their case, it does seem true that if Conservatism has had a "historic mission" in terms of preventing the complete alienation and religious disorganization of the East European-derived Jew, that task has been completed. Perhaps Conservatism will not rest upon this accomplishment but will come to play a new and as yet unforeseeable role in the Jewish life of the future.

Recent Developments
in Conservative Judaism

CONSERVATIVE Judaism has flourished during the past two decades. Conservatism's prosperity is particularly noteworthy in its stark contrast to developments in Protestantism and Catholicism: Conservatism has experienced none of the reductions-in-force which have characterized the Christian community. To be sure, most recently the budgets of Conservative institutions have had to be scrutinized, plans for certain programs have had to be deferred, and the viability of some Conservative synagogues located in changing Jewish neighborhoods has had to be re-evaluated. But retrenchment, when it occurred, has been on a minor scale.

The recent prosperity of Conservatism also suggests that Conservative Judaism is much more than a temporary resting place on the road from Orthodoxy to Reform. Rather, it has come to occupy a permanent place in Jewish life. In fact, the group's progress in the 1950's and 1960's was so rapid that Conservatism overtook Orthodoxy and Reform and went on to achieve primacy on the American Jewish religious scene. Considering the recency of its establishment, the victory of Conservatism was remarkable.

A.

THE PRIMACY OF CONSERVATISM

Religious prosperity during the past two decades has not been confined to Conservatism alone—Orthodoxy and Reform have also made progress. But if Jewish religious groups have fared better in the secular city than Christian groups have, it is apparent that Conservatism has fared particularly well. Thus, during recent years more American Jews have come to consider themselves "Conservative" than either "Orthodox" or "Reform."

The trend to Conservatism is particularly evident in cities of substantial Jewish population, especially cities located in the Northeast. For example, a survey conducted in 1965 in Boston found that 44% of the Jews of that community thought of themselves as Conservative, some 27% thought of themselves as Reform, and 14% as Orthodox.[1] In smaller cities in the same geographical area the triumph of Conservatism has been even more overwhelming. Thus a survey conducted in 1963 in Providence, R.I., discovered that as many as 54% of the Jews of that community considered themselves Conservative, while only 21% thought of themselves as Reform and 20% as Orthodox.[2] Furthermore, Conservative strength has also become evident even in the Midwest, which has long been a center of Reform. In 1964 as many as 49% of Milwaukee Jews considered themselves Conservative, in contrast to only 24% who considered themselves Reform.[3]

Statistics for New York City are unavailable; the presumption of most observers is that Orthodoxy is stronger in New York than elsewhere. Nevertheless, it is apparent that even in the New York metropolitan area more Jews would describe themselves as Conservative than as either Orthodox or Reform.[4] And inasmuch as some 64% of American Jewry is concentrated in the Northeast, Conservatism's predominance in the Middle Atlantic and New England states means that it has won a plurality in the nation. Thus, while Reform remains strong in the South, the Middle West, and the West, Conservatism's growth in the East, together with its penetration into all areas of the nation, has resulted in its primacy. The victory of Conservatism is particularly remarkable if we bear in mind that until recently it was generally assumed that the dominance of Reform was inevitable: Reform is, after all, the form of Judaism most in tune with the norms of the general society.

The new predominance of Conservatism is still imperfectly reflected in synagogual affiliation, for not every individual who describes himself as Conservative is affiliated with a synagogue. In Boston, for example, some 39% of those who describe themselves as Conservative are unaffiliated.[5] The problem of non-affiliation cuts across all groups; there are also unaffiliated Reform and, to a smaller degree, Orthodox Jews. But the presence of so many unaffiliated Conservative Jews is in one sense especially advantageous to Conservatism—it means that there is a large pool of individuals to draw upon for future expansion.

Conservatism has made good use of its reservoir of potential recruits. The last two decades have witnessed a noticeable increase in the number of Conservative synagogues, as well as a sharp rise in the membership of those Conservative synagogues located in areas of expanding Jewish population. Furthermore, the type of synagogue that the Conservative movement pioneered—the "synagogue center" offering social and recreational activities in addition to the classical functions of prayer and religious study, and which conceives of itself as the central Jewish address in the geographic area it serves—has become predominant on the American Jewish scene.[6] As a consequence, Reform and Orthodoxy have come to look to Conservative models in fashioning their own religious institutions.[7]

The rising influence of Conservatism can be traced, in part, to the suburbanization that has occurred during the past two decades among Jews living in the largest cities. Suburbanization brought with it the problem of the maintenance of Jewish identity, and it was to the synagogue that the new Jewish suburbanite tended to look for identity-maintenance. The result was that the synagogue emerged in the 1950's and 1960's as the crucial institution in Jewish life. And Conservatism exemplified the type of synagogue that was most appealing to the new suburban Jew.

The vitality of individual Conservative synagogues had actually been clear prior to the development of the newer suburbs. During the 1940's there were any number of Conservative synagogues that had surpassed their Reform competitors. But Conservatism's predominance was not apparent at the time: the past achievements of Reform lived on in the monumental temples which had been constructed in the 1920's and earlier. In the newer suburbs, however, the predominance of Conservatism became visible to all.

Philadelphia provides the clearest example of the process. In the 1950's, Beth Sholom, one of the leading Conservative congregations of the city, decided to move to suburban Elkins Park. The congregation chose no less an architect than Frank Lloyd Wright for its new edifice.[8]

Considering Wright's imperial manner and demands, the decision was an act of daring. But Beth Sholom was amply rewarded: the building Wright designed was visible for miles, and it immediately established itself as the most striking synagogue in Philadelphia. It was so definitive a statement that no Reform or Orthodox congregation in the area felt capable of exceeding it. Even today Beth Sholom remains the most widely known of the nation's newer surburban synagogues; it is a magnet for tourists, architects, and of course for devotees of the Wright mystique who wish to study the master's only synagogue.

Prior to the 1950's, the emerging strength of Conservative Judaism on the local level was not reflected on the national scene. While the United Synagogue of America —the union of Conservative congregations—had been established as early as 1913, it remained a paper organization for many years.[9] The only group that visualized Conservatism in national terms was the rabbis, organized as the Rabbinical Assembly of America. However, in the past two decades a sharp change has occurred: the laity have transmuted their loyalty to local congregations into attachment to a national movement.

The rapid development of the United Synagogue, which now has a membership of 832 congregations, is an index to the new sense of constituting a movement. During the 1950's and 1960's, the United Synagogue emerged as an important Jewish agency. In contrast to its older status as a paper organization, the United Synagogue currently maintains some seventeen field offices in addition to its national headquarters. The conventions of the United Synagogue, held every two years at the Concord Hotel, have grown in size to the point where they tax the facilities of what is the largest kosher hotel in the country. The United Synagogue would long have surpassed its

Reform counterpart—the Union of American Hebrew Congregations established in 1873—but for the fact that it has been under the control of the Jewish Theological Seminary of America. Fearful of the centrist and left-wing influence of the laity and of many congregational rabbis, Seminary officials—all of whom belong to Conservatism's right wing—have discouraged aggressive growth. Their influence over the United Synagogue is symbolized by the fact that the agency makes its national headquarters in the buildings of the Seminary.[10]

Despite discouragement from influential quarters, the feeling of constituting a distinctive movement has become an increasingly pervasive sentiment in Conservatism. The growth of the United Synagogue is not the only sign of this development: the establishment in 1959 of the World Council of Synagogues is another illustration of the same trend. The organization's name bears no relationship to reality, for the World Council consists of the Conservative congregations of the United States and Canada plus only a handful of synagogues located in other countries. The World Council is consequently barely more than a paper organization, but it nevertheless serves an important symbolic fuction: its existence serves to imply that Conservative Judaism is characterized by irresistible force, wide scope, and enduring permanence. Furthermore, the existence of the World Council conveys the message that Conservatism is more than simply an American idiosyncrasy—a group of local congregations which happen to have evolved a common synagogual pattern at a single point in time.

The symbolic significance of the World Council has been complemented by the establishment of other Conservative agencies, whose unanticipated effect has been to

add to the feeling that Conservative Judaism is a movement. Ramah—a chain of Conservative summer camps
conducted under the supervision of the Teachers Institute
of the Seminary—is the best example of the process. While
the idea had long been discussed on the national level,
Ramah is a grass-roots development initiated by a group
of Conservative laymen and rabbis from Chicago who
opened a camp in the woods of northern Wisconsin in
1947. The purpose of the enterprise was to train an indig-
enous Conservative leadership—both lay and rabbinical—
and thereby to assure the perpetuation of the movement.
As Rabbi Ralph Simon—the spiritual leader of Congregation Rodfei Zedek of Chicago and the chairman of the
camp's program committee—phrased it, the purpose of
Ramah was to "bring out and develop those qualities in
boys and girls which will best prepare them for leadership
in the American-Jewish community." [11]

During the first year only 89 youngsters were enrolled;
in its early period Ramah was an obscure experiment.
However, it developed rapidly during the 1960's, and by
1970 it had grown to a network of seven camps. In addition, there were programs in South America and Israel,
as well as other activities such as a day camp and a training camp. In 1970 Ramah enrolled 2,833 youngsters in
its seven American camps, 350 in an Israel program, and
52 in a special training program. The staff totalled 1,321
individuals.

The extent to which Ramah has succeeded in fulfilling
its original objective need not concern us. For our purposes what is significant about Ramah is that it brings
together Conservative youngsters from many different areas
in a setting where they necessarily constitute a community.
As a consequence, Ramah campers develop close associa-

tions with each other—associations which flow from their common Conservative origins. Inevitably the feeling of a shared Conservatism is nurtured.

Ramah also serves to bring Conservative adults into a closer bond. Visiting Day, for example, serves as an opportunity to meet peers from other congregations. Again, the feeling of a shared Conservatism is reinforced. The effect of Ramah, however, goes much beyond the campers and their parents. The Ramah ideal is that every camper graduate to a staff position. With the exception of Israeli specialists who are hired to enrich the camp program, the majority of the staff are in fact ex-campers, or individuals who are otherwise connected with Conservatism. The staff constitutes a kind of Conservative society in miniature, and interaction is intense. The "Ramah marriage" has become a well-known phenomenon in Conservative circles.[12]

In summary, the recent development of Conservative Judaism is characterized by: (1) the emergence of Conservatism as the favored religious self-designation of the American Jew and its consequent achievement of primacy on the American Jewish religious scene; (2) the emergence of Conservative synagogues, particularly in surburban areas in the East, as the leading congregations in their communities; (3) the emergence of national agencies that reflect the strength of Conservatism on the local level; and (4) the emergence of a sense of constituting a movement—a sense of a shared Conservatism on the part of the Conservative laity.

These developments appear to portend a brilliant future for Conservatism. The continued growth of Conservative Judaism seems assured: in the large metropolitan centers there are significant numbers of unaffiliated Jews who identify themselves as "Conservative." All that seems necessary to further augment the primacy of Conservatism is that such individuals be induced to activate a commitment they already hold.

B.

THE PROBLEM OF CONSERVATIVE MORALE

Despite brilliant achievements and excellent prospects for future growth, the morale of the Conservative movement is on the decline. Seemingly, present-day Conservative leaders are less satisfied with their movement than they have a right to be; they are less sanguine about its future than the facts would appear to indicate. Paradoxically, during the period when the movement was overshadowed by Reform and Orthodoxy, Conservatism's élan was high. But when Conservatism came into its own, morale began to sag.

Doubts about the movement are most frequently expressed by the rabbis. As religious professionals, they have a heightened interest in Conservatism, a special sensitivity to its problems, and a sophisticated set of standards by which to judge its success. The following statement illustrates the doubts felt by some Conservative rabbis:

During these past decades we have grown, we have prospered, we have become a powerful religious establishment. I am, however, haunted by the fear that somewhere along the way we have become lost; our direction is not clear, and the many promises we made to ourselves and to our people have not been fulfilled. We are in danger of not having anything significant to say to our congregants, to the best of our youth, to all those who are seeking a dynamic adventurous faith that can elicit sacrifice and that can transform lives.[13]

This statement emanates from an esteemed leader of Conservatism, Max Routtenberg. As the rabbi of the Kesher Zion Synagogue in Reading, Pa., from 1932 to 1948, Routtenberg helped to establish Conservatism in eastern Pennsylvania. After a period during which he served as a leading official of the Seminary and Rabbinical Assembly, Rabbi Routtenberg went on to become the spiritual leader of B'nai Sholom of Rockville Center, N.Y. He was instrumental in developing B'nai Sholom into an important suburban synagogue in the prime area of Long Island. In 1964 Routtenberg was elected to the presidency of the Rabbinical Assembly. He was viewed by his colleagues as a kind of ideal Conservative Jew: he succeeded in combining the scientific methodology he had encountered as a student at the Seminary with the approach to learning he had assimilated during his earlier years at a *yeshiva*. Furthermore, Routtenberg was a man of the world—he sought in his person to combine Jewish and Western culture. However, in his presidential address to the Rabbinical Assembly from which we have quoted, Rabbi Routtenberg spoke in accents far different from those that characterize the man of success.

Why this disparity between achievement and satisfaction? Why the decline in morale among Conservative leaders? The proper starting point for an analysis of these questions is the world of Orthodoxy. More specifically, it is the attitude of Conservatism toward Orthodoxy.

The founders of Conservatism believed that Orthodoxy was fated to disappear. While some Orthodox Jews might persist, Conservatism held that such individuals would be relatively few in number and insignificant in social status. The founders of Conservatism did not relish the passing of Orthodoxy: they had strong sentimental ties with their Orthodox childhood, they had friends and relatives who had remained Orthodox, and they admired Orthodoxy's persistence in the face of seemingly overwhelming odds. However, while conceding Orthodoxy's historic contribution, they were convinced that it had run its course. As Rabbi Routtenberg put it:

I think back to the period when my fellow students and I, at the *yeshivah,* decided to make the break and become Conservative rabbis . . . We were breaking with our past, in some cases with our families who had deep roots in Orthodoxy. We broke with beloved teachers who felt betrayed when we left the *yeshivah.* It was a great wrench . . . but we had to make it. . . . We loved the Jewish people and its heritage, and as we saw both threatened we set out to save them. We saw the future of Judaism in the Conservative movement.[14]

Orthodoxy, then, was viewed as a kind of *moshav z'kenim*—a home for the aged, and for those old in spirit. Accordingly, Conservatism was destined to supplant Orthodoxy. Furthermore, Conservatism was seen as a contemporary expression of what was most vital and creative in the Orthodoxy of old—that is, in the Orthodoxy of the pre-modern era:

In spite of the claims made in other quarters it is we [Conservative Jews] who are the authentic Jews of rabbinic Judaism. . . . Many of those who attack our movement as "deviationist"—a term totally repugnant to the authentic Jewish tradition—and who demand unswerving adherence to the written letter of the Law are actually the Sadducees of the twentieth century. Had they lived in the days of Hillel, Rabbi Johanan ben Zakkai, Rabbi Akiba, Rabbi Meir or Rabbi Judah Hanasi, they would have condemned every creative contribution that the Sages made to the living Judaism of their age.[15]

In a sense, then, Conservatism is conceived by its elite as twentieth-century Orthodoxy. Or, to put it another way, if Orthodoxy had retained the ability to change it would have evolved into Conservatism.

The Conservative movement's understanding of its relationship to Orthodoxy has been best expressed in the many books, articles, and addresses of the man whom we have just quoted: Robert Gordis. Gordis is considered by his colleagues to be the most powerful mind in Conservatism. From 1931 until his recent retirement into academic life, he served as the rabbi of Temple Beth El of Rockaway Park, N.Y. He also taught on a part-time basis at the Seminary as well as at other institutions. Gordis recalled his traditional upbringing with great affection; but at the same time he stressed Orthodoxy's rigidity and resistance to change. He maintained that Conservatism had adopted what was best in Orthodoxy. And although he avoided making the painful declaration that Orthodoxy was doomed to a lingering senility, the conclusion was inescapable.

In recent years it has become clear that Conservatism is incorrect in its diagnosis of Orthodoxy and especially in its prognosis of Orthodoxy's future. Unaccountably, Orthodoxy has refused to assume the role of invalid. Rather, it has transformed itself into a growing force in American Jewish life. It has reasserted its claim of being *the* authentic interpretation of Judaism.

Having achieved a new sense of élan, Orthodoxy has proceeded to implement a policy of strict non-cooperation with Conservatism. Orthodox policy has called for the rejection of all changes proposed by Conservatism—even changes that might be acceptable if they emanated from a different quarter. Furthermore, the tolerance of individual Orthodox rabbis toward Conservatism, characteristic of the 1920's and 1930's, has become only a dimming Conservative memory, especially on the Eastern seaboard.

While the Orthodox rabbi of yesterday might successfully resist a Conservative takeover of his congregation,[16]
he was prepared to concede that Conservatism represented
the wave of the future. Today's Orthodox leaders, however, proceed on the assumption that Conservatism is a
hollow shell—that its seemingly strong synagogues are peopled by weak Jews who are fated to assimilate. Only
Orthodoxy will have the tenacity to survive the tempta-
tions of the open society.

The Orthodox offensive against Conservatism has been
waged on two fronts simultaneously: Israel and the United
States. Orthodox leaders in the United States have stimulated their colleagues in Israel to attack Conservatism.
Inasmuch as Orthodox leaders in Israel are in firm control of their country's religious establishment, have considerable political leverage, and are not inhibited by a
tradition of church-state separation, they have been able
to implement anti-Conservative policies inconceivable in
the United States. Accordingly, Conservative rabbis have
been disqualified from performing any rabbinic functions
in Israel. The few Conservative institutions that have
managed to gain a foothold in Israel are barely tolerated.
The fugitive position occupied by Conservatism in Israel
has been a particularly bitter blow for the American
movement. To Conservative leaders it appears that, instead
of being rewarded for its long history of support for the
Zionist cause, Conservatism is being penalized.[17]

The full story of the renaissance of American Orthodoxy has yet to be written. One scholar has ably analyzed
the disorganization of the older Orthodoxy as well as the
new spirit of confidence which emerged after World War
II.[18] Nevertheless, the reasons for the resurrection of what
was seemingly a dead religious movement are still imperfectly understood. If by the 1960's the editors of the *Amer-*

ican Jewish Year Book were struck by the renewal of
Orthodoxy and commissioned a study (they termed Orthodoxy "a vital but hitherto neglected area of American
Jewish life"), Conservative leaders had noticed the resur-
gence a decade earlier. However, the latter were unsure
of what their response should be, for the Orthodox renaissance played havoc with their understanding of the balance of power in the American Jewish community as well
as with their prognosis of the American Jewish future.

To Conservative leaders, each new Orthodox success
seemed to provide another instance where the laws of
religious gravity had been repealed. Orthodoxy did not
satisfy itself with serving those Jews who continued to
reside in decaying central-city neighborhoods. Rather it
began to push outward. It proceeded to establish congregations in the better residential areas. In the Midwood
area of Brooklyn, for example, the giant East Midwood
Jewish Center—which had once dominated the neighborhood—found itself surrounded by a network of smaller
Orthodox synagogues whose dynamism recalled its own
exuberant past. In Boston there was the example of the
Orthodox synagogues of Roxbury, Dorchester, and Mat-
tapan. Unaccountably, when these areas became black,
their Orthodox synagogues refused to die. Rather, they
relocated in new neighborhoods. And some of the congregations were not satisfied to establish themselves even in
such solid middle-class areas as Brookline and Brighton.
Instead, they proceeded to relocate in Newton, the most
desirable Jewish area in Boston. It had always been assumed that Newton—with its upper-class reputation—was
a Conservative and Reform preserve.

During the 1950's and 1960's the *yeshivoth* multiplied
in number, size, and fundamentalism; the Orthodox rab-

bis became ever more intransigent; the influence exercised by Orthodoxy in Israel became clearer; and Orthodox synagogues established themselves in upper-class and upper-middle-class areas. Even Hassidism was transformed from an antediluvian curiosity into a movement which, it was said, had much to teach modern man. The net result was that the Conservative understanding of the American Jewish present, together with the Conservative expectation of the American Jewish future, became confounded. The ground was prepared for the development of a kind of Conservative *anomie*. The problem was particularly aggravated in the case of one segment of the Conservative elite —the rabbis. Many rabbis had a deep sympathy with Jewish traditionalism. Thus on the one hand they admired and identified with the Orthodox advance. But on the other hand they were filled with dismay and hostility toward this totally unexpected development.

C.

THE CRISIS IN CONSERVATIVE OBSERVANCE

While the renewal of Orthodoxy has been an important cause of the decline in Conservative morale, developments internal to the Conservative movement have also been an important influence. Conservatism is a religious movement. As such, it is subject to evaluation from the vantage point of suprasocial achievement. Thus, Conservative Jews may measure the progress of their movement in terms of its success in bringing man closer to God, or, as Rabbi Routtenberg phrases it, by its ability to "transform lives." Conservative Jews, if they are strong religionists, not only have this option but are impelled to embrace it. That is, they must give preference to suprasocial achievement and disregard, or even disvalue, such social achievements as monumental synagogue buildings and prosperous congregations.

All religious traditions have several yardsticks to measure suprasocial achievement, but each tends to stress a particular yardstick. The one that predominates in Judaism is that of the performance of the *mitzvoth maasiyoth,* the commandments of the Jewish sacred system. True to this thrust, Conservatism uses a ritualistic yardstick in gauging its effectiveness. While at times it has been attracted to the moralistic-ethical yardstick in measuring religious growth, it has nevertheless remained close to the sacramental approach of rabbinic Judaism.[19]

Conservative Judaism believes that it possesses a unique approach to the *mitzvoth,* and especially to the problem of maintaining their observance. Conservatism holds that it is possible to advocate change in *halachah* (Jewish law) and simultaneously to be loyal to *halachah.* Change is seen as essential. From the Conservative standpoint, the maintenance of observance has been immensely complicated, if not rendered impossible, by what is regarded as Orthodoxy's ossification. While the modern Jew must be responsive to the requirements of *halachah,* such loyalty cannot reasonably be expected unless *halachah* is responsive to the needs of the modern Jew. Thus, in the Conservative view, Orthodox authorities who refuse to sanction change, much less to stimulate it, bear part of the responsibility for the lamentable decline of observance. As Rabbi Simon puts it in a presidential address to the Rabbinical Assembly: "We have felt that Reform Judaism abandoned Halahah while Orthodoxy permitted Halahah to abandon us." [20]

As Conservatism sees it, certain *mitzvoth* are outmoded or even offensive to the modern spirit. In the interest of promoting observance, as well as out of a desire for intellectual honesty, such *mitzvoth* should be declared null and void. Furthermore, emphasis must be placed on the promotion of the essential requirements of the sacred system. Minutiae of the Jewish code can safely be disregarded. *Mitzvoth* that are "fences around the Torah" rather than central to the Torah itself may be allowed to fall into disuse. Change can be effected by proper interpretation of the halachic system, and, where necessary, by legislation.

The essence of the Conservative position, then, is liberalization. While Conservatism believes that liberalization is its own justification, it also holds that liberalization makes possible the promotion of observance. As religious authorities come to differentiate between major and minor —between what is required and what is elective, between what is in keeping with the modern temper and what is offensive to it, between what can be reinterpreted in the light of new needs and what is beyond rescue—the ground for a renewal of observance of the *mitzvoth* is prepared.[21] In addition to liberalization, the Conservative platform has two additional planks. One is "innovation," the development of new observances or procedures that are required when there is a need to substitute for, modify, or extend the traditional *mitzvoth*. The other is "beautification," the requirement that the *mitzvoth* be practiced in as esthetic a manner as possible—"the Jewish home beautiful." In sum, the Conservative position is that liberalization—in combination with innovation and beautification— will succeed in averting the evil decree of non-observance.

The dominant Orthodox position on the *mitzvoth* differs radically from the Conservative stance. From the Orthodox perspective, liberalization is seen as severely limited, due to restraints internal to the halachic system.

But even more to the point, liberalization is viewed as self-defeating. From the dominant Orthodox perspective, the net result of seeking to make the *mitzvoth* more modern and appealing, more rational, more internally consistent, and more discriminating between major and minor requirements of the Jewish code will not be more observance. Rather it will be lessened observance, and ultimately complete non-observance.

If liberalization is viewed not only as subversive but as counterproductive, innovation is also rejected. (To be sure, there has been some acceptance of innovation when promulgated by the Israeli rabbinate.) And while beautification is viewed as more acceptable than liberalization and innovation, it too is under suspicion: the essence of observance should be the desire to serve God rather than the appeal to the esthetic sense.

The crucial aspect of the Conservative position on observance is not its acceptability to Orthodoxy, however, but its success in promoting religious growth among the Conservative laity, and specifically in advancing their observance of the *mitzvoth*. Judged from this vantage point, Conservatism has been an abysmal failure: there has been a steady erosion of observance among Conservative Jews. And despite a strong desire to encourage observance, Conservatism has not succeeded in arresting the decline in observance among its adherents, much less in increasing their level of conformity to the Jewish sacred system. The belief among Conservative leaders that the movement's approach to *halachah* had the power to maintain observance, as well as to inspire its renewal, has proved illusory.

The decline in observance is in part traceable to the changing composition of the congregations. Religious observance among Jews in the United States has generally tended to decline with each succeeding generation. Thus, observance has dropped as the membership of Conservative congregations has come to be composed of Jews of more advanced generation. To be sure, in each Conservative synagogue there are some families that are as observant as those of the preceding generation. Furthermore, there are cases in Conservative congregations of increased performance of the *mitzvoth*: for example, men who recite *Kiddush* on the Sabbath more regularly than did their fathers, and women who light Sabbath candles more faithfully than did their mothers. But such instances of retention and growth have not been frequent enough to offset the sharp trend toward diminished observance.

In recent years it has become increasingly clear that Conservative Jews have broken with *halachah* as a system. Not only has this meant a steep decline in observance, but it has also brought about a new personalism. Resulting incongruities include the fact that lesser observances, such as the lighting of the menorah on Hanukah, have become more widespread than major observances, such as the lighting of candles on the Sabbath.[22]

Conservatism's defeat on the ritual front can be demonstrated in almost every area of Jewish observance. Sabbath observance is a case in point. After World War II there was a good deal of optimism in Conservatism with respect to Sabbath observance. The influences that seemed to portend a renewal included the rising prosperity of Conservative Jews and the increased popularity of the five-day work week. The new life style of the suburban Jew, which stressed the building of a meaningful pattern of identity for one's children, constituted an additional factor. And the need for surcease from the increasingly hectic pace of life appeared to offer new justification for Judaism's stress on the sanctity of Sabbath rest.

Encouraged by these prospects, the Conservative rabbis pushed for liberalization. In 1950 the Law Committee of the Rabbinical Assembly proceeded to make a daring innovation. On a split decision it voted to permit travel on the Sabbath—travel specifically for the purpose of attending services. It also voted to permit the use of electricity on the Sabbath.[23]

What these decisions were saying was that the traditional concept of prohibited work was outmoded and counterproductive. Thus, driving an automobile was not intrinsically bad, and if the machine was employed to transport the individual from his home in the sprawl of suburbia to the synagogue on the Sabbath, it was a positive good. In any case the emphasis should be not on prohibitions as much as on positive acts that would promote the holiness of the seventh day: attending services, lighting candles, making *Kiddush,* reciting the blessing over bread, and serving special Sabbath meals. Furthermore, such an emphasis would inevitably lead the congregant to refrain from following his accustomed routine on the Sabbath. Thus the emphasis on positive acts constituted a more profitable approach to building Sabbath observance than would harping on a detailed list of prohibited activities.

In addition to the technique of liberalization, the Conservative approach to building Sabbath observance stressed the role of beautification. Thus the congregational gift shops conducted by the sisterhoods were stimulated to promote the sale of candlesticks, *Kiddush* cups, *hallah* covers, *hallah* knives, Sabbath napkins, and other such items. Finally, innovation was utilized. Innovation was in fact a long-standing Conservative tradition in respect to Sabbath observance—late Friday evening services had been one of the movement's most significant innovations.[24]

The available evidence suggests that the Conservative strategy of liberalization, innovation, and beautification has been a failure; it underlies the fact that the majority of Conservative Jews do not follow even the most basic Sabbath observances. To cite the example of Conservative-dominated Providence, R.I., only 12% of those who designate themselves as "Conservative" attend services once a week or more. And what is even more serious, attendance at Sabbath worship declines with each generation: while some 21% of the first generation attend, only 2% of the third do so.[25] The lighting of Sabbath candles fares somewhat better, in part because the ritual is a female obligation. But despite the fact that lighting the candles is required of the Jewish woman, it is observed in only 40% of Conservative households. And while the ritual is observed in 52% of first-generation households, it is followed in only 32% of third-generation households.[26]

Kashruth is another area of observance that constitutes a problem for Conservative Jews. Only 37% of Conservative households in Providence buy kosher meat. Furthermore, in only 27% of the households are separate dishes utilized. And true to the pattern we have already encountered, observance declines in each generation: while 41% of the first generation maintain two sets of dishes, only 20% of the third generation do so.[27]

If anything, the level of observance in Providence tends to be higher than among Conservative Jews in the nation at large—a result due to the fact that Jews in the Middle Atlantic and New England states are more traditionalistic than those who reside in other parts of the country. However, it might be contended that since a community-wide survey includes respondents who do not have sufficient commitment to join a synagogue, it is to be expected that their level of observance would be well below the ideal norms. But the fact is that there is not a Conservative synagogue in the country where most congregants practice the *mitzvoth* according to the Conservative regimen.

The observance of the membership of the Har Zion Synagogue of Philadelphia illustrates the problem. Har Zion is located in the city where Conservatism has made its deepest impact. And if Beth Sholom of Elkins Park is Conservatism's architectural showcase, Har Zion is its religious standard-bearer. Har Zion's pre-eminence is traceable to the influence of powerful laymen, but more especially to Simon Greenberg who served as its rabbi from 1925 to 1946. A strong personality, talented organizer, and determined opponent of left-wing thinking in Conservatism, Greenberg developed Har Zion into a model of Conservative traditionalism. He was so successful that he was invited to join the staff of the Seminary and exercise his influence on the national level. Despite Greenberg's removal to New York, Har Zion continued to look to him for inspiration.

A recent study of this model congregation has uncovered the fact that, despite its seeming traditionalism, the level of observance of the *mitzvoth* is strikingly low. Sabbath candles are lit in only 52% of Har Zion households. The practice of *kashruth* is limited to a minority: only 41% purchase kosher meat, and only 33% utilize separate dishes for meat and dairy foods. A bare majority —51%—attend services other than on the High Holidays, and only a segment of this group—perhaps a quarter—are regular Sabbath worshipers.[28]

For understandable reasons, the Conservative elite have avoided publicizing the painful evidence contained in the congregational and communal surveys. Aware of how far its followers deviate from Conservative norms, the movement has felt in recent years that it can do little more than provide a source of information and inspiration for those who might somehow find their way back to the *mitzvoth*.[29] While a "National Sabbath Observance Effort" was sponsored by the United Synagogue in the early 1950's when there was hope of a renewal of observance, the campaign has not been repeated.

In recent years it has become increasingly clear that the problem of observance constitutes a permanent crisis in Conservatism—that the religious derelictions of Conservative Jewry are much more than a temporary condition traceable to the trauma of removal from the closed society of the *shtetl* to the open society of the American metropolis. The elite are losing faith in their belief that through liberalization, innovation, and beautification the mass of Conservative Jews can be persuaded to return to the observance of the *mitzvoth*. In lieu of a solution to the crisis, the movement has sought to insure the observance of the *mitzvoth* in public: in the synagogue, at the Seminary, at Ramah, and during the tours and pilgrimages of U.S.Y. Although such conformity is gratifying to the elite—particularly to the older men who were reared in Orthodoxy and who have a strong need to justify their defection—it does not serve to erase the suspicion that the movement has been a failure. And Conservatism's failure in the area of the suprasocial is heightened by its brilliant achievements in the social arena: its success in building synagogues, in promoting organizational loyalty, and in achieving primacy on the American Jewish religious scene.

There is one final aspect to the observance crisis: the disillusionment among the Conservative elite with the very possibility of liberalization. The cause of this disillusionment is not so much Orthodox intransigence as the fact that, whatever the validity of liberalization in theory, the principle has proved to be difficult to implement in practice within the Conservative movement itself. During the 1950's and 1960's, sharply divergent opinions on almost every halachic problem were encountered in the Rabbinical Assembly. Consensus could not be attained. Important halachic opinions of the body's Committee on Jewish Law and Standards were seldom unanimous: they commonly consisted of a majority and a minority opinion. The result was that, in an effort to achieve a workable approach to liberalization, Conservative rabbis were accorded the privilege of following the minority opinion, if they were so inclined. However, such latitudinarianism succeeded in promoting further dissension rather than in building greater unity. By 1970 an impasse had been reached, with the result that the majority of the members of the Committee on Law and Standards resigned. In an effort to salvage decades of effort in the field of Jewish law, a special committee, with Rabbi Gordis as chairman and Rabbi Routtenberg as co-chairman, was appointed.[30] But whatever the outcome, there is no possibility of a return to the old Conservative faith in the principle of liberalization.

D.

THE NEXT CONSERVATIVE GENERATION

Although Conservative Judaism was not a creation of the young, its rise in the 1920–50 era was closely connected with its appeal to young marrieds who were in the process of establishing independent households and developing a pattern of Jewish living that would be distinctive to their generation. Younger Jews who wished to retain continuity with their past and at the same time integrate with American middle-class culture found Conservative Judaism to be the perfect solution to their dilemma. Conservatism was traditional yet flexible; Jewish yet American. Its religious services were based on the Hebrew liturgy but also included prayers in English. Its rabbis appeared as authentic representatives of an age-old tradition yet were accepting of the culture of the larger environment. Conservatism stood for religious observance without rejecting the less observant.

The élan of Conservative Judaism during the period of its rise was in no small measure due to the fact that the elite of the movement felt their formula was precisely the one acceptable to younger age-groups in the Jewish population—groups whose connection with traditional Jewish culture was less firm than their own. In 1949 a leading Conservative layman in the Midwest, Julian Freeman, neatly summarized the appeal of Conservatism when he commented: "A generation ago the young architect, the young engineer, the young doctor, the young lawyer, the young businessman saw in Conservative Judaism a chance for religious self-expression integrated with the best of thinking in the world at large." [31]

The present-day Conservative elite, however, is no longer so confident that its formula will be attractive to the younger generation. There are two aspects to this crisis of confidence. One is the problem of Jewish continuity—the problem of whether the battle against assimilation can be won. This question, most commonly perceived in terms of the threat of intermarriage, began to preoccupy the Jewish community in the 1960's. The *American Jewish Year Book* published its first study on intermarriage in

1963, and the following year *Look* magazine published its famous article ominously entitled "The Vanishing American Jew." [32]

The ensuing discussion deeply affected the Conservative movement. Although the intermarriage rate was highest among Reform-affiliated Jews, its incidence among the offspring of Conservative-affiliated families was frequent enough to generate considerable anxiety. The confluence of individual instances of intermarriage and communal discussion of the problem soon produced a feeling of anxiety. It seemed to many that the very physical survival of the group was at stake. The threat inevitably spilled over into feelings about the prospects for Conservatism: if group continuity was in doubt, how much less was there a future for Conservative Judaism?

In addition to pessimism about whether the battle against intermarriage could be won, Conservatism in recent years has lost its older confidence of being in possession of a formula that can win the support of younger Jews. Despite interest in the *shtetl* and the East European milieu, many younger Jews—including those reared in Conservative congregations—have little connection with the Jewish culture of the immediate past. Inasmuch as Conservatism assumes some continuity with the East European past and some familiarity with Jewish culture generally, it has been deeply affected by such Jewish deculturation. If the mission of Conservatism has been to show how it was possible to practice selected aspects of Jewish culture in an American milieu, the result of Jewish deculturation has been that the movement no longer has its older foundation of Jewish culture on which to build its synagogual loyalties. Rather than having an assured constituency as before, Conservatism finds itself placed under the uncomfortable necessity of winning adherents to its cause, and having to do so without the undergirding of cultural compulsions. Thus, if Conservative leaders seem less assured by Conservative prosperity than they have a right to be, in one sense they are justified in their insecurity.

To win a constituency rather than merely to inherit one is difficult enough, particularly if a movement has the feeling that years of devoted labor and sacrifice entitle it to a loyal following. But Conservatism labors under the further doubt that it can prevail in its battle to win the loyalty of young people. The reason for Conservative pessimism resides in the disjunction between its cultural system and that of younger American Jews. Many Conservative young people not only lack Jewish culture, but they have been influenced by youth culture—some are card-carrying members of the "Woodstock nation," others are fellow travelers, and still others have inchoate sympathies with the counterculture. While the problem of enlisting the loyalty of such young people is encountered by all Jewish religious movements, the issue is a particularly knotty one for Conservatism, with its stress on cultural reconciliation and the blending of Jewish and general culture.

Despite the fact that the so-called *havuroth* originated among Conservative young people, Conservatism has not been notably successful in enlisting the loyalties of those who are part of the youth culture, who have little connection with East European culture, or who are antagonistic to the type of American culture on which the movement is based. The most notable demonstration of the difficulties involved in Conservative efforts at cultural reconciliation took place, appropriately enough, in the communitarian setting of Ramah—specifically at the Ramah camp in Palmer, Mass., during the summers of 1969 and 1970.[33]

The greening of the Ramah program was inspired by
Rabbi Raphael Arzt, a member of one of Conservatism's
first families and the son of Rabbi Max Arzt, a veteran
Seminary administrator and a beloved figure in the Conservative movement. What Raphael Arzt sought to do was
to integrate the Ramah program into youth culture. He
sought thereby to provide a Jewish alternative for campers
of high school and college age who were attracted to youth
culture.

There has been considerable controversy in Conservatism as to what actually happened at Palmer: the extent
of drug use, the degree to which campers absented themselves from religious services, the extent of laxity about
the dietary laws, the amount of non-attendance at classes,
and the implications of an English-language presentation
of "Hair." Some claim that the outcome of the Palmer
experiment was a greater Jewishness, while others contend
that it resulted in heightened alienation.[34] Whatever the
case, the movement decided not to open Palmer in 1971.
Palmer represented the first closing in Ramah's history;
it was understood that the experiment was not to be continued at any other Ramah camp.

Sensitive leaders in Conservatism are aware of how
deeply the movement is rooted in an older American
middle-class culture which is currently out of favor with
a significant segment of Conservative youth. The problem
was presented to the Rabbinical Assembly by Rabbi
Edward Gershfield in an address which celebrated the
organization's seventieth anniversary. According to Gershfield,

Our services of readings in fine English, correct musical ren-
ditions by professional cantors and choirs, and decorous and
dignified rabbis in elegant gowns arouse disdain and con-

tempt in our young people. They want excitement and noise, improvisation and emotion, creativity and sensitivity, informality and spontaneity. On the other hand, they feel guilty about the spending of large sums of money for synagogue buildings rather than for social services (generally for non-Jews). And they are "turned off" by the very beauty and decorum which we have worked so hard to achieve.

Of course, the youth do not wish to go into the reasons why these aspects of our life have been created. They are impatient with our explanations that most people are not dynamic and creative, and look to religious leaders for directions and instructions; that we who have managed to survive the rigors of youth appreciate regularity and stability in life, that we honestly want to endow our heritage with dignity and beauty, and that a congregation of a thousand persons cannot have a prayer service in a coffeehouse to the accompaniment of a guitar . . . we seem to be doomed to having to watch as our youth relive the same self-destructive impulses that we have seen long ago, and have thought could not happen again. Our appeals to reason and history . . . go right past them and we are for the most part helpless.[35]

As Gershfield intimates, the fact that the American culture for which Conservatism has stood is under attack is profoundly upsetting to the movement. In the years immediately ahead, it will become apparent whether Conservatism has retained sufficient flexibility to deal with such cultural challenges.

In summary, the immediate reasons for the drop in Conservative morale at the very zenith of Conservative influence include the emergence of Orthodoxy, the problem of Conservative observance, and the widespread alienation among Conservative young people from the American culture to which their movement has been strongly attached. But on a deeper level the Conservative crisis —if that be the word—represents a questioning of whether the Jewish people and its "chain of tradition" can long endure on the American continent. Since Conservatism's future is predicated upon such survival, its fears are understandable. *Yisrael v'oraitha had hu*: the Jewish people and its tradition are indissolubly linked. There cannot be an authentic Jewish people without the continuity of Jewish tradition, even as there cannot be meaningful continuity of Jewish tradition without the maintenance of the integrity of the Jewish group. It is to this momentous issue that the Conservative movement, in its present mature phase, has been moved to address itself.

Notes

ABBREVIATIONS

CJSA   *Conservative Judaism: A Sociological Analysis,* by Marshall Sklare (Ph.D. dissertation, Columbia University, 1953)

J.T.S.   Jewish Theological Seminary, or Jewish Theological Seminary of America

R.A.   Rabbinical Assembly of America

U. Syn. United Synagogue of America

Introduction

1. Will Herberg, "The Postwar Revival of the Synagogue," *Commentary*, IX (1950), 317.

2. Moshe Davis, "Jewish Religious Life and Institutions in America," *The Jews: Their History, Culture, and Religion,* ed. by Louis Finkelstein (2 vols., New York: Harper & Brothers, 1949), I, 430.*

3. The following books and articles touch upon some historical or contemporary aspect of Conservative Judaism: Robert Gordis, *Conservative Judaism* (New York: Behrman House, 1945); Louis Ginzberg, *Students, Scholars, and Saints* (Philadelphia: Jewish Publication Society of America, 1928); Mordecai M. Kaplan, *Judaism as a Civiliza-*tion (New York: The Macmillan Co., 1935)**; Moshe Davis, *Yahadut Amerikah Be-Hitpathutah* (New York: J.T.S., 1951); and Herbert Parzen's series in *Conservative Judaism* running from Vol. III, No. 4 (July, 1947) to Vol. VIII, No. 2 (January, 1952).

All of these writers are rabbis of Conservative congregations, scholars teaching at the Conservative rabbinical school, or officials of the Conservative movement. Although these Conservative functionaries are not all in agreement with each other, considered as a whole they present what may be called the "sectarian" interpretation of their movement. Most of them feel that Conservatism represents the "au-

---

* Paperback edition: 3 vols., New York: Schocken Books, 1970-71.

** Paperback edition: New York: Schocken Books, 1967.

tonomous" development of a religious *ideology* whose innovations justified a secessionist movement and the consequent establishment of a new American-Jewish religious group. Their approach was summarized by Clark when he said: "In the sectarian mind the causes of [religious] divergence are theological." (Elmer T. Clark, *The Small Sects in America* [rev. ed., Nashville: Abingdon - Cokesbury Press, 1949], p. 18.)

While the present work attempts the first *sociological* interpretation of Conservative Judaism in monographic form, the treatments of previous investigators who have studied Jewish communities, and thus have encountered Conservatism on the local level, are suggestive. See particularly Arthur T. Buch, "The Jewish Community of Scranton," (Unpublished Ph.D. Dissertation, New School for Social Research, 1945); Uriah Z. Engelman, "Medurbia," *Contemporary Jewish Record,* IV (1941), 339-48, 511-21; Samuel Koenig, "The Socioeconomic Structure of an American Jewish Community," *Jews in a Gentile World,* ed. by Isacque Graeber and Steuart H. Britt (New York: The Macmillan Co., 1942), pp. 200-42; and W. Lloyd Warner and Leo Srole, *The Social Systems*

of American Ethnic Groups (New Haven: Yale University Press, 1945).

For a detailed analysis of the varying perspectives involved in the sectarian and the sociological approaches, see *CJSA*, pp. 52-63. It is worthwhile to point out that some of the "sectarians," like Parzen for example, have a less rigid approach than others of their group. Upon occasion Conservative rabbis have made remarks indicating their deviation from the sectarian approach. See the comment by Ira Eisenstein in *The Reconstructionist*, XII, 8 (May 31, 1946), 28-31; and Max Kadushin in R.A., *Proceedings*, I (1927), 60ff., as well as his article "Conservative Judaism—Customs and Ceremonies," *The Sentinel* (Chicago), LXVI, 9 (May 27, 1927), 10, 34. (Note: Reference to R.A., *Proceedings* is to year of publication, rather than to date of convention.)

4. Note the series of monographs sponsored by the Institute of Social and Religious Research. Since there is much repetition, only one of them needs to be cited: H. Paul Douglass and Edmund DeS. Brunner, *The Protestant Church as a Social Institution* (New York: Harper & Brothers, 1935).

Chapter I

1. With increasing research, the three waves of immigration scheme has come under criticism as constituting an oversimplification. For our purposes, however, its very simplicity is its chief virtue.

2. It should be pointed out that the Sephardim pronounce some Hebrew vowels and consonants differently than do the Ashkenazim

(the German and East European Jews). Also, the Sephardic prayer book differs in certain details from the Ashkenazic.

3. Note how Dr. David de Sola Pool, the prominent Sephardic rabbi, differentiates historically between his congregation and others, who practiced what he calls "American Orthodoxy," and Ashkenazic

Jewry with their "East European Orthodoxy" (David de Sola Pool, "Judaism and the Synagogue," *The American Jew*, ed. by Oscar I. Janowsky [New York: Harper & Brothers, 1942], p. 50).

4. Ethical Culture may be considered an offshoot of German-Jewish Reform. It is significant that for some, affiliation with this movement did not mean the end to their Jewish identification.

5. Oscar I. Janowsky, *The JWB Survey* (New York: The Dial Press, 1948), p. 239.

6. See United States Bureau of the Census, *Religious Bodies, 1936*, (2 vols., Washington: Government Printing Office, 1941), II, pp. 756-72; Harry S. Linfield, *Statistics of American Jews* (New York: Jewish Statistical Bureau, 1944); and Linfield, *The Jewish People in the Federal Census of Religious Groups* (New York: Jewish Statistical Bureau, 1948). For information about the public relations aspect, see the report in the *New York Herald Tribune*, June 23, 1950, p. 17. For a critical analysis of the field, see Uriah Z. Engelman, "Jewish Statistics in the U.S. Census of Religious Bodies (1850-1936)," *Jewish Social Studies*, IX (1947), 127-74. Note also H. L. Lurie, "Jewish Social Research," *Freedom and Reason; Studies in Philosophy and Jewish Culture in Memory of Morris Raphael Cohen*, ed. by Salo W. Baron, Ernest Nagel, and Koppel S. Pinson (Glencoe: The Free Press, 1951), pp. 383-96.

7. See Herbert Parzen, "Religion," *American Jewish Year Book*, LII (1951), 86-87.

8. Starting with 16 founding congregations in 1913, the United Synagogue of America (which is the congregational union of Conservative Judaism) totalled 420 affiliates in 1952.

9. The poll to which we make reference was done for the National (then Federal) Council of Churches of Christ. See their bulletin *Information Service*, May 15, 1948. For interpretations of this and similar studies, see Jessie Bernard, *American Community Behavior* (New York: Dryden Press, 1949), pp. 197-98; Eli E. Cohen, "Economic Status and Occupational Structure," *American Jewish Year Book*, LI (1950), 53-70; and Liston Pope, "Religion and the Class Structure," *The Annals of the American Academy of Political and Social Science*, CCLVI (March, 1948), 84-91. A study of American college graduates also presents interesting confirmatory evidence: see Ernest Havemann and Patricia S. West, *They Went to College* (New York: Harcourt Brace & Co., 1952), pp. 187-89.

10. Warner and Srole, *op. cit.*, pp. 61, 203.

Significantly, there is a disparity between the *class* level and the *status* level of Jews. While the problem is outside of our purview at present, it must at least be mentioned here for it has important effects on the structuring of Jewish communal life. See Bernard, *op. cit.*, pp. 388-408.

11. For an excellent illustration of the disintegrative effects of social mobility in a Norwegian Lutheran church, see W. Lloyd Warner, *Democracy in Jonesville* (New York: Harper & Brothers, 1949), esp. pp. 176-77.

12. However, there now exists a small group of synagogues (the majority of which are located in New York City) whose leaders are younger, somewhat acculturated,

and generally middle-class individuals who are determined to remain Orthodox. This is the "Young Israel" movement, a group which has set up its own congregations in response to the fact that the typical Orthodox synagogue is an institution administered for and by a closed group of elders. Young Israel synagogues are characterized by greater decorum than is typical of most Orthodox houses of worship, by the use of English, by the avoidance of certain administrative practices characteristic of the immigrant and East European synagogue, and by an institutional youth work program. See Milton Richman, "A Descriptive Analysis of a Local Orthodox Jewish Synagogue" (Unpublished Master's thesis, New School for Social Research, 1943), and Young Israel, *President's Report, 1950-51* (New York: National Council of Young Israel, n.d.).

13. For our purpose it is necessary to emphasize dissimilarities rather than similarities. By so doing we do not mean to deny that many parallels or resemblances may exist. Actually, if one looks closely, it becomes clear that certain constellations of Jewish *attitudes* (if not practices) are highly modern and Western.

On the "foreignness" of Jewish practices, note the comments by Robert M. MacIver, in his *Report on the Jewish Community Relations Agencies* (New York: National Community Relations Advisory Council, 1951), pp. 33-34, 47. It is important to note that some Near Eastern Christians continued with "Easternness," but characteristically they have lived in their native lands until very recent times.

14. However, since many of the laws regulate the preparation of food, as well as other aspects of homemaking, the occupational role of woman means that for all practical purposes it is she—and not her husband—who must see to the observance of many commandments other than simply the three "womanly" ones.

15. For a description of *shtetl* life, see Mark Zborowski and Elizabeth Herzog, *Life Is With People* (New York: International Universities Press, 1952).*

16. Warner and Srole, *op. cit.,* p. 204.

17. See Mhyra S. Minnis, "Cleavage in Women's Organizations: A Reflection of the Social Structure of a City," *American Sociological Review,* XVIII (1953), 47-53.

18. Note Arnold and Caroline Rose, *America Divided* (New York: Alfred A. Knopf, Inc., 1948), pp. 178-82. These writers stress rejection as the causative factor for minority group identification.

19. Earlier theorists had equated ethnic group identification with cultural deviation. As a consequence the tendency to discard old-world traits was taken as an index of assimilation: cultural assimilation meant group assimilation. The possibility that social differentiation might continue in spite of a high rate of acculturation was neglected. Robert E. Park, for example, considered the problem almost completely from the standpoint of the social processes working to destroy the integrity of immigrant communities. He and others saw ethnic persistence as an imbalance or temporary stage which would be righted as the operation of social processes inevitably levelled these groups.

* Paperback edition: New York: Schocken Books, 1962.

See Robert E. Park and Herbert A. Miller, *Old World Traits Transplanted* (New York: Harper & Brothers, 1921), pp. 303-08, as well as a more recent statement by Maurice R. Davie, "Our Vanishing Minorities," *One America*, ed. by F. J. Brown and J. S. Roucek (third ed., New York: Prentice-Hall, Inc., 1952), pp. 545-57. For a contrasting view, see Peter A. Munch, "Social Adjustment among Wisconsin Norwegians," *American Sociological Review*, XIV (1949), 780-87.

20. Cf. Louis Wirth, "Education for Survival: The Jews," *American Journal of Sociology*, XLVIII (1942-43), 682-91. For a significant development in the Yankee City Jewish community which illustrates the operation of the desire for survival, see Warner and Srole, *op. cit.*, pp. 205-17.

21. Charles F. Marden, *Minorities in American Society* (New York: American Book Co., 1952), p. 427.

22. *Ibid.*, pp. 415-16. Note that our treatment of American Jewry as constituting an *ethnic* group follows that of many present-day sociologists. In addition to Marden, see R. A. Schermerhorn, *These Our People* (Boston: D. C. Heath & Co., 1949), and Warner and Srole, *op. cit.* This designation should be taken as an approximation. We do not deny the possibility that Jews can also be studied with profit by the employment of a special category necessitated by the presence of certain features unique to the group, e.g., their intermarriage taboo and consequent endogamy.

23. I am grateful to Mark Zborowski for pointing up this factor in the course of discussions conducted about another piece of re-

search. It is hoped that it will be fully documented and developed in a future publication.

24. In order that the Negroes may be included, some prefer the term "minority church" instead of "ethnic church." See Stanley H. Chapman, "New Haven Churches" (Unpublished Ph.D. dissertation, Dept. of Sociology, Yale University, 1942). Chyz and Lewis, on the other hand, use the term "nationality church." See Y. J. Chyz and Read Lewis, "Agencies Organized by Nationality Groups in the United States," *The Annals*, CCLXII (March, 1949), 149-53. For an analysis of some of the main distinguishing marks of the ethnic church, see Ch. I of *CJSA*.

25. Of course in the broadest sense all denominations, in contrast with sects, are descent groups. Furthermore, by distinguishing between "ethnic" and "non-ethnic" churches we mean only to imply that the non-ethnic churches represent the dominant group. Thus ultimately they are also "ethnic," and possess ethnic functions.

The classic statement of the relationship between *religio* and *ethnos* is Emile Durkheim's, *The Elementary Forms of the Religious Life*, trans. Joseph Ward Swain (Glencoe: The Free Press, 1947). Aside from the functionalists, interesting contemporary examples of the problem can be found in a historical treatment such as Salo W. Baron, *Modern Nationalism and Religion* (New York: Harper & Brothers, 1947). Another significant application is made by Werner Cahnman, "Religion and Nationality," *American Journal of Sociology*, XLIX (1943-44), 524-29.

26. Some Lutheran churches, it should be noted, exhibit ambiva-

lence about their ethnicity and would prefer to be identified as non-ethnic churches. See Erich C. Knorr, "The Adjustment of the Lutheran Church to Social Change in the Modern World" (Unpublished Ph.D. dissertation, Dept. of Sociology, University of Washington, 1946). On the other hand, the Jewish group may well constitute the "ideal type" in the ethnic church category. If one wishes to remain a Jew, except in certain special cases the only church to which he may belong is the Jewish one. Thus in Judaism *religion* and *ethnicity* are perfectly articulated. The following case cited by Baron illustrates the process: "The first Czechoslovak census of 1921 [revealed] that eleven residents of Prague and hundreds more throughout the country registered as belonging to the Jewish 'nationality' and the Roman Catholic 'religion'. . . . Six other Prague Jewish 'nationals' stated that they professed Protestantism or Greek Orthodoxy. The Zionists [the group which tended to de-emphasize religion by their very stress on ethnicity and who, as nationalists, might be expected to welcome everyone who was of Jewish descent] had long received with open arms Jews having no religious affiliation, but they drew the line in the case of converts to another faith." (Baron, *op. cit.*, p. 241). For a detailed analysis of Jewry as an "ideal type," see *CJSA*, pp. 27-34.

27. Robin M. Williams, Jr., *American Society* (New York: Alfred A. Knopf, Inc., 1951), p. 307. See also J. O. Hertzler, "Religious Institutions," *The Annals*, CCLVI (March, 1948), 1-13.

28. See Chyz and Lewis, *op. cit.* When an international church is

resistant to special ethnic purposes, or favors one ethnic group as over against another, schisms may result. This has been the case with the Catholic Church in the United States, and may be illustrated by the relationship between the Church and the Polish-American group. While the Catholic Church in Poland had been very sympathetic to nationalistic aspirations, the Poles found that here it was controlled by the Irish. This group favored a policy of de-Polonization and discriminated against Polish priests in the making of clerical appointments above the parish level. Hence starting in 1904 we find the growth of a secessionist movement under the name of the "Polish National Independent Catholic Church."

29. H. R. Niebuhr, *The Social Sources of Denominationalism* (New York: Henry Holt & Co., 1929), pp. 223-24. Cf. Robert M. MacIver and Charles H. Page, *Society* (New York: Rinehart & Co., 1949), p. 493.

30. They will be documented in a forthcoming publication by the author and others of a study of the attitudes of some two hundred Jewish families residing in a middle-sized Eastern city.

31. *Opinion News,* V, 13 (December 25, 1945). Cf. Havemann and West, *op. cit.*, pp. 105-07. Some would doubt whether attendance at services is a valid criterion of religiosity for the Jewish group. They would hold that the home is as important as the synagogue as a *locus* of religious observance. Even if this approach were a correct one, these figures would still be highly significant.

32. Abraham G. Duker, *Outline of Comprehensive Introductory*

Course for Adult Jewish Studies (New York: American Jewish Congress, 1951), p. 25. Some significant interpretations of trends in Jewish communal life can be found in H. B. Grinstein, "Communal and Social Aspects of American Jewish History," *Publications of the American Jewish Historical Society,* XXXIX (1949-50), 267-82.

33. M. M. Kaplan in *Jewish Communal Register,* 1917-18 (New York: Kehillah of New York City, 1918), p. 122. While Kaplan stresses the factor of Jewish ethnicity in his writings, at the same time he generally compares Jews to Catholics and Protestants (see, for example, *The Reconstructionist,* XVI, 15 [December 1, 1950], 29). In addition, note Samuel Margoshes in R.A., *Proceedings,* X (1947), 261-62. That the synagogue - centered forces in the Jewish community appeal for support on the basis of their actual or potential contribution toward bettering group rela-

tions can be gathered from the documents quoted by Rabbi Ahron Opher in *American Jewish Year Book,* XLVIII (1946-47), 133-35. As a non-Jew, MacIver's general agreement with Opher's viewpoint is particularly significant (see MacIver, *op. cit.,* passim).

34. F. S. Mead, *Handbook of Denominations in the United States* (Nashville: Abingdon-Cokesbury Press, 1951), p. 103.

35. These conclusions need to be qualified by the realization that since the end of World War II, some Jewish religious groups *have* opened field offices which assist local congregations, and that in recent years a few subsidies to congregations have been granted due to certain special circumstances. See Union of American Hebrew Congregations, *Seventy - fourth — Seventy-sixth Annual Reports* (New York: Union of American Hebrew Congregations, 1950), pp. 27, 29, 64, 256; and Young Israel, *op. cit.*

Chapter II

1. Cf. MacIver and Page, *op. cit.,* pp. 489-90. Parsons notes that ". . . religious systems have a tendency to stabilization and crystallization which is stronger than that of empirical action systems." Talcott Parsons, "The Institutionalization of Social Science and the Problems of the Conference," *Perspectives on a Troubled Decade: Science, Philosophy, and Religion* [10th Symposium of Conference on Science, Philosophy, and Religion], ed. by Lyman Bryson, Louis Finkelstein, R. M. MacIver (New York: Harper & Brothers, 1950), p. 233.

2. For the purpose of this analysis, we choose to disregard the impact of the social trends which

existed in the larger Jewish communities of Eastern Europe, as well as the changes introduced in the entire area by late 19th-century industrial development. Since we are speaking in terms of ideal types (the *Gemeinschaft* of the *shtetl* as distinguished from the *Gesellschaft* of the American metropolis), we can ignore the growth of non-Orthodox Jewish ideologies. Should we have wished to grasp the *actual* evolution of East European Jewry, such developments would form an essential part of the story.

3. This is the program of the so-called "neo-Orthodox" school. Since a consideration of this development is hardly essential for

an understanding of the *growth* of Conservatism, we shall not treat "neo-Orthodoxy" in any systematic way.

4. Some of the factors helping to preserve Orthodoxy require mention. First, the continued residence of Jews in urban areas works to the advantage of Orthodoxy. Secondly, due to the destruction in Eastern Europe, some leading Orthodox figures have come to the United States recently. The destruction of the East European community has helped prepare the ground psychologically for some small revivalistic tendencies here. The passing of the immigrant era has also lessened somewhat the identification of Orthodoxy with foreignness. In connection with this, the growth of a sentimental or intellectual Orthodoxy in certain circles should not be overlooked. Lastly, the fact that the numbers of the group have been reduced until in some neighborhoods only the "hard core" remains, means that there is increased stabilization and presumably a slowing down of the rate of defection.

5. In view of the concentration of Jewish population in New York City (about 43% of American Jewry reside in this city and its environs), no one "typical" Jewish community exists. Not only does New York have very special characteristics because of the large absolute size of its Jewish population as well as the unusually high ratio of Jews to non-Jews, but the necessary data are lacking. The vast size of the Jewish population and the absence of an over-all community organization has served to discourage publication of the basic

materials except for the earliest periods.

Source material for some of the small communities is more readily available, and in such cities field work and community study are feasible procedures even on a limited budget. But inasmuch as Conservative Judaism first developed in the larger cities, data obtained from smaller communities would be of limited value. Under the circumstances it seemed wisest to study community patterns in one of the 23 largest cities other than New York. Approximately 35% of the total Jewish population reside in such centers.

We had compiled some research materials on Chicago for a previous study and found that these constituted a foundation for further observations. Also it was discovered that the historical materials and demographic data on this community were adequate for our purposes. Chicago was particularly advantageous since it has been studied intensively by urban sociologists who have used its variegated life as their social laboratory. Our observations could be fitted into the framework developed by previous researchers. While the institutional structure of Chicago lacks the variety of New York, many well-established Conservative **congregations** are located in the community as well as a good representation of Orthodox and Reform synagogues. During a large part of the century Chicago contained the second largest Jewish community in the country. By choosing Chicago we do not claim that the particular developments which took place in this community are found in other places. However, we *do* think that the underlying *processes* which we highlight have very strong elements of typicality.

6. Since different types of synagogues are found in each area, this migration on the basis of a three-fold (or more) change of residence gives added clarity to our analysis. In smaller communities the three-step pattern is frequently reduced to only two steps. Thus the transition from Orthodoxy is not so clearly reflected in the ecological situation (see the example of Minneapolis as described by Albert I. Gordon, *Jews in Transition* [Minneapolis: University of Minnesota Press, 1949]).

7. The character of these areas is given extensive treatment in Charles S. Bernheimer (ed.), *The Russian Jew in the United States* (Philadelphia: John C. Winston Co., 1905), as well as in the volume by Louis Wirth which is cited below. Fictional treatments of life in these areas, as well as volumes of reminiscences, are legion. In his book *A Walker in the City* (New York: Harcourt Brace & Co., 1951), Alfred Kazin brilliantly succeeds in evoking much of the "atmosphere" of the Jewish immigrant neighborhood.

8. The area of first settlement in Chicago is known as the Near West Side. The second settlement, to which we shall make frequent reference, is the community area of North Lawndale, and the adjacent sections of East and West Garfield—the entire district being popularly referred to as "Lawndale." A smaller second settlement district is located in the community area of West Town. This neighborhood at one time had much the same character as that of Lawndale, but its Jewish life has

been less intensive due to the smaller proportion of Jews to non-Jews. Third settlement districts include areas to the north of Lawndale such as Humboldt Park, Logan Square, Lakeview, North Park, and Rogers Park; neighborhoods to the west such as Austin and Oak Park; and communities to the south such as Hyde Park and South Shore. Information about these districts can be found in Louis Wirth and Eleanor H. Bernert, *Local Community Fact Book* (Chicago: University of Chicago Press, 1949). To simplify our analysis we will not consider one complication: a neighborhood such as Albany Park which is essentially transitional in that it incorporates elements of Lawndale together with the characteristics of third settlement areas.

9. We place quotation marks around *ghetto* to draw attention to the fact that the employment of this word in the present context differs from the exact historical usage of the term.

10. Although we have not attempted to draw any distinctions, it is well to point out that synagogues in Eastern Europe were not all of a single type. Although a few Germanized congregations could be found in the largest cities, the really significant division was **between Hassidic and non-Hassidic** institutions (relatively few Hassidic synagogues were organized here). In addition to separation on such "ideological" grounds, occupation served as an additional distinction. All of these types, as well as a wide variety of private and semi-private synagogues, can be found in New York City. The desire for personal gain on the part of some cantors and kosher caterers has motivated

the establishment of many private synagogues here of a type unknown in the *shtetl*.

11. Louis Wirth, *The Ghetto* (Chicago: University of Chicago Press, 1928), p. 206. While the Wirth volume is quoted very frequently, it has several limitations for our purposes: the material on the "ghetto" was gathered when that area was on the decline, the data on Lawndale is not extensive and contains inaccuracies, and the third settlement areas are hardly touched upon. Although Wirth realized that different types of synagogues characterize each area, his assertion that: "In the ghetto the synagogue . . . is predominantly orthodox; in the area of second settlement it becomes 'conservative'; and on the frontier it is 'reformed' " *(ibid.,* p. 256), is mistaken except for the first category.

For other materials on the Chicago Jewish community see *The Chicago Jewish Community Blue Book* (Chicago: Sentinel Publishing Co., 1918); H. L. Meites (ed.) *A History of the Jewish Community of Chicago* (Chicago: Jewish Historical Society of Illinois, n.d.); Philip Bregstone, *Chicago and its Jews* (Chicago: Privately Published, 1933); Morris A. Gutstein, *A Priceless Heritage* (New York: Bloch Publishing Co., 1953); and Simon Rawidowicz (ed.), *The Chicago Pinkas* (Chicago: College of Jewish Studies, 1952).

12. Our description of the second settlement area synagogue is a generalized composite picture of such Lawndale congregations as Anshe Kneseth Israel (the "Russishe schul"), Anshe Sholom, Beth Hamedrosh Hagadol (the "Lukniker schul"), Kehillath Jacob, and Kneseth Israel Nusach Sfard (the "Sfardishe schul") during the 1920's and 1930's. For information on the history of each congregation, see Meites, *op. cit.,* pp. 486ff. All are large institutions by American-Jewish standards. Their buildings generally consist of a large main hall for weekly and holiday services (the "synagogue" or sanctuary), a smaller hall for daily services and religious study, and a social hall. Some also provide other facilities such as classrooms.

13. Zborowski and Herzog, *op. cit.,* p. 56.

14. Cf. Abraham J. Feldman, "The Changing Functions of the Synagogue and the Rabbi," *Reform Judaism; Essays by Alumni of the Hebrew Union College* (Cincinnati: Hebrew Union College Press, 1949), pp. 206-20. Feldman states that the modern rabbi has seven institutionalized roles: serving as a preacher, a Jewish educator, a pastor, a priest, a leader in Jewish life, a leader of general social movements, and as a representative of his people to the non-Jews. It is obvious from this listing that the Lawndale rabbi serves in only a few areas, and that even in these his role is a limited one. For the function of the rabbi in the *shtetl,* see Zborowski and Herzog, *op. cit.,* pp. 63, 218-20.

15. Cf. Zborowski and Herzog, *op. cit.,* pp. 100-102.

16. While daily and Sabbath services may be repeated, this is not done on the High Holidays. However, some Reform congregations have modified this practice upon finding their facilities overtaxed.

17. The second settlement illustrates the situation of what one sociologist calls that of "Israel" in America: the lack of any deeply

felt problem in regard to Jewish identification. This typically occurs in those areas of large cities which are rather solidly Jewish. Factors such as the constant use of non-Jews as a reference group and the exertion of community pressure on individuals who are apathetic to ethnic values is generally not found in such places; the psychological correlates of minority living seem to be strongly modified in these neighborhoods. When an inactive member of the Lawndale community, for example, moves to a town where Jews are strongly in the minority, he may soon demonstrate attitudes toward Jewishness which were hardly apparent before. Studies of such individuals would be of great value in furthering understanding of the components of Jewish identification.

18. See Ralph Linton, "Nativistic Movements," *American Anthropologist*, XLV (1943), 230-40.

19. Typically there is little antireligious agitation in the area of second settlement. Such was not the case, however, in the first settlement. The Yom Kippur day banquets which were held in first settlement areas (where the prohibition against eating was *publicly* flaunted) are now exotic historical phenomena. Also, in contrast to former years, anti-religious agitation has all but disappeared from the Yiddish press.

20. The Jewish population of Lawndale, but a handful at the turn of the century, reached almost 100,000 by 1922 (Wirth, *op. cit.*, p. 278). Between 1930 and 1947, North Lawndale lost 15% of its Jewish population. The two adjacent districts declined by 31% and 35%, respectively (Erich Ro-

senthal, "The Jewish Population of Chicago, Illinois," in Rawidowicz, *op. cit.*, p. 78).

For Jews, first settlement neighborhoods do not appear to hold the same symbolic quality as for others. There is much less localization of ethnic solidarity. It is significant, for example, to compare the history of Jewish first and second settlements with similar Italian areas (see Walter Firey, *Land Use in Central Boston* [Cambridge: Harvard University Press, 1947]).

21. For the greater part of its history the Temple has been considered by the other local Reform institutions to be one of the weakest congregations in the city. It has been forced to call upon the (Reform) Union of American Hebrew Congregations for financial assistance (see Union of American Hebrew Congregations, *op. cit.*, p. 143).

22. *U. Syn. Recorder*, VII, 4 (October, 1927), 18.

23. The executive director of the local Council of Conservative Synagogues—apparently unaware that this previous effort had been made —was troubled by the fact that a Conservative synagogue had never been opened in Lawndale. It was felt that responsibility for this situation could be traced to the Conservative movement which had "neglected" the community and that Conservative rabbis apparently did not care to lead congregations located in the area:
"The people on the West Side are in our lowest economic brackets. They want to be Jews . . . even more so than the economically better situated Jews. I think it will be the responsibility of the United Synagogue and the Seminary to provide this kind of a community

with a rabbi who will represent
the very best we have. I feel that
until now our best talent, our most
effective men, have gone to high-
class congregations." (Rabbi Jacob
Hochman in U. Syn. *National
Board Minutes,* January 18, 1947
[Typescript], p. 57.) ". . . the Conservative movement in Chicago . . .
has . . . neglected the very heart
and core of the community, the
Lawndale section—50,000 Jews."
(Rabbi Gershon Rosenstock in
R.A. *Proceedings,* XI [1947], 347.)
24. This is a very unusual procedure, for almost invariably a
charge—either in the form of an
annual membership fee which entitles the individual to a specific
number of seats, or by direct sale
of admission tickets—*is* made for
seats at the High Holiday services.
This system of pew rentals seems
to be most highly developed in
the Jewish community. Perhaps it
functions, in part at least, as a
modern equivalent of the old Jewish communal tax. Notice that
when seats are sold they commonly
vary in price according to location.
Also, many of the congregations
which rely chiefly on the annual
membership plan do not have a
flat rate, but use a progressively-
scaled schedule of dues.
25. For some information on the
adherence to avoidance patterns in
the *shtetl,* see Zborowski and Herzog, *op. cit.,* pp. 132-38.
26. Williams, *op. cit.,* p. 355.

27. It is possible to over-empha-
size the disintegrating effect of
American norms. Few students of
ethnic problems consider the opposite result: the situation in
which American norms work toward *reinforcing* a traditional religious system. For example, secularization took place among some
Jewish workers and members of
the intelligentsia while they were
still in Eastern Europe. As previously noted, this movement took
a strongly anti-religious direction
and flourished here for a time. To
the extent that these attitudes were
a reflection of class position, we
would expect them to diminish as
the group became more middle-
class. However, the rapid decline
in militant anti-religion among
Jews is more than merely a reflection of a shift in social class.
Among other factors, it also represents the impact of Americanization. The cultural system of our
society may encourage the separation of religious organizations
from other institutional structures
and there is much secularization,
but militant atheism is in extreme
disfavor. For a significant case in
point, note the situation among
the Czechs where Americanization
has worked toward reducing their
once widespread atheism (see the
comment in Murray Leiffer, *City
and Church in Transition* [Chi-
cago: Willett Clark & Co., 1938],
p. 203).

Chapter III

1. See U. Syn., Women's League,
and Young People's League, *Directory* (New York: U. Syn., 1926).
See also Wirth, *op. cit.,* pp. 255,
278. Third settlement community
areas during this period are as

follows: Uptown, Lakeview, Humboldt Park, Albany Park, Rogers
Park, Grand Boulevard, Englewood, Hyde Park, Logan Square,
and Washington Park.
2. Thus a Conservative congre-

gation was started in Rogers Park in 1918-19, and one in Logan Square originated at the same time (see Meites, *op. cit.*, pp. 508, 539). This is apparently rather typical of the situation found in many other cities. One questionnaire distributed among Conservative rabbis in the early 1940's included a query regarding the age of their congregations, and the following is the conclusion which was drawn from the data: ". . . the majority of our congregations have been established for about a quarter of a century. . . ." (R.A., *Proceedings*, VIII [1944], 156.) Thus the typical synagogue was founded around 1917. Cf. Gordon, *op. cit.*, pp. 152-53, 162.

These congregations are of two types. In one category are those synagogues originally organized in third settlement areas, and which recognized from the start that they were not fully Orthodox. They either called themselves "Conservative," or since this term was not too widely used at the time they employed other designations such as "traditional" or "modern Orthodox." The other type of congregation was founded earlier and originated in the first or second settlement area. It started as an Orthodox synagogue and was relocated finally in a third settlement area. It is difficult to date with exactness the Conservatism of these congregations, but by the time they reached the third settlement area they were generally fully Conservative. These congregations are much fewer in number than those in the first category.

3. According to Rosenthal, Jews constituted 67% of the total population of North Lawndale in 1931. In third settlement areas the ratios are very different during the same period: 8% for Uptown, 6% for Lakeview, 12% for Humboldt Park, and 19% for Hyde Park (Rosenthal, in Rawidowicz, *op. cit.*, p. 76). It should be noted that these percentages are typical for only about the first twenty years in the development of the third settlement area. After this, frequently the ratio of Jews to non-Jews begins to approach more closely the figure for Lawndale. Thus there was a 339% increase in the Jewish population of Lakeview between 1930 and 1946, and a 149% increase in Hyde Park (*ibid.*, p. 78). (Part of this increase represents the arrival of German-Jewish refugees rather than East Europeans.) This increase is not of great significance in the present context, for the institutional structure of the area is established chiefly during the early years. Although Orthodoxy profits somewhat from this constant in-migration, the characteristic responses found in the third settlement area remain much the same. That a low ratio of Jews to non-Jews favors Conservatism is borne out by the case of Albany Park. By 1931 this area was 42% Jewish (*ibid.*, p. 76). While Conservative synagogues exist in the area, they have not been particularly strong institutions in comparison to similar congregations in other neighborhoods.

4. For the purpose of discussion we assume that other ethnic groups follow the first- second- third-settlement scheme.

5. Apparently the East European Jew was highly aware of the character of these districts; he considered them well-differentiated from first and second settlement areas and sought behavior patterns

which would be in conformity with newly achieved position. One of the South Side Conservative institutions describes its synagogue as follows: "In the *well-to-do* Hyde Park section of Chicago, where *wealth* and *dignity* combine Rodfei Zedek Synagogue . . . stands majestically as an institution dedicated to modern Orthodoxy." (*U. Syn. Recorder*, VII, 1 [January, 1927], 23.) (Emphasis supplied.) A congregation on the North Side states that: "The dream of a beautiful synagogue . . . to be erected on Pratt Boulevard in the *fashionable* district of Rogers Park is nearing realization" (*ibid.*). (Emphasis supplied.)

6. As the "classical" Jewish language, Hebrew can be preserved while Yiddish is relinquished. Since Hebrew has been traditionally employed for sacred purposes only, it is not—like Yiddish—in competition with English. It hardly creates any problems of adjustment, for it is not spoken on the street nor is it commonly read in public places. (Cf. Warner and Srole, *op. cit.*, pp. 231-33.)

7. The few empirical studies on this subject bear out these observations but they generally require respondents to answer on an "either-or" basis rather than giving them opportunity of checking one of the many possible permutations. They also fail to run cross-correlations with their data. Cf. Jacob S. Golub and Noah Nardi, "A Study in Jewish Observance," *The Reconstructionist*, XI, 9 (June 15, 1945), 10-16; Gordon, *op. cit.*, pp. 84-85, 97; and the literature cited by I. Steinbaum, "A Study of the Jewishness of Twenty New York Families," *YIVO Annual of*

Jewish Social Science, V (1950), 232-55.

8. In addition to those groups with ostensibly Jewish purposes, there are also organizations with non-sectarian aims whose membership is largely Jewish. Also, some groups whose total national membership is mixed have local lodges or affiliates which are self-segregated.

9. Note the figures on participation in voluntary associations given by Golub and Nardi, *op. cit.*

10. It should be stressed that our analysis here refers chiefly to the era from the start of World War I to the close of World War II, the period during which Conservatism was firmly established. With the rapid post-war decline of Jewish second settlement areas in Chicago, Detroit, and other cities where Negroes live in large numbers, the pattern becomes more complicated. The desire to move is not provided by the "pull" of the third settlement, but rather by the "push" from the second settlement. Characteristically, Jews do not employ violence to defend their second settlements against Negro invasion as is the case with other groups, and this situation suggests some interesting research problems.

11. Bregstone, *op. cit.*, p. 143.

12. In addition to the resistance toward welcoming the East Europeans into the already existing Reform congregations, apparently the movement as a whole was not too eager for the formation of new congregations. Note the remarks of Dr. Maurice N. Eisendrath, President of the Union, about what he terms "snobocracy" in Reform (see Union of American Hebrew Congregations, *op. cit.*, pp. 297, 320).

In spite of this, a study made between 1928-30 of forty-three temples in the eleven cities whose Jewish population was over 50,000 at the time, revealed that: "About equal proportions of temple members are of German parentage and of East European parentage. However, considering the foreign-born responders by themselves, the proportion of those born in Germany proves to be considerably less than of those born in East European countries (33% of foreign-born responders were born in Germany; 57% were born in East European countries). This is indicative of a marked increase in the enrollment of Jews of East European origin in the ranks of Reform within the space of one generation." (Union of American Hebrew Congregations, *Reform Judaism in the Larger Cities—A Survey* [Cincinnati, Union of American Hebrew Congregations, 1930], p. 10.)

Chapter IV

1. A comment by Joseph Weinstein in U. Syn., *Proceedings of the 1950 Biennial Convention* (New York: U. Syn., n.d.), p. 86. Weinstein adds: "Here is where special problems presented themselves and the Ritual Committee came into being." (*Ibid.*) We will cover the major innovations introduced by these Committees; they have also instituted a great number of minor changes designed to bring the service into adjustment with the new aesthetic norms.

2. According to the rationale developed for the sacred system, division of labor in the religious area was calculated to strengthen the system itself. The woman, by virtue of her household responsibilities, presumably lacked the required leisure for prayer and study —her participation in such activities would have been a threat to family life. Thus the assumption by the males of these duties *promotes* religious values. Such a point of view, while typical of the East and expressing its mores, entails severe dysfunctional consequences in the West.

3. Robert S. and Helen M. Lynd, *Middletown* (New York: Harcourt Brace & Co., 1929), p. 355. Note that this relationship holds true even for college-trained individuals: see Havemann and West, *op. cit.*, p. 105. Since synagogue membership is recorded by families rather than by individuals, no valid comparison with Christian denominations based on the sex ratio of the membership can be made.

4. Murray Leiffer, *The Effective City Church* (New York: Abingdon-Cokesbury Press, 1949), p. 186. Cf. Gerhard E. Lenski, "Social Correlates of Religious Interest," *American Sociological Review*, XVIII (1953), 533-44.

5. Joseph H. Fichter, *Southern Parish*, Vol. I, *Dynamics of a City Church* (Chicago: University of Chicago Press, 1951), p. 254. The only spiritual activity in which men were represented in equal or better proportion was in attendance at retreats, an enterprise in which women find it difficult to participate because of their family responsibilities.

6. This is obviously related, among other things, to the fact that since these women confine themselves largely to domestic du-

ties, they hardly have the opportunity for culture contact open to males by virtue of the masculine occupational role. Another factor is that the proper observance of the sacred system presupposes a certain degree of leisure, or at least the possibility of self-regulation of working hours. It would be safe to assume that, in contrast to Eastern Europe, here it is the females rather than the males who have the most leisure, and also the greatest opportunity for self-scheduling.

7. For a report on one of the few Conservative congregations which have not permitted mixed seating, see the *National Jewish Post*, VII, 3 (April 18, 1952), 1. In recent years mixed seating has become an issue in some Orthodox, or so-called "traditional," congregations. It is significant to note that the separation of the sexes in the Greek Orthodox church has continued: see Warner and Srole, *op. cit.*, p. 110.

8. Data about this, and some subsequent points in this chapter, are taken from U. Syn., *National Survey* (New York: U. Syn., 1950). (Hereafter this reference will be footnoted simply as *Survey*.) This study, done under the technical direction of the Bureau of Applied Social Research of Columbia University, consists of four sections. The first part, which is the longest, is entitled "Charting Synagogue Attendance"; the second, "Taking Stock of Children's Jewish Education"; the third, "Target: Adult Jewish Education"; and the fourth, "Spotlight on Youth Work." Two different questionnaires were employed for the *Survey*. The first, of a fact-finding character, was distributed to congregations. Forms

were mailed to the 387 synagogues then in good standing; 200 institutions, or 52% of the total group, returned the questionnaires. (While there are some non-affiliated Conservative congregations, they are comparatively few in number.) According to the instructions, they were to be filled out by one of the ranking officials of the institution. The second form, in the nature of a public opinion poll, was directed to the laity. Of the 5,800 questionnaires mailed, 1,145, or about 20%, were returned in sufficient time for tabulation.

A second study along the same general lines was done several years later: U. Syn., *National Survey on Synagogue Leadership* (New York: U. Syn., 1953). For this study questionnaires were sent to 9,100 officers and board members in 443 congregations; 1,787 individuals, or about 20% of the group, replied.

8a. *Survey*, I, p. 9.

9. Thus services like the one held on Saturday morning where the attendance ratio is still highly in favor of the males (see *ibid.*, p. 36), or in which females do not participate (as in the daily service), represent the weakest links in the worship program. Of course many other factors, in addition to the present one, are involved in the decline of these services.

10. Julian Freeman, "Address," delivered before Conference of National Association of Jewish Men's Clubs, New York City, April, 1949. Note the experiment in advancing the position of woman which took place in one congregation: See *U. Syn. Review*, V, 5 (January, 1950), 4. Cf. Women's League of the U. Syn., *Proceedings—1950* (New York: Women's League of the U. Syn., n.d.), p. 135.

11. *U. Syn. Recorder,* IV, 1 (January, 1924), 14.

12. It is also necessary that the worshiper does not attempt to address the Deity in the traditional style, for this would constitute a breach in decorum. The Conservative Jew prays while the Orthodox worshiper "davens" (*daven* in Yiddish means "pray," but it connotes worship of a particular character). The difference in mood conveyed by the two terms illustrates the transition from the individualistic, informally conducted, worshiper-centered Orthodox service, to the disciplined, mannered, and pulpit-centered rites of the Conservative synagogue.

13. *U. Syn. Recorder,* V, 3 (July, 1925), 20.

14. U. Syn., *High Holiday Planning for Your Congregation* (New York: U. Syn., n.d.), p. 20. This publication presents much material on the decorum problem in Conservatism. It is in effect a catalogue of the methods which have been used in the modification of Orthodox worship patterns. It includes an interesting "test" entitled: "How Good Are You on Your Synagogue Etiquette?"

15. Cf. Zborowski and Herzog, *op. cit.,* pp. 54-56, 206-7.

16. U. Syn., *Sabbath Observance Kit—Number 2* (New York: U. Syn., 1951-52). The quotation is from pamphlet 4 in the *Kit,* entitled, "Yours Is the Honor: A Guidance Manual for Torah Honors," p. 6.

17. Also, there is less psychological motivation for the procedure inasmuch as the honorific worth of participation in the Torah honors has been devalued. Some of the services at which they are distributed, such as on the Sabbath

and festivals, are now attended by only a relatively small group of worshippers.

18. U. Syn., *High Holiday Planning for Your Congregation, op. cit.,* p. 39.

19. *Ibid.,* p. 37.

20. A comment by Joseph Eister in U. Syn., *Proceedings of the 1948 Biennial Convention* (Typescript), pp. 194-97.

21. U. Syn., *National Survey on Synagogue Leadership, op. cit.,* p. 51.

22. U. Syn., *High Holiday Planning for Your Congregation, op. cit.,* p. 36.

23. A comment by Joseph Goldberg, Executive Director of the Brooklyn Jewish Center, in U. Syn., *Proceedings of the 1948 Biennial Convention, op. cit.,* p. 160. (Emphasis supplied.)

23a. Cf. Zborowski and Herzog, *op. cit.,* p. 198.

24. Golub and Nardi, *op. cit.,* p. 11. This congregation does not stress the type of membership plan which automatically entitles one to High Holiday seats.

25. *Survey,* I, pp. 45-52, gives some information about promotional techniques. Much of the literature issued by the United Synagogue deals with such matters. Promotional techniques are used most frequently in connection with the Friday evening services rather than with the traditional services.

26. *Ibid.,* p. 3, and U. Syn., *Proceedings of the 1950 Biennial Convention, op. cit.,* p. 87. For techniques sometimes employed to gather the quorum required for public worship, see *Survey,* I, pp. 3-5. That a number of congregations have cancelled their daily services during the last decade

seems clear from the figures printed in R.A., *Proceedings*, VIII (1944), 151. The Sunday morning breakfast and *Tefillin* clubs conducted by a number of synagogues are interesting examples of attempts to reinforce the daily services. See *Survey*, I, pp. 4-5.

27. *Survey*, I, p. 35. There are a few congregations in the East (the section of the country where tradition is strongest) which make the Saturday morning service the main weekly service. A few do not even conduct a late Friday night service. Congregations of this type help account for the 7% whose Saturday worshipers number 300 or more. But note Arzt's statement: "With the virtual disappearance of the pious grandfather of yesteryear, the Sabbath morning service is on the verge of being abolished. Only the artificial stimulus of a socially popular *Bar Mitzvah* ceremony enables it to show sporadic signs of life." (Max Arzt, *Increasing Effectiveness of Our Synagogues* [New York: U. Syn., n.d.], p. 3.) Some congregations are already incorporating aspects of the *Bar Mitzvah* ceremony into the Friday night service, although the main ritual is still generally scheduled for Saturday morning. The boy may be assigned some part in the Friday night service, and his participation helps to increase attendance. At the same time the significance of the occasions for the candidate is multiplied since he appears at one of the more popular and well-attended services.

28. *Survey*, I, pp. 40-41.

29. *Ibid.*, p. 53. While *Yizkor* is also recited on Yom Kippur, it is not needed as a High Holiday attendance-builder. The same principle applies to the Friday night service: while the *Kaddish* prayer is read, it also does not represent a vitally needed reinforcement.

30. U. Syn., *Proceedings of the 1950 Biennial Convention, op. cit.*, p. 58. Other services, such as *Selihoth*—prayers said before the High Holidays and serving as a prelude to them—are on the decline in Conservative congregations: "Throwing in the sponge and writing off Selihoth Services from the congregational calendar altogether and just letting them go on for the 'few old-timers' as a perfunctory gesture of keeping up a venerable custom, does not reflect any credit to imaginative High Holiday planning." (U. Syn., *High Holiday Planning for Your Congregation, op. cit.*, p. 13.) A plan has been proposed to revive the interest of young people in *Selihoth* by holding a social prior to the start of worship. (*Ibid.*, pp. 13-14.)

31. U. Syn., *Shavuoth Planning for Your Congregation* (New York: U. Syn., n.d.), p. 1.

32. See *Survey*, I, p. 10. According to the slogan which many congregations seek to popularize: "Friday night is synagogue night." Ninety-five percent of all Conservative congregations schedule a Friday evening service. (*Ibid.*, p. 8.) Note that many Orthodox synagogues now conduct Friday evening services. In some cases this is currently their main weekly service. It should be noted that by the time Conservative congregations were founded, a considerable number of Reform temples had already switched their main Sabbath service to Friday night. This shift in Reform from Sunday morning to Friday evening constitutes a significant trend in Jewish reli-

gious life which cannot, however, be detailed here.

33. The most thought-provoking volume published in recent years which deals with such trends is David Riesman, *The Lonely Crowd* (New Haven: Yale University Press, 1950). We speak here of the general tenor of the Conservative service; it is true that laymen are still encouraged to perform the various duties involved in the holding of public worship.

33a. *Survey,* I, p. 23.

34. *Ibid.,* p. 26.

35. Anonymous comment quoted in *ibid.,* p. 33.

36. *Ibid.,* p. 30.

37. *Ibid.* In only 6% of the congregations is an organ used for the Saturday morning services.

38. *Sabbath and Festival Prayer Book* (New York: R.A., and U. Syn., 1946).

39. *Survey,* I, p. 12.

40. See *ibid.,* pp. 46-47. This is sometimes referred to by the Hebrew expression *Oneg Shabbat.*

41. *Ibid.,* p. 8.

42. See *ibid.,* p. 47. There is also the practice of arranging "special Sabbaths" for the congregational auxiliaries.

43. *Ibid.,* pp. 50-51.

44. See *ibid.,* pp. 35-44 and R.A., *Proceedings,* VIII (1944), 153-55. See also Elias Charry, "Baruch Adonoi Yom Yom," *Conservative Judaism,* VIII, 1 (November, 1951), 14-19. Rabbi Charry points out that ". . . the daily service is the last stronghold of the 'orthodox' in the Conservative congregations. . . . the 'old-timers' have here retained control." (*Ibid.,* 16.)

45. Anonymous comment quoted in *Survey,* I, p. 42. At times the division between the Orthodox periphery and the Conservative core

group is explicitly recognized. During the High Holidays in some congregations the "old-timers" do not participate in the service held in the main sanctuary, but rather are allowed to hold their own Orthodox service in another part of the building.

46. Charry, *op. cit.,* 15.

47. *U. Syn. Recorder,* VIII, 1 (February, 1928), 25. (Emphasis supplied.)

48. This point was made by Ismar Elbogen. It is cited by Robert Gordis in his significant article "A Jewish Prayer Book for the Modern Age," *Conservative Judaism,* II, 1 (October, 1945), 1-20. Rabbi Gordis concludes that ". . . practical considerations rather than philosophical ideals were at the roots of the objections to the traditional liturgy." (*Ibid.,* 5.)

49. Cf. Eugene Kohn, " 'Conservative Judaism'—A Review," *Conservative Judaism,* II, 4 (June, 1946), 12.

50. Gordon, *op. cit.,* p. 166. While most Orthodox worshipers pray in their street-hats, many Conservative congregations insist that the male worshiper check or store his street-hat and wear the more inconspicuous and "tasteful" skull cap. This is just one of the many minor readjustments to the new aesthetic norms which is part of the Conservative pattern. While each one is minor, in sum they make the "atmosphere" of the Conservative service very different from that of Orthodoxy.

51. *S.A.J. Review,* VI, 2 (September 17, 1926), 3.

52. *Ibid.* See also *S.A.J. Review,* VII, 2 (September 23, 1927), 14.

53. *High Holiday Prayer Book,* Vol. II, *Prayers for Yom Kippur*

(New York: Jewish Reconstructionist Foundation, 1948), p. 2.

54. *Sabbath Prayer Book* (New
York: Jewish Reconstructionist
Foundation, 1945).

55. Letter from Hannah L. Goldberg, Executive Secretary, Jewish
Reconstructionist Foundation, February 6, 1952. It is possible that
all of these synagogues are not
Conservative. In contrast to the Reconstructionist volumes, the more
traditional *Sabbath and Festival
Prayer Book* has been widely
adopted. See *Survey*, I, p. 15.

56. The "Adler Machzor" was
originally prepared for the congregations of Great Britain by H. M.
Adler and Arthur Davis. It was re-
published here under the title,
Service of the Synagogue (2 vols.,
New York: Hebrew Publishing Co.,
n.d.). It features an English translation of the liturgy. The two most
important volumes edited by Silverman are: *High Holiday Prayer
Book* (Hartford, Conn.: Privately
published, 1939), and *Sabbath and
Festival Services* (rev. ed., Hartford, Conn.: Fox Press, 1937). On
the variety of prayer books used in
Conservative congregations, see *Survey*, I, p. 14.

57. Samuel Cohen, "Jewry in the
West," *Jewish Theological Seminary of America Students Annual*,
Vol. I (New York: J.T.S., 1914),
pp. 76-77. (Emphasis supplied.)

58. It is important to note an
exception. The Jewish intellectuals
who, like their counterparts in
Protestantism and Catholicism,
have recently been attracted to religion, are a new type. They are
relatively uncritical of traditional
forms and content and are almost
exclusively concerned with finding
their way "back" to religion. Ex-
piation for previous adherence to

beliefs such as pragmatism and
materialism is a prominent motif.
Will Herberg is the outstanding
representative of this trend in
Judaism. See his *Judaism and
Modern Man* (Philadelphia: Jewish
Publication Society of America,
1951). Although it is too early to
assess the impact of the trend, it is
perhaps safe to say that it will
have more effect in the area of
Jewish religious philosophy than
on the Conservative movement as
such.

59. A comment by Rabbi Simon
Greenberg in U. Syn., *Proceedings
of the 1948 Biennial Convention,
op. cit.*, p. 135.

60. Excerpted from a wall poster
in the U. Syn., *Sabbath Observance
Kit—Number 1.* (New York: U.
Syn., 1951-52).

61. Williams, *op. cit.*, p. 337.

62. *Survey*, I, p. 18. On the basis
of personal observation, we feel
that even this figure represents an
over-estimation.

63. In addition to the publica-
tions of the Reconstructionist
Foundation, Kaplan was responsi-
ble for *Supplementary Prayers
and Readings for the High Holi-
days* (New York: U. Syn., 1934).
See also Solomon Goldman and
Harry Coopersmith, *Songs and
Readings* (Chicago: The Anshe
Emet Synagogue, 1938).

64. Although many readings are
by modern authors, some are from
the classical literature such as the
Psalms and the medieval ethical
writings.

65. Gordis, "A Jewish Prayer
Book for the Modern Age," *op. cit.*,
p. 17. Note the proposal made by
the Prayer Book Commission: ". . .
[that] great latitude be permitted
the Commission in the preparation
of the English texts of the prayer

book and that it not be confined to a literal translation or even paraphrase of the original Hebrew." R.A., *Proceedings,* VIII (1944), 158.

66. Several thinkers, Kaplan in particular, have pointed out that reinterpretation has a long history in Judaism. They note, however, that until modern times it was *unconscious:* interpretations of the traditional texts were made on the assumption that the new meanings had always been implicit. The view, therefore, was that nothing really new was being added and that the revised concept was inspired by "the living God." The modern, with characteristic sophistication and employing the insights of scientific scholarship rather than the kind of classical learning typical of the scholastics of all religions, can no longer proceed in this naive fashion. In sum, contemporary ("conscious") reinterpretation is fundamentally different from the ancient and medieval ("unconscious") reinterpretation.

Kaplan's method of reinterpretation is explained in his: *The Meaning of God in Modern Jewish Religion* (New York: Behrman's Jewish Book House, 1937). See also his *Judaism as a Civilization, op. cit.,* pp. 386ff.; his article, "Revaluation of Jewish Values," *S.A.J. Review,* VIII, 3 (September 28, 1928), 4-11; and comments in R.A., *Proceedings,* VIII (1944), 266-67. Cf. Maurice H. Farbridge, *Judaism and the Modern Mind* (New York: The Macmillan Co., 1927); and Horace M. Kallen, *Judaism at Bay* (New York: Bloch Publishing Co., 1932), pp. 215-16.

67. Gordis, "A Jewish Prayer Book for the Modern Age," *op. cit.,* p. 13.

68. *Ibid.,* p. 14.

69. *Sabbath and Festival Prayer Book, op. cit.,* p. ix.

70. *Sabbath Prayer Book, op. cit.,* p. xxiii. To avoid what he considers to be intellectual dishonesty, Kaplan even provides two translations in some cases for some prayers: ". . . the literal version [and] what we call [the] 'interpretive version'." (*Ibid.,* p. xvii.)

71. *Festival Prayer Book* (New York: U. Syn., 1927). Since some argued that the petition for the restoration of the sacrificial system should be revised, two different editions were permitted: the official one retained the standard version of the prayer, and individual rabbis were allowed to publish an unofficial edition incorporating a revised wording. See *U. Syn. Recorder,* III, 2 (April, 1923), 3; and Gordis, "A Jewish Prayer Book for the Modern Age," *op. cit.,* p. 8.

72. *Sabbath and Festival Prayer Book, op. cit.,* p. i.

73. Gordis, "A Jewish Prayer Book for the Modern Age," *op. cit.,* pp. 9-11.

74. *Sabbath and Festival Prayer Book, op. cit.,* p. ix.

75. Gordis, "A Jewish Prayer Book for the Modern Age," *op. cit.,* p. 17. In this article Gordis provides a detailed summary of the changes. The notes to the *Sabbath and Festival Prayer Book,* found on pp. 377-85, give interesting sidelights on the revision problem. A remark made by Rabbi David Aronson is particularly illuminating: "We wouldn't consider it a spiritual advancement to restore animal sacrifices; yet when we prepared a new prayer book, it required years . . . to muster the courage to change the reference to animal sacrifices from a future

wish to a past experience. It's not easy." (Woman's League of the U. Syn., *Proceedings—1950, op. cit.,* p. 29).

76. Rabbi Max Arzt in R.A. *Proceedings,* XIV (1951), 57-58.

77. W. J. Goode, *Religion Among the Primitives* (Glencoe: The Free Press, 1951), p. 49. Even the liberals admit that ". . . great numbers of our people are attached to the traditional prayer book by sentiments of deep and sincere piety and deplore any deviation from its time-honored text." (*Sabbath Prayer Book, op. cit.,* p. xvii.) See also Eugene Kohn,

"Prayer and the Modern Jew," *The Jewish Reconstructionist Papers,* ed. by Mordecai M. Kaplan (New York: Behrman's Jewish Book House, 1936), pp. 101-11. Kohn states that: ". . . most people have a sentimental attachment to the traditional text based on habit and pleasant association." (*Ibid.,* p. 108.) As a Reconstructionist he stresses that ". . . our prayers [should] be a true expression of our faith." (*Ibid.,* p. 105.)

78. U. Syn., *Proceedings of the 1948 Biennial Convention, op. cit.,* p. 141.

Chapter V

1. MacIver and Page, *Society, op. cit.,* p. 491.

2. See Paul J. Tillich, "The Social Functions of the Churches in Europe and America," *Social Research,* III (1936), 90-104.

3. Note, for example, the description of the Lutheran youth group in A. B. Hollingshead, *Elmtown's Youth* (New York: John Wiley & Sons, 1949), pp. 261-64; and the comments about the Irish Catholic Church in Yankee City found in Warner and Srole, *op. cit.,* esp. pp. 173-74.

4. The compromise with secularism and the attempt on the part of the church to maintain itself by sponsoring leisure-time activities was noted by the Lynds when they compared the Middletown churches of the 1920's with the religious institutions characteristic of the same city some three decades earlier: see Lynd and Lynd, *op. cit.,* pp. 398-401.

5. See J. B. Maller and Joseph Zubin, "The Temple Center," *Jewish Center,* XI, 3 (September,

1933), 9-15. Cf. Philip D. Bookstaber, "The Place and the Function of the Temple Center in Congregational Life," Central Conference of American Rabbis, *Yearbook,* XXXV (1925), 280-85; and S. D. Schwartz, "The Place and Function of the Temple Center," *ibid.,* 286-94. See also Horace M. Kallen, *Judaism at Bay, op. cit.,* pp. 221ff. It should be noted that a few of the Reform "temple houses" functioned in part as social settlements.

6. Philip D. Bookstaber, *Judaism and the American Mind* (New York: Bloch Publishing Co., 1939), p. 57.

7. A. H. Silver, "Synagogue versus Synagogue Center," *American Hebrew,* CXXV (1929), 204. Cf. Abraham J. Feldman in *Reform Judaism: Essays by Alumni of the Hebrew Union College, op. cit.,* pp. 211-12.

8. Note the statement made in the 1920's by Rabbi Kadushin: "Today, our conception of God is vague, and what is worse for our

group consciousness, highly individualized. The culture, lacking its core, is powerless. . . . the chaos of the various parties in Jewry is the result of groping attempts to find a new point of reference for the group culture." (Max Kadushin, "The Place of the Jewish Center in American Jewish Life," *The Sentinel*, LXIII, 13 [September 24, 1926], 8.)

9. Mordecai M. Kaplan, "The Way I Have Come," *Mordecai M. Kaplan: An Evaluation*, ed. by Ira Eisenstein and Eugene Kohn (New York: Jewish Reconstructionist Foundation, 1952), p. 311. Kaplan's leadership was helpful to some of the rabbis who required an intellectual orientation which would assist them in accepting changes in synagogue structure. Kaplan was not too widely known among the laity in the early period, and it must be emphasized that reforms were instituted independently of his influence. Some think of Kaplan and his group as leading a movement, but in reality their role was confined chiefly to reflecting some of the contemporary developments. Cf. Davis, *The Jews*, ed. by Louis Finkelstein, *op. cit.*, I, p. 429, and Harry L. Glucksman, "The Synagogue Center," R.A., *Proceedings*, IV (1933), 267-79.

10. *U. Syn. Recorder*, VI, 4 (October, 1936), 19. Cf. Solomon Goldman, *A Rabbi Takes Stock* (New York: Harper & Brothers, 1931), p. 20.

11. Gordon comments that: "The synagogue in Minneapolis has become the center of Jewish life and activity. It is definitely the house of assembly of the Jewish people. . . . It is, however, less a house of worship than it was around the turn of the century." Gordon, *op.*

cit., p. 169. For comparative purposes, note the situation in the Anglican Church of Quebec. Here the English Canadians, though having substantial economic power, are inferior numerically and have developed a minority psychology. Their church has consequently started to incorporate recreational activities in its program: see Everett C. Hughes, *French Canada in Transition* (Chicago: University of Chicago Press, 1943), pp. 115-16.

12. Because the synagogue stresses ethnicity and schedules a variety of activities, members are quite variable in their attitude toward Judaism. Gordon, writing out of years of experience in the Conservative rabbinate, comments that: "At present one finds Jewish religionists, culturists, and nationalists, and some antinationalists, within the synagogue fold. Though there are many varieties of Jewish opinion and belief, somehow the synagogue in Minneapolis manages to . . . hold them all." (Gordon, *op. cit.*, p. 172.)

13. For an example of synagogue-center activities during the early period in a community outside of New York City, see the description of the Cleveland Jewish Center found in the *U. Syn. Recorder*, V, 3 (July, 1925), 20-21. Another description of the institution in the same publication demonstrates how ethnic as well as religious loyalties are cultivated. It is reported that each Saturday night three separate and distinct groups use the facilities of this Center. They are as follows: A group of aged men who studied the Talmud; a group of Phi Beta Kappa members who ". . . rationalize over Bergson and Dewey . . ."; and the young people who play basketball

in the gymnasium. According to the report: "It is this reconciliation of the generations that is the great achievement of the Cleveland Jewish Center." Furthermore: "Three generations of Jews meet under the same roof and each is drawn closer to the other by the common bond of Jewishness." (*U. Syn. Recorder*, IV, 2 [April, 1924], 18.)

14. Cf. William W. Sweet, *The American Churches* (Nashville: Abingdon-Cokesbury Press, 1948), pp. 106-7. For a description of the typical Protestant congregational pattern, see Charles Lee Wilson, "A Social Picture of a Congregation," *American Sociological Review*, X (1945), 418-22.

15. See Mordecai M. Kaplan, "The Jewish Center," *American Hebrew*, II (1917-18), 529-31; Janowsky, *The JWB Survey, op. cit.*, esp. pp. 244-45, 266; and U. Syn., *Proceedings of the 1950 Biennial Convention, op. cit.*, pp. 105ff.

Numerous articles in the publication *Synagogue Center* illustrate some of the compromises made between the competing demands of the congregational and the communal approach. It is worthy of note that even Kaplan, the *leader* of the communal school, never was able to implement his ideas successfully. After a comparatively brief career at the Jewish Center in New York City, he resigned this post over a policy dispute. The institution (presumably the prototype of the synagogue center) then changed its character. At the Society for the Advancement of Judaism, Kaplan was able to experiment with some of his proposals for innovations in the ritual, but this institution also resisted a communal approach. To all intents

and purposes, it has become just another synagogue hardly distinguished from others except by some of its ritualistic innovations. Note Kaplan's pleas for a communal approach in *S.A.J. Review*, VI, 23 (February 11, 1927), 3-5.

Parenthetically, the threefold typology of Conservative synagogues based on the extent of their recreational activities, as suggested by Louis Katzoff (*Issues in Jewish Education* [New York: Bloch Publishing Co., 1949], p. 146), relies somewhat on artificial distinctions which can hardly be observed in the field.

16. See Glucksman, *op. cit.*, p. 271; and Janowsky, *The JWB Survey, op. cit.*, pp. 317ff.

17. See R.A., *Proceedings*, IX (1949), 39, 90ff. The base membership fee in most Conservative congregations is now about $100 per family per year. It is frequently graduated in the larger congregations to somewhere between $500 and $1,000. (Cf. U. Syn., *Proceedings of the 1950 Biennial Convention, op. cit.*, p. 63.) Active participation requires many expenditures in addition to the membership fee; see Engelman, "Medurbia," *op. cit.*, pp. 514-15.

There is an interesting example in Chicago of center-synagogue cooperation: see *J.W.B. Circle*, VII, 5 (May, 1952), 11-12, 14.

18. On the early attempts in the 1920's to win back Jewish youth, see Israel Goldstein, "The Synagogue and the Youth," *Jewish Center*, VI, 1 (March, 1928), 2-9; and Herbert S. Goldstein, "From the Synagogue Back to the Synagogue," *Jewish Center*, II, 3 (June, 1924), 29-32. For criticisms of the young adult groups, see R.A., *Proceedings*, XI (1947), 216ff; and U. Syn. *National Board Minutes*, Jan-

uary 19, 1947, pp. 146ff. The general problem of youth work in the Conservative synagogue is suggested in Part IV of the *Survey*. On pp. 8-9 and 11, data is given on the number of children of non-members participating in synagogue youth groups. See also U. Syn., *Proceedings of the 1950 Biennial Convention, op. cit.*, p. 103.

19. U. Syn., *Three Pillars of Synagogue Administration*, (New York: U. Syn., n.d.), p. 5.

20. *Ibid.*, p. 2. See also Aaron Weiss, *Over-All Problems of Congregational Management* (New York: U. Syn., n.d.), p. 6; Douglass and Brunner, *op. cit.*, pp. 90-97; and the description of the B'nai Jeshurun Center of New York City, *U. Syn. Recorder*, II, 2 (April, 1922), 15. Notice the charge of secularization contained in *U. Syn. Recorder*, VIII, 2 (April, 1928), 5.

21. Simon Greenberg, "Looking Behind the Pilot-Plant Stage," *U. Syn. Review*, V, 1 (October, 1951), 3.

22. U. Syn., *Three Pillars of Synagogue Administration, op. cit.*, pp. 3-4.

23. Comment by Joseph Abrahams in U. Syn., *Proceedings of the 1948 Biennial Convention, op. cit.*, pp. 178-79. See also the Comment by the Honorable H. P. Kopplemann, *ibid.*, p. 208.

24. *American Jewish Year Book*, LII (1951), 102.

25. American Association for Jewish Education, *Jewish Education Register and Directory* (New York: American Association for Jewish Education, 1951), p. 35.

26. U. Syn., *Report of the Second Annual Meeting* (New York: U. Syn., 1914), p. 34. This quotation may be misleading unless we recognize that different educational goals can exist in the same family

depending on the sex of the child. The son may be sent to Hebrew school while the parents may be satisfied with a Sunday school education for their daughter.

27. On the contrast and transition from the Talmud Torah to the congregational school, see Judah Pilch, "Is the Talmud Torah Doomed?" *Jewish Education*, XVIII, 1 (November, 1946), 21-28. For the hours of instruction see *Survey*, II, pp. 7-8. Cf. U. Syn.,*Proceedings of the 1950 Biennial Convention, op. cit.*, p. 96, and Katzoff, *op. cit.*, pp. 42, 151. Also M. H. Lewittes, "Three-Day-a-Week Hebrew School," *Synagogue Center*, VI, 1 (June, 1945), 4-6.

28. See Katzoff, *op. cit.*, pp. 70, 78-79.

29. *Survey*, II, p. 15, and Katzoff, *op. cit.*, pp. 78, 135-36.

30. *Survey*, II, pp. 22-24.

31. U. Z. Engelman, *Hebrew Education in America* (New York: Jewish Teacher's Seminary and People's University Press, 1947), p. 34.

32. Cf. Katzoff, *op. cit.*, and Ira Eisenstein, "The Synagogue High School in the Metropolitan Community," *Synagogue School*, X, 2 (December, 1951), 51. On the problem of size see R.A., *Proceedings of Second Annual R.A. Conference on Jewish Education* (December 22-23, 1947) (New York: R.A., n.d.), p. 100. (Hereafter this publication will be referred to as *Proceedings of Second J.E. Conference.*) Cf. Katzoff, *op. cit.*, pp. 42-43.

33. Engelman in R.A., *Proceedings of Second J.E. Conference, op. cit.*, p. 109. Note also the statement in R.A., *Proceedings*, XIV (1951), 55.

34. See R.A., *Proceedings*, IV

(1933), 144ff.; and A. E. Millgram, "Implementing a Program of Intensive Jewish Education in the Congregational School," *Conservative Judaism*, V, 4 (June, 1949), 8-9.

35. U. Syn. Commission on Jewish Education, *The Objectives and Standards for the Congregational School* (rev. ed., New York: U. Syn. Commission on Jewish Education, 1948), p. 4.

36. *Ibid.*, pp. 3-4. Cf. R.A., *Proceedings of Second J.E. Conference, op. cit.*, p. 135. On the various aspects of the Talmud Torah and congregational school problem, see *U. Syn. Recorder*, VII, 1 (January, 1927), 35; Engelman, *Hebrew Education in America, op. cit.*, pp. 37-39; Samuel Dinin, *Judaism in a Changing Civilization* (New York: Bureau of Publications, Teachers College, Columbia University, 1933), pp. 15-17, 86ff.; Katzoff, *op. cit.*, pp. 143ff.; Éugene Kohn in R.A., *Proceedings*, V (1939), 13-29; and A. E. Millgram in U. Syn., *Proceedings of the 1948 Biennial Convention, op. cit.*, pp. 82ff.

37. Louis M. Levitsky in R.A., *Proceedings*, VIII (1944), 295.

38. See U. Syn., *Synagogue Dues Assessment Plans* (New York: U. Syn., n.d.), p. 5; and R.A., *Proceedings of Second J.E. Conference, op. cit.*, p. 118.

39. U. Syn., *Three Pillars of Synagogue Administration, op. cit.*, p. 4.

40. Sidney Greenberg in U. Syn., *Proceedings of the 1950 Biennial Convention, op. cit.*, p. 43. The problem of possible advantages derivable from membership in a synagogue is not a new question in the American Jewish community: see Salo W. Baron, "American Jewish History: Problems and Methods," *Publications of the American Jewish Historical Society*, XXXIX (1949-50), 249-50.

41. "A Program for Conservative Jewish Education," *Synagogue Center*, V, 1 (June, 1944), 6.

42. Katzoff, *op. cit.*, p. 43; see also p. 152. In addition, note Mordecai M. Kaplan, "The First Step Toward Organic Jewish Community," *The Reconstructionist*, XV, 1 (February 18, 1949), 22. Some coordination has taken place on the high school level and for an analysis of a few of the problems that arise, see R.A., *Proceedings of the Second J.E. Conference, op. cit.*, p. 61; and Eisenstein, "The Synagogue High School in the Metropolitan Community," *op. cit.*

43. These quotations are from an analysis written for this study by the rabbi of the local Conservative synagogue. Material on the formal structure of the plan has appeared in educational publications. In cities like Minneapolis, where there has been a long history of communal efforts in the field of Jewish education, congregations have employed some of the same devices described above in order to assure self-maintenance. Minneapolis Conservative synagogues also conduct their own Sunday schools. In addition, an expansion in social activities may compensate for the decrease in educational work. See Gordon, *op. cit.*, esp. pp. 184-85, and cf. Samuel Dinin, "General Trends in Jewish Education," *Jewish Education*, XVIII (1946), 14.

44. Robert Gordis, "The Tasks Before Us," *Conservative Judaism*, I, 1 (January, 1945), 4. See also R.A., *Proceedings of R.A. Conference on Jewish Education, 1946* (New York: R.A., 1946), *passim*.

To an increasing degree Conservative officials are recognizing that they are reckoning with the requirements of institutional maintenance but are doing so at the sacrifice of educational standards.

45. See *Survey*, II, p. 10.

46. *Ibid.*, p. 10; see also, R.A., *Proceedings of Second J.E. Conference, op. cit.*, pp. 118-19; and R.A., *Proceedings*, V (1939), 294. On the progress made with this ceremony in one middle-sized Jewish community, see Gordon, *op cit.*, p. 128-29. The *Bas Mitzvah* ceremony is of special interest in the light of our discussion of the position of the woman in Orthodoxy and in Conservatism.

47. R.A., *Proceedings of Second J.E. Conference, op. cit.*, p. 42. See also *ibid.*, pp. 21ff., and *Survey*, II, pp. 3-5.

48. While no detailed study of the Ramah Camps has been made, we suggest that more is involved than an improved knowledge of Hebrew language and Jewish content. Campers are made familiar, through drama and story, with the leading figures in the "history" of Conservatism and there appears to be some stress on the differences between Conservative Jews and non-Conservative Jews. The program of the Camps shows strong tendencies toward institutionalization.

The ambivalence of the movement in regard to Hebrew needs further investigation. Some Conservative adherents are satisfied to confine use of the language to prayer, religious rites, and Bible study; others believe that there is intrinsic value in the language. Also, the rabbis and teachers in Conservative congregations appear to have somewhat different goals.

The varied emphases ("religionists" vs. "'nationalists") are reflected to some extent by the different textbooks used in the schools: see Katzoff, *op. cit.*, pp. 58, 63, 91, 138.

49. See R.A., *Proceedings of Second J.E. Conference, op. cit.*, pp. 43ff.; R.A., *Proceedings*, X (1947), 82, 159, 277-78; Moshe Davis, "The Ladder of Jewish Education," *Conservative Judaism*, IV, 3 (May, 1948), 7-8; and Jeremiah J. Berman, "The Return to the Jewish Day School," *Conservative Judaism*, VII, 2 (January, 1951), 1-13. Cf. *U. Syn. Review*, IV, 8 (April, 1951), 4.

50. This quotation is excerpted from a document prepared for this study by a supervisor in one of the leading bureaus of Jewish education. It is of interest to note that several Conservative congregations have already established day schools. In a pioneer institution of this type, according to one study, the parents of the day school students are less observant religiously than are the parents of the Hebrew school students. See Golub and Nardi, *op. cit.*

The "foundation school" arrangement, embodied in the *Bet Hayeled* located in New York City, has not been widely copied. This institution has been supported and guided in large part by people affiliated with Conservatism. The school enrolls the child at the usual nursery school age and the student continues at the institution on a full-time basis until he has reached the start of the intermediary grades in elementary school. The course of study ends at this point, and the child transfers to the public school; he continues his Jewish education in the afternoon Hebrew school. Thus the period of parochialism is comparatively short, but presumably the child has acquired a solid foundation in Hebrew language and Jewish knowledge to which he can add in subsequent studies.

51. Albert Lewis, "Report on Preliminary Survey," *Synagogue School,* X, 2 (December, 1951), 8.

52. These points will be extensively documented in a forthcoming study by the author and others of the attitudes of Jewish teen-

agers and their parents.

53. See *U. Syn. Recorder,* VI, 4 (October, 1926), 50. Douglass and Brunner (*op. cit.,* p. 163), estimated that 20% of the total Protestant Sunday school enrollment is composed of young people aged 15 to 21, and that an additional 25% of the student body are adults over the age of 21. These percentages were calculated for urban, rather than rural, churches.

54. See *Survey,* III, *passim.*

Chapter VI

1. *U. Syn. Recorder,* V, 2 (April, 1925), 15. See also *ibid.,* V, 3 (July, 1925), 17, 19; and VII, 2 (April, 1927), 23.

2. Because of the operation of the acculturation process as well as other factors, it may be that the problems posed in the following pages do not trouble the present generation of Conservative rabbinical students to the same extent as they did their predecessors. Our description is meant to apply chiefly to the period 1900-50.

3. The Seminary actually began to operate in 1887. After 1902 it was popularly known for some years as "Schechter's Seminary" or simply as "Schechter's."

4. On the financial problem see Cyrus Adler, *Lectures, Selected Papers, Addresses* (Philadelphia: Privately Published, 1933), p. 242. More generally, see the annual reports and registers of the Seminary and Cyrus Adler (ed.), *The J.T.S., Semi-Centennial Volume* (New York: J.T.S., 1939). Note also Robert Gordis, *The Jew Faces a New World* (New York: Behrman's Jewish Book House, 1941), p. 198. The existence of the "Old Semi-

nary" brings up the question of whether or not a Conservative movement existed in the 19th century. This is treated in *CJSA,* Chapter II and Appendix A.

5. One book which attempts to describe changes in Jewish group status in America is Carey McWilliams, *A Mask for Privilege: Anti-Semitism in America* (Boston: Little, Brown & Co., 1948). Although frequently one-sided in approach and undoubtedly subject to revision in many details, this volume is still a significant one. Some interesting material on the status-threat problem can be found in Irving A. Mandel, "The Attitude of the American Jewish Community Toward East European Immigration as Reflected in the Anglo-Jewish Press, 1880-1890," *American Jewish Archives,* III, 1 (June, 1950), 11-36.

6. Hon. Joseph Blumenthal in J.T.S. Association, *Proceedings of the Second Biennial Convention* (New York: J.T.S. Association, 1890), pp. 8-9. Apparently the majority of those who registered in the earlier classes did not come from families belonging to congre-

gations which supported the institution. Over half of the student body in 1888 was Russian-born, and most were said to be from poor homes: see J.T.S. Association, *Proceedings of the First Biennial Convention* (New York: J.T.S. Association, 1888), pp. 17, 22.

7. H. P. Mendes in J.T.S. Association, *Proceedings of the Sixth Biennial Convention* (New York: J.T.S. Association, 1898), p. 32.

8. For details on the reorganization, see J.T.S. Association, *Proceedings of the Eighth Biennial Convention* (New York: J.T.S., 1904); and J.T.S., *Biennial Report, 1902-04* (New York: J.T.S., 1906). Cf. Norman Bentwich, *Solomon Schechter* (Philadelphia: Jewish Publication Society of America, 1938), pp. 169-71. Note that although rabbis played an important part in the founding of the Seminary (see Adler (ed.), *J.T.S., Semi-Centennial Volume, op. cit.*, pp. 3-5), rabbinical influence was absent in the reorganization. Since the Americanization interest was not made explicit by the new board, some of the old group were puzzled about the reasons behind the sudden interest in the institution: see Bernard Drachman, *The Unfailing Light* (New York: Rabbinical Council of America, 1948), p. 253.

On Schiff, see Cyrus Adler (ed.), *Jacob H. Schiff: His Life and Letters* (2 vols., Garden City: Doubleday, Doran & Co., 1929), esp. II, pp. 53-58. Marshall was perhaps less concerned than were the others in regard to the Americanization problem: note the comment in Central Conference of American Rabbis, *Yearbook*, XLI (1931), 333. Adler has left a significant record of his activities in the form of an autobiography: *I Have Considered the Days* (Philadelphia: Jewish Publication Society of America, 1941).

9. Cf. Davis in *The Jews*, ed. by Louis Finkelstein, *op. cit.*, I, p. 401; and Davis, *Yahadut Amerika Be-Hitpathutah, op. cit.*, pp. 286ff. Our analysis should not be taken as implying that Americanization was the only motivation present—doubtless there was a desire on the part of many donors to aid in the perpetuation of Judaism and to support Jewish scholarship. See, for example, the statement by Schiff in J.T.S., *Biennial Report, 1902-04, op. cit.*, p. 103.

10. See Jacob Mann, "Modern Rabbinical Seminaries and Other Institutions of Jewish Learning," Central Conference of American Rabbis, *Yearbook*, XXXV (1925), 295-310; and Adler, *Lectures, Selected Papers and Addresses, op. cit.*, p. 258.

11. Schechter in J.T.S., *Biennial Report, 1902-04, op. cit.*, pp. 98-99. Cf. the remark of Louis Ginzberg in *U. Syn. Recorder*, III, 4 (October, 1923), 5. Even supporters of the "Old Seminary" felt that the school should not bother to instruct those who were unfitted for the ministry: see *Proceedings of the Third Biennial Convention* (New York: J.T.S. Association, 1892), p. 17.

12. The non-denominational type of seminary common in Protestantism has not been popular in the Jewish community. There has been only one school which adhered to such a policy for any length of time. It has now been merged with the Hebrew Union College and thus is no longer non-denominational in character.

13. See Bentwich, *op. cit.,* pp. 213-14.

14. J.T.S., *Biennial Report, 1902-04, op. cit.,* p. 70. There has been little stress along these lines in recent years, for an adequate knowledge of English can now be assumed.

15. *Ibid.,* p. 34.

16. It was tacitly understood that whatever their own inclinations, the rabbis would not make much reference in their pulpits to observances considered outmoded by the majority of the laity. Cf. Louis Epstein in R.A., *Proceedings,* X (1947), 142.

17. See Max Weiner, "The Ideology of the Founders of Jewish Scientific Research," *YIVO Annual of Jewish Social Science,* V (1950), 184-96.

18. See Louis Ginzberg, *A Commentary on the Palestinian Talmud* (3 vols., New York: J.T.S., 1941), esp. I, pp. xxiii, xxv.

19. Louis Finkelstein, *The Pharisees* (2 vols., Philadelphia: Jewish Publication Society of America, 1938), I, p. 2.

20. *Ibid.,* I, p. 101. See also I, pp. 43-53, 145, 216, 261, 344. Note the review of the book by Morris R. Cohen in *Jewish Social Studies,* III (1941), 81-87. Cohen found himself unable to accept this analysis for he felt that Finkelstein is overly materialistic in his approach!

21. On Schechter, see Bentwich, *op. cit.,* and A. S. Oko, *Solomon Schechter—A Bibliography* (Cambridge: Cambridge University Press, 1938). Material in *Louis Ginzberg; Jubilee Volume on the Occasion of His Seventieth Birthday* (New York: American Academy for Jewish Research, 1945) gives adequate information on the background of this famed scholar. On Israel Davidson, see Carrie Davidson, *Out of Endless Yearnings* (New York: Bloch Publishing Co., 1946). Alexander Marx (whose background was different from the others) sketched the life of Israel Friedlaender in an article reprinted in his *Essays in Jewish Biography* (Philadelphia: Jewish Publication Society of America, 1948), pp. 280-89. Note also the profile of Louis Finkelstein in *Time Magazine,* LVIII, 16 (October 15, 1951), 52-59.

22. Solomon Goldman, "The Portrait of a Teacher," in *Louis Ginzberg; Jubilee Volume on the Occasion of His Seventieth Birthday, op. cit.,* p. 7.

23. Finkelstein in U. Syn., *National Board Minutes,* January 19, 1947, *op. cit.,* p. 185. Note also the statement of another faculty member, Boaz Cohen: "We cannot and dare not be swayed, in our interpretation of Jewish Law, by considerations from the study of comparative religion, or take cognizance of the data of the anthropologists . . ." (R.A., *Proceedings,* XI [1947], 60-61).

24. See *U. Syn. Recorder,* VII, 1 (January, 1927), 2.

25. According to Jerome E. Carlin and Saul H. Mendlovitz ("The Rabbi: A Sociological Study of a Religious Specialist" [Unpublished M.A. Thesis, Dept. of Sociology, University of Chicago, 1951], p. 192), the situation is as follows: " 'Build membership', 'construct educational facilities and supervise them', 'reorganize the dues structure', 'plan a budget' . . . are the core of the Conservative rabbi's description of what he actually does in any position."

26. Although he is indispensable, rapid role changes mean

that the rabbi is confronted with a good deal of ambiguity on the part of congregants in regard to his functions. In such a semi-structured situation, it is necessary that he be prepared to gain loyalty on the basis of manipulation of personality rather than strictly on the grounds of performance of the duties of his office.

27. See Gordon, *op. cit.*, pp. 171-72. Note the plan evolved by the Conservative group in Philadelphia where a local rabbi, if notified by an out-of-town colleague that a congregant has come to the city for medical treatment, will himself visit the patient. Thus the surrogate pastor is not an anonymous individual exercising a routinized function as with the hospital chaplain, but he is a chosen representative of the congregant's own spiritual leader. (See U. Syn., *National Board Minutes*, January 18, 1947, *op. cit.*, p. 120.) So great is the demand for pastoral service and so unprecedented is this in the role constellation of the rabbinate, that many spiritual leaders are unprepared to deal with the problem with full effectiveness. See Jeshaia Schnitzer, "Religious Counseling and the American Rabbinate," *The Reconstructionist*, XVI, 13 (November 3, 1950), 10-15.

In an attempt to increase congregational affiliation, it has frequently been proposed — particularly among the Reform group— that rabbis serving congregations be barred from performing religious ceremonies for non-congregants. The idea has not gained much support, although some rabbis practice it informally; there are financial, religious, and legal reservations. In middle- and large-sized cities there already exists a class of rabbis who have little or no congregational affiliation, and who derive most—if not all—of their income from fees in payment for the performance of rituals.

28. From an interview with a Conservative rabbi.

29. See J.T.S., *Biennial Report, 1902-04, op. cit.*, pp. 32, 68-69. Note the Seminary commencement address as reported in *U. Syn. Recorder*, V, 4 (October, 1925), 7, in which the speaker advises the graduating class (who were reared in Orthodoxy where regular preaching is looked upon as befitting only to a person of inferior scholarship) to drop such attitudes and to accept the preaching role without reservations.

30. The description of these seven roles, plus the "rabbi" one, are adapted from a typology worked out during 1951 by the "University Seminar in the Professions in Modern Society," meeting at Columbia University.

31. The term is used by Carlin and Mendlovitz, *op. cit.*

32. This results in a neat reversal. It was mainly laymen who served in former times as pastors, rectors, etc. Now these roles are numbered among the preeminent responsibilities which the rabbi must assume. On the other hand, the function which had once served as the chief rabbinical occupational role is now actually in the hands of the laity.

33. Of course the rabbi may still do some teaching and interpreting, but he no longer claims authority for his declarations. He does not attempt a legitimation in terms of the divine system and he acts more like the secular teacher who communicates a body of knowledge

which the listener is free to accept or reject on the merits of content.

34. Thus Carlin and Mendlovitz state that all the rabbis in their sample (which was drawn from both the Reform, the Conservative, as well as the Orthodox wings), ". . . aspire to a scholar-saint role." (*Op. cit.*, p. 229.) (It should be noted that most Reform rabbis still come from families which are East European in background.) They state: "The contemporary rabbi still falls within the shadow of Emancipation and therefore still faces in varying degrees the problem of loss of authority." (*Ibid.*, p. 224.)

35. Thus it is the laity, whose sentiments are expressed through local synagogue boards and ritual committees, who guide the rabbi in major policy decisions. Issues in the religious area which are of *minor* importance tend to remain more exclusively within rabbinical jurisdiction. But note Carlin and Mendlovitz: "The Conservative rabbi looks upon these changes [in Jewish customs and synagogue rituals] as minor. He handles these changes from the point of view of satisfying his membership." (*Op. cit.*, p. 203.)

36. Eugene Kohn in R.A., *Proceedings*, V (1939), 361-62.

37. Note the remark of Simon Greenberg about the curriculum of the Rabbinical Department of the Seminary as contrasted with its Teachers Institute in "A Tribute to Professor Alexander Marx," *Conservative Judaism*, IV, 2 (February, 1948), 3. Seminary professors have tended to adopt a biographical approach in dealing with the modern Jewish scene, as for example Ginzberg, *Students, Scholars, and Saints, op. cit.*, and Marx,

Essays in Jewish Biography, op. cit.

38. Goldman in *Louis Ginzberg; Jubilee Volume on His Seventieth Birthday, op. cit.*, p. 18. See also p. 15. Cf. letter from Mordecai M. Kaplan to H. H. Rubenovitz, January 31, 1921 (in American Jewish Archives at Hebrew Union College Library, Cincinnati).

39. Bentwich, *op. cit.*, pp. 281-82. See also pp. 343-44. The author of another study doubts that Schechter believed in revelation: see Myer S. Kripke, "Solomon Schechter's Philosophy of Judaism," *The Reconstructionist*, III, 12 (October 22, 1937), 9.

40. The tendency of Conservative thinkers to indulge in compartmentalism has aroused their Reform colleagues, for the Conservative group seems to agree with them in scholarly publications but refuses to follow Reform principles in regard to personal behavior and observance.

41. Mortimer J. Cohen, "Mordecai M. Kaplan as Teacher," in *Mordecai M. Kaplan: An Evaluation*, ed. by Ira Eisenstein and Eugene Kohn, *op. cit.*, pp. 5-6.

42. Alexander Burnstein, "Kaplan's Contribution to Conservative Judaism," in *ibid.*, p. 226. Cf. Adler (ed.) *The J.T.S., Semi-Centennial Volume, op. cit.*, p. 172.

43. See Stephen S. Wise, *Challenging Years* (New York: G. P. Putnam's Sons, 1949), p. 136; and various items in the collection of Kaplan Letters.

44. On some of these points as well as those contained in the following section, see the documentation presented by Parzen in his series of articles in *Conservative Judaism*. The student wishing fuller biographical details about the teachers and administrators

will find Rabbi Parzen's articles to be helpful.

45. Goldman in *Louis Ginzberg; Jubilee Volume on His Seventieth Birthday, op. cit.,* pp. 9-10. Cf. the addresses in R.A., *Proceedings,* IX (1949), memorializing Israel Friedlaender.

46. Cf. Goldman in *Louis Ginzberg; Jubilee Volume on His Seventieth Birthday, op. cit.,* p. 14. This factor in particular is diminishing in importance because of the greater degree of acculturation of the present generation of students.

47. While only a small part of Talmudic study had practical value even in Eastern Europe, status was nonetheless granted on the basis of accomplishments in this field. The Conservative congregant, however, is relatively unconcerned—for example—about either that part of the code which relates to worship in the Temple and hence is of purely antiquarian interest, or to the technical problems of Sabbath observance which are still relevant to the contemporary Jew who wishes to celebrate the holiday in the traditional manner.

48. Louis Levitsky in R.A., *Proceedings,* VIII (1944), 281-82. See also pp. 308ff. In addition, note the statement by Boaz Cohen in *ibid.,* VI (1940), 140.

49. See David Aronson in R.A., *Proceedings,* XIII (1950), 126.

50. Morris Adler in *ibid.,* XII (1949), 149. For trenchant criticisms of the unrealistic nature of rabbinical curricula, see Mordecai M. Kaplan, *Judaism in Transition* (New York: Covici Friede, 1936), pp. 158-84; Kallen, *op. cit.,* pp. 203-20; and Central Conference of American Rabbis, *Yearbook,* LX (1950), 328-57.

It is highly significant to note that during one year over 40% of the rabbis who held Conservative pulpits applied to the Placement Commission of the R.A. for recommendations to new positions: see R.A., *Proceedings,* XIV (1951), 35. Functionaries have asked for more careful screening of Seminary candidates, and also that the "Committee of Selection" of the institution include a rabbi in congregational work. The fact that Conservative rabbis are chiefly recruited from the large communities where the Jewish lower class and lower-middle class live, and that many of the pulpits are located in the smaller communities due to the large middle-class and upper-middle-class representation in such areas, makes for further complications in addition to difficulties already suggested.

51. William Greenfeld in R.A., *Proceedings,* XII (1949), 138. For further insight into the approach of the teacher to the student and practicing rabbi, see the address of Israel Davidson in J.T.S., *Commencement Address,* June 8, 1930 (New York: J.T.S., 1930). Seminary students are not awarded the *semichah* (ordination which allows the recipient to render authoritative judgments in questions of Jewish law) upon graduation, and thus few Conservative rabbis possess real rabbinical authority: see Isaac Klein in R.A., *Proceedings,* XII (1949), 138-39.

52. Note the statement made before a Seminary audience by Felix Warburg: "I feel the best bringing up that you can receive is to be acquainted with Jewish matters and philosophies . . . and then leave it to you to observe or ask for observance of these [customs]

that you and your people consider essential." (*U. Syn. Recorder,* IV, 3 [June-July, 1924], 11.)

53. Cf. J.T.S., *Heritage* (New York: The Semi-Centennial Committee of the J.T.S., 1937), esp. p. 13. Note the desire of Cyrus Adler and others that the students take their undergraduate work (except during the early years, one of the requirements for admission to the institution has always been a Bachelor's degree from a recognized college or university) at one or another of the leading private Eastern universities, and that the Seminary itself maintain relationships with such schools. But most of the early aspirants had to matriculate at public institutions, or at colleges outside of the Ivy League type. See J.T.S., *Biennial Report, 1902-04, op. cit.,* pp. 105-06 and J.T.S., *Students Annual,* Vol. II (1915), pp. 14-29, 54-56.

54. See Adler (ed.), *The J.T.S., Semi-Centennial Volume, op. cit.,* p. 15.

55. On Schechter's position, see Bentwich, *op. cit.,* pp. 309ff. Note the items cited in Oko, *Solomon Schechter—A Bibliography, op. cit.,* p. 54; and see also Solomon Schechter, *Seminary Addresses and Other Papers* (Cincinnati: Ark Publishing Co., 1915), pp. xi-xiii, 92-103. On Schiff's attitude, see Adler (ed.), *Jacob H. Schiff: His Life and Letters, op. cit.,* II, p. 168; also II, pp. 164-67, 297-313.

56. *Ibid.,* I, pp. 369, 378-81; II, p. 291. On Schechter's view that board members were more interested in what he termed "civics" rather than in rabbinical learning, see the statement found in Bentwich, *op. cit.,* p. 190.

57. Note Schechter's statement found in Bentwich, *op. cit.,* p. 194;

and see also Schechter, *op. cit.,* pp. 230-31.

58. See Bentwich, *op. cit.,* p. 192.

59. *Ibid.,* p. 190. But note the statement of Rabbi Max Davidson, who commented recently about: ". . . the miracle we witnessed a generation ago—the fascinating case of theological genetics, that happy marriage, whereby a Seminary faculty which was Orthodox and a board of directors which was Reform, gave birth to Conservative Judaism." (R.A.. *Proceedings,* XV [1952], 96.)

60. Bentwich, *op. cit.,* p. 191.

61. *Ibid.,* p. 195. It was during this period that Schechter resigned from the board of the Educational Alliance in protest against the concept of Americanization held by the German Jews. The specific conflict which led to his withdrawal was a proposed modification in the work of the religious department of the institution. The change was designed to lessen the Jewish aspects of the program and to speed up the tempo of Americanization. It was Schechter's feeling that the immigrant was as much in need of what he termed "Judaisation" as he was of Americanization—in fact more strongly so, since the newcomer was quickly shedding his traditions. Moreover, Schechter resented the attitude that the East European Jews needed "civilizing." The text of his letter of resignation is found in *ibid.,* pp. 215-19. See also Educational Alliance, *Annual Report, 1916* (New York: Educational Alliance, 1917), esp. p. 49. Cf. Israel Friedlaender's essay, "The Americanization of the Jewish Immigrant," in his volume *Past and Present* (Cincinnati: Ark Publishing Co., 1919), pp. 353-69.

62. As the Americanization ob-

jective declined in importance, a number of donors hesitated to contribute to an institution whose religious outlook differed from their own. Hence the Seminary Library was given separate corporate status so that donations could be made directly to it; philanthropic moneys would thus support strictly scholarly purposes and donors would not be involved in any ideological commitments.

63. See J.T.S., *Heritage, op. cit.,* esp. pp. 7-8, 17-20. The older Americanization appeal is mentioned obliquely on p. 12.

64. On the work of the gradu-ates, see R.A., *Proceedings,* X (1947), 207.

65. Moshe Davis in R.A., *Proceedings,* X (1947), 180-81.

66. See *ibid.,* VIII (1944), 358, and III (1929), 117.

67. In addition, Hebrew is now taught in some public high schools in New York, Chicago, and other cities.

68. It is reported that of the 503 students enrolled in Marshallia, a leading New York City Hebrew High School, only 94 come from Conservative congregations. See R.A., *Proceedings of Second J.E. Conference, op. cit.,* p. 54.

Chapter VII

1. The study to which we make reference is one done by the Department of Scientific Research of the American Jewish Committee. Thanks are due to the Committee for permission to use certain of the interview data which have a bearing on our problem. Of course, the conclusions drawn from the data are solely the responsibility of the author.

2. While we do not claim typicality for the opinions of the Conservative Jews of Eastville, it is significant to note that their community is located in a geographical area where Conservatism is very strong. Furthermore, while the Eastville Jewish community is a small one by metropolitan standards, it is located between two very large cities. Not only are its Jews influenced by these communities, but some of the adult respondents were born and reared in the large centers. Thus, Eastville would appear to be much more representative of "big-city" public

opinion than are communities of similar size in other areas.

3. Kadushin, emphasizing the "desire for survival," pointed out how this factor served to produce a loose but nonetheless coherent movement in the American synagogue: "Conservative Judaism is a movement of the laity and not of the rabbi. . . . Conservatism is primarily a movement which has arisen spontaneously among those who, because of their early training . . . are tied by habit and profound emotional attachment to Judaism and the Jewish people. They recognize that if Judaism is to remain potent in their lives it must become adjusted to entirely new social, economic, and intellectual conditions. They want to 'conserve' Judaism. . . . in a groping way each community tries to discover methods that would accomplish this purpose. The completely spontaneous character of this movement . . . is responsible for the wide differences in ritual

and service found among those calling themselves 'Conservative.'" (Max Kadushin, "Conservative Judaism, A Creation of the Jewish Laity," *S.A.J. Review*, VII, 23 [February 17, 1928], 4-5.)

4. For a similar analysis of Reform Judaism as a lay-created movement see Central Conference of American Rabbis, *Yearbook*, XXXVIII (1928), 386-560, and Louis I. Egelson, *Reform Judaism: A Movement of the People* (Cincinnati: Union of American Hebrew Congregations, 1949).

5. Cf. Israel Goldstein, "A Survey of Conservative Judaism," *American Hebrew*, CXXVI (1929-30), 26.

6. Cf. Buch, *op. cit.*, p. 138.

7. U. Syn., *National Board Minutes*, January 18, 1947, p. 40.

8. Julian Freeman in U. Syn., *Proceedings of the 1948 Biennial Convention, op. cit.*, pp. 128-29.

9. Contrast, for example, the data in Nathan Glazer, Herbert Hyman, and S. M. Lipset, "Characteristics of New York City Jews—A Report on the Analysis of Sample Polls for Demographic Data," (Unpublished memorandum, 1952), with the material in David and Adele Bernstein, "Slow Revolution in Richmond, Va.," *Commentary*, VIII (1949), 539-46.

10. There is also a tendency for institutional loyalties to develop—this serves to inhibit the crossing of "denominational" lines in spite of social mobility. Some prosperous Orthodox Jews in the larger communities, for example, have held fast to their affiliation. Also, one Conservative rabbi pointed out to us how his synagogue, a nationally known institution, was managing to retain those of its members who had succeeded in raising them-

selves above the level of the middle class during the era of World War II.

11. Israel Goldstein in R.A., *Proceedings*, I (1927), 34-35.

12. Rabbi Morris Adler in U. Syn., *Proceedings of the 1948 Biennial Convention, op. cit.*, pp. 26-27.

13. Max Arzt, in R.A., *Proceedings*, X (1947), 206. In speaking about the new interfaith program of the Seminary, Arzt makes it clear that this development also mirrors denominational rivalry: "The field of inter-faith relationships must no longer be monopolized by Reform Judaism." (*Ibid.*, 210.)

14. Gordis in U. Syn., *National Board Minutes*, January 19, 1947, pp. 200-01.

15. Julian Freeman, Address delivered before National Association of Jewish Men's Clubs, *op. cit.*, p. 13.

16. Gordon in U. Syn., *National Board Minutes*, January 19, 1947, pp. 209-16.

17. See Dr. Emanuel Neumann in R.A., *Proceedings*, XI (1947), 170.

18. A member of the staff of the Zionist Organization of America placed at our disposal a number of documents which explain the plan and related to us his experiences in this area.

19. Cf. Gordis, *The Jew Faces a New World, op. cit.*, pp. 206-8. Although Kaplan did much writing on this subject, it was Israel Friedlaender who was chiefly responsible for introducing the ideas of Achad Haam, the leader of the "cultural Zionism" school, in Conservative circles. A typically optimistic Conservative statement (demonstrating the trend of opinion during the 20's and 30's) as to

the expected effect of Israel on American-Jewish culture, is to be found in Israel H. Levinthal, *Judaism* (New York: Funk and Wagnalls Co., 1935), p. 256.
20. Cf. Rabbi Morris Adler in U. Syn., *Proceedings of the 1948 Biennial Convention, op. cit.,* pp. 31-33.
21. See Gordis in R.A., *Proceedings,* X (1947), 73; Ralph Simon in *ibid.,* XII (1949), 244; and Norman Shapiro in *ibid.,* XII (1949), 248-49. On how the Conservative movement believes it may benefit from the decline of Zionist activity, note the remark of William Greenfeld in *ibid.,* XII (1949), 245-46 and David Aronson in *ibid.,* XIII (1950), 130. Significantly, Conservative functionaries are—rabbinically speaking—*personae non gratae* in Israel.
22. See Max Weine, "Facing a New Era," *The Reconstructionist,* XIV, 17 (December 24, 1948), 24-30.
23. This development has taken place in Reform Judaism. It had seemed for a time that the Seminary was interested in a strong lay movement: "There are certain factors that seem to me to be making for a revitalization. . . . One of them is the fact that the . . . Seminary has a very real desire to see that the United Synagogue will grow in strength. . . ." (Gordon in U. Syn., *Proceedings of the 1948 Biennial Convention, op. cit.,* p. 53.)
24. Cf. Louis Finkelstein in R.A., *Proceedings,* XIII (1950), 117-22.
25. William Greenfeld, in *ibid.,* XII (1949), 138.
26. Julian Freeman in U. Syn., *Proceedings of the 1948 Biennial Convention, op. cit.,* pp. 131-32. Note the statement of another layman: "The men and women of our

Movement have been seeking guidance, clarification and formulation of the philosophy and program of the Conservative Movement. They have felt that the United Synagogue must become . . . the spokesman for the laity in the creation of the program and philosophy of Conservative Judaism. The feeling has been prevalent amongst our laity that both the Rabbinical Assembly and the Jewish Theological Seminary have thus far failed to clarify the point of view of Conservative Judaism. . . ." (Samuel Rothstein in U. Syn., *Proceedings of the 1950 Biennial Convention, op. cit.,* pp. 19-20.)
27. Gordon's viewpoint is summarized in his farewell message published in *U. Syn. Review,* V, 4 (December, 1949), 1.
28. It is significant to note that the Seminary group controls the budgets of both the United Synagogue and the Rabbinical Assembly. It also has some influence in the recommendation of rabbinical candidates to congregations.
29. Milton Steinberg, *A Partisan Guide to the Jewish Problem* (Indianapolis: Bobbs-Merrill Co., Inc., 1945), p. 165. In an earlier formulation Steinberg emphasized that: "They [the Conservative movement] are content . . . with a pragmatic approach. This consists largely in attempting to strike a 'happy medium' between the two extremes . . ." (Steinberg, *The Making of the Modern Jew,* [Indianapolis: Bobbs-Merrill Co., Inc., 1933], p. 286). Steinberg, who died in 1950, was both an important Conservative rabbi and a leading expositor of Jewish religious thought.
On the rabbi's conception of

himself as an intellectual, see Carlin and Mendlovitz, *op. cit.*

30. Goldman, *A Rabbi Takes Stock, op. cit.*, pp. 4-5.

31. Report of Max Routtenberg, in R.A., *Proceedings*, XIII (1950), 36.

32. Max Davidson in *ibid.*, XV (1952), 95.

33. See Simon Greenberg in Preface to Katzoff, *op. cit.*, p. xix. One prominent Conservative rabbi, in describing his movement to us, said that a number of his colleagues "want separatism without the ideology that would justify it." Some rabbis stress that the movement is still too young to have a philosophy, while others state that rigid ideological systems are characteristic of "foreign"—rather than American—movements.

34. Clarence Gross in U. Syn., *Proceedings of the 1948 Biennial Convention, op. cit.*, pp. 169-70.

35. Max Routtenberg in R.A., *Proceedings*, XIII (1950), 38.

35a. The volume to which we make reference is Joseph Zeitlin, *Disciples of the Wise* (New York: Bureau of Publications, Teachers College, Columbia University, 1945). Zeitlin found that the views of 81% of the Conservative rabbis in his sample indicated a naturalistic rather than a supernaturalistic bias; 80% of the Reform rabbis who responded were classified in the same category (*ibid.*, p. 83). Other material in this volume confirms the view that Conservative and Reform rabbis are frequently paired in their attitudes on religious problems, as over against Orthodox rabbis.

Although published in the mid-1940's, the data for this study was gathered in 1937. One would suspect that a follow-up of the Zeitlin study might show a somewhat different distribution of opinion.

36. Julian Freeman, Address delivered before National Association of Jewish Men's Clubs, *op. cit.*, p. 13. Note also that the United Synagogue has not established any standards to which its affiliated congregations must adhere.

37. Steinberg, *A Partisan Guide to the Jewish Problem, op. cit.*, p. 166. This statement, written in the 1940's, does not take the latest developments into account.

38. Samuel Rosenblatt in R.A., *Proceedings*, XIV (1951), 175.

39. Hyman D. Cohen in U. Syn., *Proceedings of the 1948 Biennial Convention, op. cit.*, p. 109.

40. Julian Freeman in *ibid.*, pp. 132-33. Note also the comment of Max Shapiro in *ibid.*, p. 121. But note that even among Catholics the ideology and practices of the laity fall far short of the standards set by the clergy: see Fichter, *op. cit.*, pp. 13, 260, 270.

41. Israel M. Goldman in R.A., *Proceedings*, XII (1949), p. 96. Cyrus Adler had previously commented: "Conservative is a general term which nearly everybody uses but which is, I believe, technically applied to those congregations which have departed somewhat in practice from the Orthodox, but not to any great extent in theory." (Adler, *Lectures, Selected Papers, Addresses, op. cit.*, p. 251.)

42. Gordis, *The Jew Faces a New World, op. cit.*, p. 199.

43. *Ibid.*, pp. 211-13.

44. Gordis, *Conservative Judaism, op. cit.*, pp. ix-x.

45. *Ibid.*, pp. 16-17.

46. Steinberg, *A Partisan Guide to the Jewish Problem, op. cit.*, p. 165.

47. Mordecai M. Kaplan, *Unity in Diversity in the Conservative Movement* (New York: U. Syn., 1947), p. 11.

48. Schechter, *Studies in Judaism* (First Series) (New York, Macmillan & Co., 1896), pp. xvii-xviii.

49. *Ibid.*, p. xix. An interesting summary and critique of this approach is given by Jacob Agus, "Law as Standards," *Conservative Judaism*, VI, 4 (May, 1950), 14-15.

50. Steinberg, *A Partisan Guide to the Jewish Problem, op. cit.*, p. 166.

51. Theodore Friedman (ed.), *What is Conservative Judaism?* (New York: National Academy of Adult Jewish Studies, n.d.).

52. We refer to Gordis' book: *Conservative Judaism*.

53. Gordis, "The Tasks Before Us," *Conservative Judaism*, I, 1 (January, 1945), 4.

54. Some of the theoretical considerations are explained by Gordis in an address printed in R.A., *Proceedings*, VIII (1944), 64-94. See esp. p. 72.

55. See *ibid.*, p. 79.

56. *Ibid.*, p. 83.

57. See Schechter in U. Syn., *Report of First Annual Meeting,* (New York: U. Syn., 1913), pp. 16-19. Schechter also stated on another occasion that: "They [the American-born generation] accept all the ancient ideas, but they want modern methods, and this, on the whole, may be the definition of Conservative Judaism." (U. Syn., *Report of the Second Annual Meeting, op. cit.*, p. 26.)

58. See, for example, Schechter's letter to Mayer Sulzberger reprinted in Bentwich, *op. cit.*, p. 301. Cf. Israel Levinthal, in R.A., *Proceedings*, IV (1933), 129-31, and

Finkelstein in *ibid.*, III (1929), 29-30.

59. References to this controversy are legion. Mention of it can be found in almost every volume of the R.A. *Proceedings*. Cf. Freehof in Central Conference of American Rabbis, *Yearbook*, LVI (1946), 283-84. Very recently a new effort along these lines has been attempted and Conservative rabbis now use a revised marriage contract form, but it is too early to gauge its effect.

60. L. W. Crohn, "A Layman Speaks Out," *The Reconstructionist*, XIV, 18 (January 7, 1949), 17.

61. See Law Committee Report in R.A., *Proceedings*, VIII (1944), 139-41.

62. See Ginzberg in U. Syn., *Report of Sixth Annual Meeting* (New York: U. Syn., 1919), p. 24.

63. R.A., *Proceedings*, XIV (1951), 98-99. Note that in contrast to the large amount of *responsa* literature published by Orthodox rabbis and agencies, no such material has emanated from the Conservative group. The material which appears in the R.A. *Proceedings*, with several exceptions, merely reports on the *responsa*. It is significant that although an R.A. *responsa* volume was projected repeatedly, no such book has yet appeared.

64. On the keeping of the traditional means of legal interpretation while the suprasocial rationale has been discarded, see Eugene Kohn, "From Theocracy to Democracy," *The Reconstructionist*, X, 12 (October 20, 1944), 8-9.

65. See R.A., *Proceedings*, XIV (1951) for the relevant documents.

66. The viewpoint of the leftist, or Reconstructionist group appears to have shifted somewhat in recent

years. It is difficult to say as yet what effect this will have on the traditional alignments in the Rabbinical Assembly.
67. Freeman, *op. cit.*, pp. 12-13.
68. William Greenfeld in R.A., *Proceedings*, XII (1949), 122.
69. David Aronson in *ibid.*, XIII (1950), 139.
70. Kaplan, *Unity in Diversity in the Conservative Movement, op. cit.*, pp. 14-15.
71. For a critical analysis of the tactical errors of the leftists, see Milton Steinberg, "The Test of Time," *The Reconstructionist*,

XVI, 1 (February 24, 1950), 20-25.
72. Of the 514 members of the Rabbinical Assembly in 1952, only 83 belonged to the Reconstructionist Rabbinical Fellowship. (Letter from Hannah L. Goldberg, Executive Secretary, Jewish Reconstructionist Foundation, February 29, 1952.)
73. These quotations are from the stenographic notes made during the course of the lectures which were delivered at the Park Avenue Synagogue, New York City, in January 1950.

Chapter IX

1. Morris Axelrod, Floyd J. Fowler, and Arnold Gurin, *A Community Survey for Long Range Planning* (Boston: Combined Jewish Philanthropies of Greater Boston, 1967), p. 119.
2. Sidney Goldstein and Calvin Goldscheider, *Jewish Americans* (Englewood Cliffs, N.J.: Prentice-Hall, 1968), p. 177.
3. Albert J. Mayer, *Milwaukee Jewish Population Study* (Milwaukee: Jewish Welfare Fund, 1965), p. 48.
4. According to a recent study by Louis Harris and Bert E. Swanson, *Black-Jewish Relations in New York City* (New York: Praeger, 1970), some 35% of New York City Jews are Conservative, 21% are Reform, 16% are Orthodox, and 28% are "non-affiliated" or "not sure" (p. xiii). It is not clear how the question on religious self-identification was asked by the Harris organization. Whatever the exact size of the Conservative plurality, it would have been appreciably increased if the study had included Jews residing in New York suburban areas.

5. Axelrod *et al.*, *op. cit.*, p. 143.
6. See *supra*, pp. 135-45.
7. On the American synagogue see Marshall Sklare, *America's Jews* (New York: Random House, 1971), pp. 126-35.
8. See Mortimer J. Cohen, *Beth Sholom Synagogue: A Description and Interpretation* (Privately Published, 1959).
9. See *supra*, pp. 218-19.
10. On the Seminary and the power of the "schoolmen," see *supra*, pp. 161-95.
11. See Abraham J. Karp, *A History of the United Synagogue of America 1913-1963* (New York: U. Syn., 1964), p. 76.
12. The effect of another youth-oriented agency, U.S.Y. (United Synagogue Youth), has also been to reinforce the feeling of a shared Conservatism.
13. Max J. Routtenberg in R.A., *Proceedings*, XXIX (1965), 23.
14. *Ibid.*
15. Robert Gordis in R.A., *Proceedings*, XXIX (1965), 92-93.
16. See *supra*, pp. 58-60.
17. See *supra*, pp. 192, 219-20.
18. See Charles S. Liebman, "Or-

thodoxy in American Life," *American Jewish Year Book*, LXVI (1965), 21-97.

19. On the problem such sacramentalism creates for the modern Jew, see Marshall Sklare and Joseph Greenblum, *Jewish Identity on the Suburban Frontier* (New York: Basic Books, 1967), pp. 45-48.

20. R.A., *Proceedings*, XXXII (1968), 160.

21. On reinterpretation, see *supra*, pp. 124-26.

22. See, for example, Goldstein and Goldscheider, *op. cit.*, p. 203.

23. See *supra*, pp. 237-38.

24. See *supra*, pp. 102-9.

25. Goldstein and Goldscheider, *op. cit.*, p. 194.

26. *Ibid.*, p. 203. See Axelrod *et al.*, *op. cit.*, p. 131, for the somewhat higher figures in Boston.

27. Second-generation Conservative Jews in Providence locate themselves between the relatively observant first generation and the highly unobservant third generation. However, the second generation tends to be positioned closer to the third generation than to the first.

28. For the Har Zion study, see Samuel Z. Klausner and David P. Varady, *Synagogues Without Ghettos* (Processed, Center for the Study on the Acts of Man, University of Pennsylvania, 1970). I am grateful to Dr. Klausner for making these figures available to me.

29. See, for example, the following publications of Conservatism's Burning Bush Press: Samuel H. Dresner, *The Jewish Dietary Laws*, and *The Sabbath* by the same author. Rabbi Dresner is singular in that he is a veteran Conservative leader of Reform background—he came to the Seminary from Hebrew Union College, the Reform rabbinical school. Since he embraced the *mitzvoth* by an act of will rather than by virtue of family inheritance, Dresner has been especially well qualified to provide information and inspiration to the exceptional individual in Conservatism who is interested in returning to the *mitzvoth*.

30. See Robert Gordis, "Toward a Revitalization of Halakhah in Conservative Judaism," *Conservative Judaism*, XXV, 3 (Spring, 1971), 49-55.

31. See *supra*, p. 90.

32. On the rate of intermarriage and the Jewish response, see Sklare, *America's Jews, op. cit.*, pp. 180-206.

33. See Stephen C. Lerner, "Ramah and Its Critics," *Conservative Judaism*, XXV, 4 (Summer, 1971), 14.

34. A doctoral dissertation being written by Uri Farrago in the Department of Sociology at Brandeis University discusses the Palmer experiment.

35. R.A., *Proceedings*, XXXIV (1970), 90-91.

Index